W9-CRL-374

Praise for *Let Them Eat Tweets*

"Sharp and thoughtful . . . The most chilling argument in [Jacob S.] Hacker and [Paul] Pierson's book is that Trump's rhetoric has focused us on the wrong authoritarian threat. . . . This is the cliff on which American democracy now teeters. The threat isn't that Donald Trump will carve his face onto Mount Rushmore and engrave his name across the White House. It's that the awkward coalition that nominated and sustains him will entrench itself, not their bumbling standard-bearer, by turning America into a government by the ethnonationalist minority, for the plutocratic minority."

—Ezra Klein, *Vox*

"With *Let Them Eat Tweets*, the political scientists Jacob S. Hacker and Paul Pierson have constructed a portrait of the Trumpian moment that, in the book's professorial way, is as terrifying as those Page 1 accounts of presidential ravings. They meticulously show how the president isn't a singular presence, but a thoroughly representative one. Hacker and Pierson are two of the most reliable and reliably creative thinkers in their discipline. . . . Persuasively and meticulously argued."

—Franklin Foer, *New York Times Book Review*

"This essential book makes clear that American democracy is threatened less by Trump than by the extreme economic inequality that set the stage for his election. Growing plutocratic power preceded Trump, and will outlast him. Unless these larger forces are reckoned with, [the authors] warn, the United States may be locked in an escalating 'doom loop.'"

—Jane Mayer, *New York Times* best-selling author of *Dark Money*

"Hacker and Pierson . . . offer a strong case that the Republican Party's dependence on its top donors explains much of its trajectory in recent decades, culminating in the rise of Trump. The authors have a knack for synthesizing complicated academic studies and explaining them concisely for popular audiences. . . . Their historical explanation of how the GOP became radicalized raises legitimate concerns that the party, its judicial appointees and its donor class will carry on 'fomenting tribalism, distorting elections, and subverting democratic institutions, procedures, and norms.' . . . Those who would resist this development should carefully consider the analysis that Hacker and Pierson lay out in such convincing and depressing detail."

—Geoffrey Kabaservice, *Washington Post*

"Jacob S. Hacker and Paul Pierson provide a persuasive and insightful explanation of the current extremes of American political polarization: it is the response to a fundamental and deep problem for conservatives, of how to enlist support for their self-interested economic policies in order to maintain a plutocratic society that benefits the few. [The authors] show that the conservative Republican Party's appeal to nativism and tribalism, while deep rooted in US history, is not inevitable. There is yet hope for American democracy. A must-read for anyone interested in understanding contemporary American politics."

—Joseph E. Stiglitz, 2001 Nobel laureate, economic sciences

"Since Ronald Reagan, Republican presidents have had to reconcile their own economic policies—which largely benefit corporations and the wealthy—with the growing populist rhetoric that their base responds to. [In *Let Them Eat Tweets*] political scientists Jacob Hacker and Paul Pierson astutely chronicle the ways that the GOP has attempted to navigate this fundamental contradiction."

—Julian Zelizer, CNN.com

"Hacker and Pierson are persuasive in contending that the Republican Party can on its own imperil the whole system by pulling everything to the right, especially if it continues to restrict voting. American mainstream politics has become profoundly out of sync with the economic realities that motivate most voters."

—Nicholas Lemann, *Nation*

"*Let Them Eat Tweets* is the perfect title for a wise and passionate book that distinguishes between a populism genuinely challenging to elites and the 'plutocratic populism' of Donald Trump, the purpose of which is to entrench the power of the already privileged. Jacob S. Hacker and Paul Pierson have an admirable record of seeing around corners and their warnings about threats to majoritarian democracy—from the right and from the way our institutions are working—are telling and worrying. In the face of this danger, [they] offer realistic hope that democratic action can rescue democracy itself. An important book for our moment."

—E. J. Dionne Jr., author of *Code Red: How Progressives and Moderates Can Unite to Save Our Country*

"This book makes intelligible how the nightmare of our current politics has happened. With their usual acuity and verve, Jacob S. Hacker and Paul Pierson confront us with an uncomfortable reality: extreme economic inequality has left America vulnerable to a right-wing extremism that has destroyed other countries' democracies in the past. Hacker and Pierson's message is not that democracy in America is doomed. But to save it, we need to come to grips with the underlying economic forces pulling it apart today."

—Daniel Ziblatt, professor of government at Harvard University and coauthor of the *New York Times* bestseller *How Democracies Die*

"Highly readable, historically grounded, analytically clear, and carefully argued, *Let Them Eat Tweets* exposes generations of Republican lawmakers who serve the narrow goals of the uber wealthy while cynically disregarding the needs of their own constituents. This book is for everyone who wants to move beyond a singular focus on the Trump presidency and gain a broader understanding of how we arrived at this political moment—and how we can move beyond it."

—Melissa Harris-Perry, Maya Angelou Presidential Chair at Wake Forest University

"A standout. . . . Highly recommended."   —Gary Day, *Booklist*

"Hacker and Pierson pull disparate pieces into a lucid narrative that goes a long way toward explaining the current iteration of the Republican Party. Liberals will be equal parts enraged and edified by this deeply sourced polemic."   —*Publishers Weekly*

"For almost twenty years, respected scholars Jacob S. Hacker and Paul Pierson have been ahead of the curve in diagnosing how the increasing concentration of wealth in America has diminished democratic accountability and threatened the underpinnings of our constitutional democracy. Now they have written a fantastic capstone volume tying together the essential elements of their story: plutocracy, asymmetric partisan polarization, counter-majoritarianism, and right-wing populism. It is a tour de force, embedded in sophisticated historical and comparative analysis yet immensely helpful in making sense of the daily headlines in these troubling times."
—Thomas E. Mann, coauthor of the *New York Times* bestseller
It's Even Worse Than It Looks

"Democracy, or plutocracy enabled by dog whistle politics? Those are the heart-stopping stakes, according to the compelling volume in your hands. Read this book and get in the fight."
—Ian F. Haney López, author of *Merge Left: Fusing Race and Class, Winning Elections, and Saving America*

LET
THEM
EAT
TWEETS

ALSO BY JACOB S. HACKER AND PAUL PIERSON

*American Amnesia: How the War on Government
Led Us to Forget What Made America Prosper*

*Winner-Take-All Politics: How Washington Made the Rich
Richer—And Turned Its Back on the Middle Class*

*Off Center: The Republican Revolution and
the Erosion of American Democracy*

ALSO BY JACOB S. HACKER

*The Great Risk Shift: The New Economic Insecurity
and the Decline of the American Dream*

*The Divided Welfare State: The Battle over Public and
Private Social Benefits in the United States*

*The Road to Nowhere: The Genesis of President
Clinton's Plan for Health Security*

ALSO BY PAUL PIERSON

Politics in Time: History, Institutions, and Social Analysis

*Dismantling the Welfare State? Reagan, Thatcher,
and the Politics of Retrenchment*

LET THEM EAT TWEETS

HOW THE **RIGHT** **RULES** IN AN AGE OF EXTREME INEQUALITY

JACOB S. HACKER
AND PAUL PIERSON

LIVERIGHT PUBLISHING CORPORATION

A DIVISION OF W. W. NORTON & COMPANY

Independent Publishers Since 1923

Copyright © 2020 by Jacob S. Hacker and Paul Pierson

All rights reserved
Printed in the United States of America
First published as a Liveright paperback 2021

For information about permission to reproduce selections from this book,
write to Permissions, Liveright Publishing Corporation, a division of
W. W. Norton & Company, Inc., 500 Fifth Avenue, New York, NY 10110

For information about special discounts for bulk purchases, please contact
W. W. Norton Special Sales at specialsales@wwnorton.com or 800-233-4830

Manufacturing by LSC Communications, Harrisonburg
Production manager: Anna Oler

Library of Congress Cataloging-in-Publication Data

Names: Hacker, Jacob S., author. | Pierson, Paul, author.
Title: Let them eat Tweets : how the right rules in an age of extreme inequality /
Jacob S. Hacker and Paul Pierson.
Description: First edition. | New York : Liveright Publishing Corporation,
2020. | Includes bibliographical references and index.
Identifiers: LCCN 2019057133 | ISBN 9781631496844 (hardcover) |
ISBN 9781631496851 (epub)
Subjects: LCSH: Conservatism—United States. | Populism—United States. |
Plutocracy—United States. | Polarization (Social sciences)—Political aspects—
United States. | United States—Politics and government—2017–
Classification: LCC JC573.2.U6 H33 2020 | DDC 320.520973—dc23
LC record available at https://lccn.loc.gov/2019057133

ISBN 978-1-63149-903-6 pbk.

Liveright Publishing Corporation, 500 Fifth Avenue, New York, N.Y. 10110
www.wwnorton.com

W. W. Norton & Company Ltd., 15 Carlisle Street, London W1D 3BS

1 2 3 4 5 6 7 8 9 0

To Oona and Tracey

CONTENTS

LET
THEM
EAT
TWEETS

INTRODUCTION

THIS IS NOT A BOOK ABOUT DONALD TRUMP.

Instead, it is about an immense shift that preceded Trump's rise, has profoundly shaped his political party and its priorities, and poses a threat to our democracy that is certain to outlast his presidency.

That shift is the rise of plutocracy—government of, by, and for the rich. Runaway inequality has remade American politics, reorienting power and policy toward corporations and the superrich (particularly the most conservative among them). In the process, it has also remade the Republican Party, transforming a mainstream conservative party into one that is increasingly divisive, distant from the center, and disdainful of democracy. From the White House on down, Republicans now make extreme appeals once associated only with fringe right-wing parties in other rich nations, stoking the fires of white identity and working-class outrage. Yet their rhetorical alliance with "the people" belies their governing alliance with the plutocrats. Indeed, the rhetorical alliance stems from the governing alliance. To advance an unpopular plutocratic agenda, Republicans have escalated white backlash—and, increasingly, undermined democracy. In the United States, then, plutocracy and right-wing populism have not been opposing forces. Instead, they have been locked in a doom loop of escalating extremism that must be disrupted.

The rise of plutocracy is the story of post-1980 American politics. Over the last forty years, the wealthiest Americans and the biggest financial and corporate interests have amassed wealth on a scale unimaginable to prior generations and without parallel in other western democracies. The richest 0.1 percent of Americans now have roughly as much wealth as the bottom 90 percent combined. They have used that wealth—and the connections and influence that come with it—to construct a set of political organizations that are also distinctive in historical and cross-national perspective. What makes them distinctive is not just the scope of their influence, especially on the right and far right. It is also the degree to which the plutocrats, the biggest winners in our winner-take-all economy, pursue aims at odds with the broader interests of American society.[1]

In all these ways, the rise of plutocracy is also an assault on our democracy. When wealth buys power, the responsiveness of government to ordinary citizens weakens, and the elected officials who are supposed to represent those citizens are pulled toward the positions of economic elites. American plutocracy has transformed both of America's two great political parties. The most profound effects, however, have been on the Republican Party. As the power of the plutocrats has increased, America's conservative party has shifted not just to the right of conservative parties in other nations, but to the right of many *right-wing* parties. And the greatest rightward movement has occurred precisely on those issues where the party's plutocratic supporters have the most radical goals.[2]

On the plutocrats' pet issues, the party has raced to the fringe. Republican leaders have become singularly focused on tax cuts for corporations and the superrich, whatever the effects on American inequality, or on the people who make up the Republican "base." When those cuts have conflicted with their traditional emphasis on fiscal restraint, they have run up huge deficits to finance them, abandoning the principle of budget balance—except as a cudgel with which to attack popular social programs, such as Medicaid, Medicare, and Social Security. They have launched an intensifying assault on environmental, consumer, labor, and financial protections. They have attempted to strip health insurance from millions of Americans. They have appointed the most consistently pro-business, anti-labor, and anti-consumer judges in the modern history of the federal courts. And they have done all this despite the fact that every one of these aims has strikingly little public support, even among Republican voters.[3]

Which raises the obvious question: How? As political scientists, we have spent many years in dialogue with fellow scholars who see a basic harmony between what citizens want and what governments do. Government responsiveness to voters should be expected, these researchers insist, because electoral competition creates strong pressures for politicians to cater to popular majorities.

But we do not see this sort of harmony today. Rather, we see a political system in which elected representatives are caught in the gravitational pull of great wealth. We see a political system in which a once-moderate party now tightly orbits the most reactionary elements of America's emergent plutocracy. And we see a political system in which, despite that party's embrace of unpopular economic policies, tens of millions of Americans of modest means don't just vote for that party but have become increasingly tribal in their loyalty to it.

As we write, the party advancing the priorities of the plutocrats holds the White House and the Senate, it has a dominant position on the federal courts (especially the Supreme Court), and it has entrenched a set of tax and regulatory policies that disadvantage ordinary workers, consumers, and citizens. More striking still, this party's voting base consists increasingly of less affluent white voters living in regions of the country devastated by these very policies—voters who favor more infrastructure spending and promises to protect Medicaid rather than more corporate tax cuts and blueprints for privatizing Social Security.

We've been struggling with the "how?" question for nearly twenty years. Our interest in the evolution of the GOP started with an article on the 2001 Bush tax cuts, which gave roughly 40 percent of their benefits to the richest 1 percent. In that article, we argued that while the cuts received surface support in polls, the contents of the new law were sharply at odds with what the majority of voters thought the nation's budget priorities should be. As the biggest policy shift of the last two decades, the tax cuts were strong evidence of declining responsiveness to voters.[4]

Some of our fellow political scientists thought that article was alarmist. If Republicans were really out of step with voters, they reasoned, the party would eventually pay the price. But they haven't paid the price, and they keep moving further to the right. Again and again, what seemed like the peak of Republican radicalism proved to be just a base camp, as the party shifted its focus toward a narrower and narrower slice at the top. The tax cuts of 2017— passed after a presidential campaign in which the Republican standard-bearer suggested he would turn the GOP into a "workers' party"—delivered more than 80 percent of their largesse to the top 1 percent. Looking back, we did make at least one error. We weren't worried enough.[5]

This book is our answer to the "how" question. As the GOP embraced plutocratic priorities, it pioneered a set of electoral appeals that were increasingly strident, alarmist, and racially charged. Encouraging white backlash and anti-government extremism, the party outsourced voter mobilization to a set of aggressive and narrow groups: the National Rifle Association, the organized Christian right, the burgeoning industry of right-wing media. When and where that proved insufficient, it adopted a ruthless focus on altering electoral rules, maximizing the sway of its base and minimizing the influence of the rest of the electorate through a variety of anti-democratic tactics, from voter disenfranchisement to extreme partisan gerrymandering to laws and practices opening the floodgates to big money. And more and more, it coupled this vote rigging with even more extreme strategies to undermine the checks and balances in our system, weakening democratic accountability and strengthening the ability of powerful minorities to dictate policy. In short, Republicans used white identity to defend wealth inequality. They undermined democracy to uphold plutocracy.

The centrality of white backlash to Donald Trump's rise has received plenty of attention. Among journalists and academics alike, the president is generally seen as an exemplar of what analysts call "right-wing populism," a transnational wave of anti-elite and anti-immigrant sentiments that has roiled rich democracies in the wake of the global financial meltdown. But America's version of right-wing populism began to surface well before Trump—in fact, well before the financial crisis. Trump turned the dial to eleven, but he did so on a machine that was already built.

Nor does America's variant of right-wing populism mirror the variant found abroad. In other rich countries where right-wing populists are challenging for power, animus toward immigrants and minorities gets coupled with fervent defense of social benefits for white citizens. Republicans—and Trump especially—have the animus part down. The defense of social benefits, not so much. On the contrary: what they have done on economic matters has been consistently, breathtakingly plutocratic. Benefits for downscale Republicans have been on the chopping block. The benefits Republicans have defended—and, in fact, expanded—are those for corporations and the superrich.

So peculiar is America's version of right-wing populism that it deserves a label of its own. In this book, we use the term "plutocratic populism" to describe the party's bitter brew of reactionary economic priorities and right-wing cultural and racial appeals. This distinctive American hybrid emerged after 1980 as the Republican Party struggled to manage the tensions between its governing priorities and its electoral strategies, between its defense of plutocracy in the face of rising inequality and its reliance on less affluent white voters in the face of growing diversity. To deliver for the plutocrats yet still win elections, Republicans reached ever deeper into parts of the nation and segments of the electorate where conservative economic policies failed to stir voters' passions but divisive appeals to identity did. The choices and alliances they made—and the opportunities to take a less destructive course they rejected—radicalized a party, divided a nation, and empowered a demagogue. They now imperil our democracy.[6]

AS THE TITLE OF THIS BOOK IMPLIES, the Republican Party has substituted division and distraction for a real response to the needs of ordinary Americans—and nothing better demonstrates this than

Donald Trump's Twitter feed. But it is not just voters who are distracted. Pundits and experts are, too. Almost everything we read today is about the president and his outrages. But focusing on Trump can obscure more than it reveals. We need to step back and understand the long road to plutocratic populism, and the degree to which Trump has reinforced, rather than challenged, the core elements of what his party had already become.

Two narratives, in particular, dominate commentary about our present crisis. Both contain crucial elements of truth, but both, in different ways, neglect the fundamental role of plutocracy.

The first and simplest account focuses on what's often called the Republican "civil war." In this analysis, Trump and his right-wing populist allies are an insurgent army that's taken over the Republican Party, emphasizing "toughness" on immigration and trade while abandoning the party's long-held (if not always upheld) commitments to limited government and fiscal responsibility. The enemy they've allegedly vanquished is the "establishment," the politicians and groups aligned with the party's national leadership and big-money lobbies. Among those supposedly toppled: Paul Ryan, the former Speaker of the House known for his hard-right budgets; the Tea Party and its grassroots warriors, who battled President Obama in the name of constitutional conservatism after 2009; and the libertarian Koch brothers and their network of conservative mega-donors. In this narrative, Trump demanded a party very different from what the Republican establishment represented, and the establishment lost.[7]

If the establishment lost, however, it's hard to know what winning would have looked like. Now that Ryan has retired from Congress, he suggests his alliance with Trump was intended to "get [Trump's] mind right." But getting Trump's mind right apparently meant ensuring his economic priorities were *to the* right. Under the leadership of Ryan and his Senate counterpart, Mitch McConnell, Republicans in Congress slashed taxes on corporations and the rich, stacked the federal courts with staunchly pro-business conservatives, and tried to repeal the most popular elements of the Affordable Care Act. Their refusal to devote resources to anything but tax cuts and the military turned "Infrastructure Week" from a popular Trump promise into a punchline. Another of Trump's pledges—to *not* cut Medicaid—did not stop Ryan and McConnell from attempting to do just that. The point isn't that they hoodwinked Trump. The supposed tribune of working-class Americans went along with all these moves, having outsourced his entire legislative strategy to economic hardliners in Congress and to a domestic policy team comprised mostly of economic hardliners who had recently been in Congress. The point is that Republicans tried to do with unified control of Washington mostly what they and their plutocratic allies had been trying to do for years—only in a more extreme form.

These policy developments are hard to square with the notion that Trump has trashed the ultra-conservative orthodoxies of the establishment. They make much more sense if we see Trump not as the victor in an intraparty civil conflict, but as both a consequence and recent enabler of the GOP's long, steady march to the right. Some of the country's most astute opinion writers have stressed this point, including Paul Krugman, Matthew Yglesias, and Jonathan Chait (and, beyond opinion writers, Jane Mayer, who has painstakingly investigated the party's plutocratic ties). But their counterpoints are too often forgotten amid breathless chatter about Trump's latest outrages. The same *New York Times* that publishes Krugman's columns also publishes story after story explaining how Trump has rolled over the Tea Party, the Koch brothers, and America's economic elite more broadly.[8]

Part of the confusion is that observers frequently assume that if *some* corporate leaders or billionaire donors are complaining, then Trump must be pursuing policies that plutocrats don't like. And certainly, neither Trump's tariffs nor his immigration policies are popular in moneyed circles. It is also true that precincts of the business community, such as Silicon Valley, find the president downright detestable, and that plenty of very wealthy people support the Democratic Party and style themselves progressives.

Still, most of the superrich are broadly aligned with the core Republican economic agenda. Few among the fabulously wealthy speak openly about these priorities, and many of the most public plutocrats are also the most progressive (think Tom Steyer and George Soros). But in those rare instances when political scientists successfully survey the views of the very wealthy, those views turn out to be much more conservative than commonly believed. For example, a 2011 poll of rich Americans—average wealth of respondents: $14 million—found that just 17 percent of these wealthy citizens said they'd support high taxes on the rich to reduce inequality, a position endorsed by over half of the general public.[9]

The most engaged and organized segments of the plutocracy are even further to the right. The typical plutocrat is a lot more conservative than the typical American: the poll just cited found twice as many Republicans as Democrats among the wealthy (among all voters, Democrats have the edge), and the self-identified Democrats in the survey were substantially more conservative on economic issues than the norm for nonaffluent voters in their party. But the typical rich American isn't nearly as conservative as the most politically engaged plutocrats are. When you look at the ultra-wealthy activists who are spending fortunes to remake American politics—especially through their huge outlays of "dark money" encouraged by the ongoing decimation of campaign finance limits—you see a plutocracy that's even more conservative. And when you look at the stances and investments of the political organizations that magnify the influence of corporations and the superrich, you see one that's more conservative still. The most effective groups representing economic elites—the Koch Network, the US Chamber of Commerce, the American Legislative Exchange Council—range from the hard right to the even harder right.[10]

By no means are conservative plutocrats happy with *everything* Trump is doing to American public policy. Yet they are playing the long game—a game that has always required trade-offs. And far from losing that game, they are winning much more than they had once thought possible. Right-wing populism hasn't derailed the extreme agenda of reactionary plutocrats. It has enabled it, accelerating the Republican Party's decades-long transit toward their hard-right priorities.

To see just how stunning this transformation has been, it helps to throw off another assumption that leads observers astray: that the two parties are more or less mirror images of each other, moving away from the center at equal speeds. In truth, Republican politicians have moved much further right than Democratic politicians have moved left, a phenomenon we call "asymmetric polarization." Republicans have also embraced rhetoric and tactics that are much more aggressive and anti-democratic, ranging from extreme obstruction—say, blocking a Democratic president's Supreme Court nominee for a year—to all-out assaults on the right to vote. Neither the extreme groups that mobilize GOP voters nor the right-wing media outlets that shape those voters' preferences and perceptions have real counterparts on the liberal side. Yes, important elements of the Democratic Party have moved leftward in recent years, but the Republican Party has moved rightward *over decades*. With increasing ruthlessness, Republican elites have embraced plutocratic priorities that lack appeal even among the party's own voters—and that embrace has only grown tighter as the party's public face has grown more "populist."[11]

THE SECOND DOMINANT ACCOUNT is more convincing, but still incomplete. This narrative, too, focuses on right-wing populism— but as a symptom of a deeper disease, rather than a manifestation of internal GOP conflicts. That deeper disease is racism.[12]

The racism-focused narrative takes various forms. Some emphasize contemporary forces: the incessant race-baiting of Donald Trump; white backlash against the nation's first black president; the anxiety generated by the ongoing shift toward a "majority-minority nation." Others emphasize the deeper historical roots of white identity. Yet all these accounts suggest that race is *the* cleavage that defines American politics. They all emphasize, too, that this cleavage reflects deep psychological attachments that are easily triggered and highly resistant to change. In this respect, they present a "bottom-up" perspective, emphasizing the underlying resistance of key parts of the white electorate to the shifts in status and power that demographic change entails.

This narrative rightly stresses the deeper forces at work in Trump's rise, which is why it is more convincing than accounts focused on recent struggles within the GOP. America's racial history is indeed unique, its legacies are often toxic, and those toxic legacies have been on vivid display in the response of many white Americans to the nation's dramatic demographic changes. In 2016, Trump won in significant part because he exploited that response. We recognize now that our previous writings paid far too little attention to the role of racial divisions in the radicalization of the Republican Party, and we have tried to grapple with those divisions and their effects much more fully in this book.

To elevate the role of race, though, does not require denying the role of plutocracy. It requires seeing how (and how fundamentally) the two are intertwined. It also requires thinking about how the psychology of race is shaped and directed by elites with their own partisan and economic motives—to see how it works from the top down as well as from the bottom up. In multiracial democracies, what scholars call "ethnic outbidding"—when parties seek to mobilize voters on the basis of race, ethnicity, religion, or citizenship—is always a temptation. Decades of research suggest that these spirals of extremism do not bubble up from below; they emerge when elites capitalize on preexisting prejudices in pursuit of political gain, forcing citizens and leaders to take sides in an intensifying battle of competing identity claims. In the absence of such elite outrage-stoking, citizens may well be receptive to more moderate party stances and strategies.[13]

As recently as 2004, for example, George W. Bush won 44 percent of the Hispanic vote on the way to reelection. Because of his ability to attract nonwhite voters without alienating white voters, he became the only Republican presidential candidate to win the popular vote in more than three decades. Subsequent Republican leaders abandoned this multiracial strategy not merely because resentful GOP voters greeted it with suspicion, but also because attracting Hispanic voters proved difficult to reconcile with the GOP's increasingly reactionary economic agenda and its growing reliance on extreme groups. The embrace of plutocratic priorities has been a powerful force pushing the Republican Party toward increasingly open and hostile racialized appeals. That choice, in turn, created powerful incentives for ethnic outbidding, as party leaders leaned more heavily on outrage-stoking organizations and ambitious Republican politicians intensified their appeals to resentful white voters.

Just as we should consider the role of top-down mobilization of racial resentments, we also should remember that Trump won over Republican voters in 2016 with a variety of appeals. He did unusually well among the most racially resentful voters. Yet he attracted these voters not only with divisive racial rhetoric, but also with liberal (for a Republican) economic pledges—pledges he mostly abandoned once in office. And Trump's victory did not just rest on the support of working-class whites in the Midwest, as journalistic accounts often imply. He swept the party, pulling in white Republicans who expressed racially tolerant views as well as those who did not. In this respect, Trump benefited decisively from what political scientists call "affective" or "negative" polarization—that is, antipathy toward the other party and its supporters. Even Republicans who viewed him with dismay couldn't bring themselves to vote for Hillary Clinton.

Prejudice has been an enormous contributor to affective polarization; the best available research suggests, for instance, that racial resentment was a bigger factor in the Tea Party movement than principled conservatism. But Republican elites have drawn on a range of themes, targets, and emotions to stoke the hostility of the Republican base to the "other side." Demeaning minorities as predatory and dependent has gone hand in hand with demonizing government as corrupt and ineffective. Fears of status decline have gone hand in hand with fears of economic decline. Untangling racism, distrust of government, and economic insecurity is so hard because GOP efforts to tangle them together have been so successful.[14]

Racial divisions are, and always have been, central to the American story. What we want to emphasize is that the particular role they now play in our politics owes much to the massive shift of wealth and power toward the top. The United States is not, after all, the only rich nation struggling with racism or white backlash to demographic change. Yet it is the only one struggling with such extreme inequalities of wealth and power. Other western democracies have seen widening economic gaps; a handful (notably, the United Kingdom and Canada) have witnessed trends that bear surface similarity to the United States'. But none has seen anything like the intensifying concentration of economic and political resources that characterizes the American political economy of the past generation. That distinctiveness, in turn, explains a good deal of what's so unusual (and dangerous) about America's peculiar version of right-wing populism.[15]

Plutocratic populism brings together two forces that share little in common except their distrust of democracy and their investment in the GOP. Plutocrats fear democracy because they see it as imperiling their economic standing and narrowly defined priorities. Right-wing populists fear democracy because they see it as imperiling their electoral standing and their narrowly defined community. These fears would be less consequential if they were not packaged together within one of the nation's two major parties. Plutocratic populism is a force multiplier, fusing hard-right economic policies that would have little future if relied on to mobilize voters with right-wing populist strategies that would have little future if they truly endangered, rather than reinforced, elite power. Yet plutocratic populism is also a threat multiplier, because neither side of the relationship feels secure despite this combined power. The result is an especially volatile and dangerous mix—a party coalition that is capable of changing policies and institutions, but fearful it will not long control them; a party coalition that is able to achieve its priorities, but only by disregarding majorities, dividing and lying to citizens, and distorting democracy.

Many have pointed to the risk of creeping authoritarianism under Trump, and we share these fears. Yet the Republican Party's marriage of plutocracy and populism also points to another risk—not rule by a single powerful man, but rule by a set of powerful minorities. This threat, which might be called "creeping counter-majoritarianism," predates Trump's election. For years, Republicans have exploited America's aging political institutions to cement their power in

Congress, the federal courts, and rural and right-leaning states—even when they cannot win the majority of the nation's votes, and even when they do not hold the country's one nationally elected office. Our distinctive constitutional system was designed to make it hard for majorities to rule, forcing compromise and broad consensus. It was not supposed to make it possible for minorities to control governance in the face of majority resistance. Yet in an age of polarization, key features of that system—from the tilt of the Senate and Electoral College toward rural states, to the growing role of the Senate filibuster, to the vulnerability of state-administered elections to partisan rigging, to the conservative capture of the courts—allow a more and more determined minority to not just resist the will of a majority but increasingly to rule over it. In our vigilance against authoritarianism, we risk neglecting the less perceptible but no less pressing threat of permanent minority rule.

AFTER AN ELECTION, journalists rush to pivotal parts of the nation to interview voters. Social scientists dig into surveys to construct a more systematic picture of what those voters thought. These stories and statistics are revealing. Yet we often invest in them more importance than they deserve. Too frequently these bottom-up investigations treat voters as unmoved movers. But they are not unmoved; they are mobilized, messaged, and sometimes manipulated. Especially because of the tilt of our democracy toward the superrich, we cannot ignore how the attitudes of citizens are refracted by the interests, investments, and actions of those with outsized power.

A top-down perspective focuses our attention on elites, and particularly on the elites so often out of view. The spectacle of right-wing populism gets all the press. But it was reactionary plutocrats who first radicalized our politics. As their interests narrowed and their power expanded, democratic politics posed a growing threat to their privileges. But to protect and augment those privileges, they had to work through democratic politics—and, in particular, through the political party most closely allied with economic elites, the Republican Party. The result was a dilemma for Republican leaders: How to side with the elites who were winning big, yet attract the support of voters losing out? The answer was plutocratic populism.

Our argument is not that the plutocrats who have allied with the Republican Party are directly engineering all the developments we will describe. The plutocrats are not Bond villains in a hidden lair inside a volcano. There is no dominant figure—intellectual or economic—who set in motion the policies and strategies that have come to define plutocratic populism. A handful of conservative plutocrats have aggressively pushed the Republican Party to link its reactionary economic agenda to racialized appeals—for example, the financier Robert Mercer and his daughter Rebekah, who bankrolled Trump's white-backlash whisperer Steve Bannon and the right-wing news source Breitbart—but they are the exceptions.

What the plutocrats have done is use their formidable resources to shift the American political terrain in their favor, encouraging politicians and leaders to adopt certain stances and pursue certain strategies. Their influence has been so consequential precisely because it was not directed by one or a few powerful players, much less by some sort of coordinated conspiracy. Embedded in institutions and organized action, their efforts tend to endure over time and across successive political leaders, raising the stakes—and the hurdles—for those who seek to challenge it. Understanding this not only helps us see where Trump's presidency came from. It also allows us to comprehend how and for whom that presidency has worked. And it shows us just how much must be done to repair our polity even if he governs for only a single term.

All along, of course, powerful people have made choices—choices that not only deserve analysis but demand accountability. Conservative plutocrats have usually remained a step removed from the divisive and anti-democratic tactics they have generated, but they have tolerated and sometimes encouraged those tactics. Nor does responsibility end with plutocrats on the conservative side of the spectrum. Even the most progressive plutocrats are much less so when wealth-defending policies are on the table. Many of the same tech executives who regularly criticize Republicans for their conservative stances on immigration and LGBTQ rights supported the 2017 tax cuts, allowing their companies to provide billions in stock buybacks to their shareholders. Conservative plutocrats may deserve the greatest share of blame, but all parts of the plutocracy are implicated in the shift of government toward business and the superrich—and the destructive politics that shift has unleashed.[16]

This shift sets our nation starkly apart from other rich democracies. Yet it does have parallels—in democracy's troubled past. Roughly a century ago, conservative parties struggled to adapt to a world with large numbers of newly enfranchised voters, a world in which their long-standing alliance with the rich and powerful was suddenly a liability. They had two basic choices. They could make concessions and craft new appeals without demonizing vulnerable groups or destroying democratic norms. Or they could take a much darker path, one that involved partnering with groups capable of riling up voters, resorting to ever more incendiary rhetoric, and rigging elections. The British Tories mostly took the first path; German conservatives, alas, the second.[17]

Conservative parties of the early twentieth century were torn between the rich and the rest because the rest were gaining the right to vote. The Republican Party has been torn in a similar way because the rest are falling behind the rich so quickly. Adding to the dilemma, the party's white voting base is becoming a smaller and smaller share of the electorate. To stay in power, Republicans have had to rally support in places and among parts of the electorate where the rise of plutocracy has brought more misery than opportunity. Meanwhile, their plutocratic allies have become richer and more powerful, their demands more at odds with those of ordinary voters, and their commitment to democracy weaker. As these trends have collided—rising inequality, growing demographic diversity, deepening ties between conservative plutocrats and Republican politicians—they have generated the same stark choices confronted by previous conservative parties. On one side are the priorities of the plutocrats. On the other, the demands of the broader electorate. In between is the Republican Party, whose response may decide our democracy's fate.

Chapter 1

THE CONSERVATIVE DILEMMA

PLUTOCRATIC POPULISM IS RATHER NEW; the political dilemma that gives rise to it is very old. For as long as the idea of democracy has existed, thoughtful observers—both those who supported democracy and those who opposed it—have asked a fundamental question: What happens when an economic system that concentrates wealth in the hands of the few coexists with a political system that gives the ballot to the many?

The question has been a central preoccupation of political philosophers and statesmen alike, including those involved in the fledgling experiment with democratic rule in the new United States in the late eighteenth century. John Adams contemplated the prospect of political equality and prophesied disaster: "Debts would be abolished first; taxes laid heavy on the rich, and not at all on the others; and at last a downright equal division of everything be demanded, and voted." In the first volume of *Democracy in America*, published in 1835, Alexis de Tocqueville had similar fears, observing that "universal suffrage really gives the government of society to the poor" and "the government of democracy is the only one in which he who votes the tax can escape the obligation to pay it."[1]

Social scientists studying the establishment of democracies across the globe have fixated on the same question. They have long seen the divide between the rich and everyone else as a fundamental challenge for every new democracy. The entrenched rich wish to hold on to the economic and political resources they have. A system that more broadly disperses political power is a threat to both. In most cases, a successful and relatively peaceful transition to democracy requires two things: a growing capacity for collective action among ordinary citizens (which makes continued repression by elites more and more costly) and a set of political commitments (perhaps enshrined in a new constitution) that reassure elites that, while they need to make concessions, their fundamental interests will not be trampled upon. Elites, in other words, ask the same question as the philosophers, though with greater urgency: What, in a democracy, is to keep the many from taking what I have? Popular pressure on elites, combined with insurance for the elite's core interests, creates the essential balance of power and constraints within which stable democracies can develop.[2]

Scholars of democracy have largely focused on how popular rule is born and secured. About the stability of established democracies, they have mostly been optimistic—at least until recently. For nearly a century, their optimism proved to be well-founded. Established democracies in affluent countries almost never broke down. Once they were up and running in societies with a broad middle class, they created a "positive-sum" environment that generated widely distributed benefits. These societies were, in general, less unequal than prior social arrangements and more capable of sustaining economic growth. They achieved considerable improvements in the quality of life for most groups across the income distribution. And while the rich lost some of their political power, they typically thrived economically, too. Political systems that encouraged investment in the nation's people and limited corruption and uncertainty fostered prosperity.

In short, once firmly established, democracies could be expected to endure because they generally made life better for most people. Considerable inequalities of economic power could be reconciled with the broadening of political power because democracies made the pie much bigger even as they allocated an increasing share to ordinary citizens.

THIS IS AN ENCOURAGING STORY, but it comes with an important and troubling corollary: extremely unequal societies have a hard time finding that delicate balance between protecting ordinary citizens and reassuring the privileged few. In the early American republic, elite observers like Adams and de Tocqueville worried about challenges to democracy from below. A century later, many American statesmen wrestled with potential threats from above. As the United States struggled with increasingly extreme inequality in the early twentieth century, the great jurist Louis Brandeis declared that "we must make our choice. We may have democracy, or we may have wealth concentrated in the hands of a few, but we can't have both."[3]

Scholars, for their part, have long seen extreme inequality as a threat to democracy. This threat takes three forms. The first is unequal power. As Frederick Douglass famously observed, "Power concedes nothing without a demand. It never did and it never will." What drove the development of democracy in the first place was the growing power of ordinary citizens. As societies became more complex and urbanized, the relative power of economic elites declined. The many found it easier to organize, and the few found it harder and costlier to deploy the brute tools of coercion. In country after country, it was this shift in social and economic power that pressured elites to make political concessions—and, when things went well, to accept democracy.[4]

Extreme concentrations of wealth have the potential to short-circuit this necessary dispersal of political power. Affluence can buy influence. Societies where the rich control vastly more economic resources than the rest are likely to be ones where the rich wield vastly more political power as well. And if the rich do enjoy these twin advantages, they may feel less urgency to make concessions in order to maintain their standing and power.

The second threat extreme inequality poses is diverging interests. Democracy rests on the notion that even in large and diverse societies where fundamental disagreements are inevitable, most citizens will come to have reconcilable economic interests. Leaving aside a few petro-states and the island city-state of Singapore, all of the world's richest nations are long-standing democracies. A stable system, based on the rule of law and with some state accountability to the citizenry, has proven to be a powerful formula for prosperity, from which the rich and middle class may both derive benefits.[5]

Extreme inequality makes it harder to reconcile these interests. If an economic system is funneling most gains to those at the very top, improvements for the majority are likely to require challenges to that system. Necessarily, those challenges will come at the expense of the beneficiaries of the status quo. "Positive-sum" games that promote cooperation become "zero-sum" games that ensure conflict. The greater the degree of inequality, the harder it is to build and sustain consensus on arrangements that work for most citizens.

The third and final threat is elite fear. There are always going to be very considerable tensions between rich and poor. A widening chasm between the interests of the wealthy and those of the less fortunate encourages the privileged to view democracy itself as a danger to their wealth and status. All the old elite worries about democracy—that it is a weapon in the hands of the many, wielded at the expense of the few—return. When combined with the growth in elite power, elite fear may lead the wealthy to believe that ceding political ground is both unnecessary and risks gravely undermining their privileges. In turn, they may become more willing to contemplate and support political alternatives to democracy that will protect those privileges.

An economic elite that is extremely powerful, separate, and fearful is likely to put considerable pressure on democratic institutions. Time and again, this pressure has taken a particular form.

IN THE SPRING OF 2014, one of us (Paul) received an irresistible invitation to do some writing in Paris. The invitation came with an unexpected bonus: a scholar of comparative democratization was assigned to share the same office. He was working on a study of European politics in the early twentieth century that would eventually win the biggest book prize in political science. Though separated from contemporary American politics by the Atlantic Ocean and roughly a century, the story he was telling nonetheless turned out to be surprisingly relevant.

That office mate was the Harvard political scientist Daniel Ziblatt. Along with his colleague Steven Levitsky, Ziblatt would later publish the influential *How Democracies Die*. Back then, however, he was examining how European democracies had taken root—or failed to do so. Ziblatt had zeroed in on the relationship between conservative parties, extreme inequality, and democratic politics. Though Ziblatt studied European history and we studied contemporary American politics, these were precisely the relationships that had animated our own collaborative work for almost two decades. The many parallels between Ziblatt's investigations and our own, despite the obvious and enormous differences in setting, point to the profound significance of extreme inequality for the contours of democratic politics.[6]

Ziblatt's central claim was that conservative political elites played a decisive role in determining whether fledgling democracies would flourish or die. Why conservatives? Because they are the politicians most closely aligned with traditional economic elites. As representative democracies emerged, conservatives had to carry that allegiance into a new kind of political contest where they needed to win the support of voters of ordinary means. The result is what Ziblatt calls the "Conservative Dilemma." To participate in democratic politics, conservative politicians had to get and maintain voters' backing even as their elite allies sought, in Ziblatt's words, "to preserve their world, their interests, and power."[7]

We use "Conservative Dilemma" more specifically to describe the tension facing conservative *parties*. A century ago, in all countries with expanding franchises, conservative parties struggled to maintain their historical defense of elite privilege in the face of electoral challenges from the masses. When suffrage was restricted, conservative parties could ignore the massive gap between the rich and the rest. But this became a losing game once the working class gained the vote. Relatively quickly, conservative parties found themselves caught between a commitment to economic elites and an expanding electorate. How, they were forced to ask themselves, do we reconcile the needs of our core constituency with the need to win elections?

One potential solution to the dilemma was to address the material needs of the newly enfranchised. Most conservative parties took at least halting steps in this direction. Famously, it was the Prussian monarchist Otto von Bismarck who, in 1883, put in place the cornerstones of the welfare state as a way to fend off competition from the emerging popular parties of the left, especially the Social Democrats. Economic concessions were, and are, an important means by which conservative parties can survive in democratic politics. Yet Bismarck and others found they had limits. For one, they often angered wealthy backers. For another, because conservatives' political competitors had weak or no ties to those same backers, they were usually in a position to offer voters more generous programs than conservatives could.[8]

In sum, moderation on economic issues was not always successful. Nor, when the economy was highly unequal and economic elites extremely powerful, was it an easy path for conservative parties to take. Inevitably, conservative parties found they had to offer something else to voters. Outflanked by the left on economic issues, their survival depended on introducing or highlighting other social divisions. And these divisions couldn't be trivial or temporary; they had to be strong enough to attract durable political support from the working and middle classes. In modern societies, the list of such "cleavages" is short, and their history unpleasant. There are racial, ethnic, and religious divisions. There is the call of nationalism or foreign military adventures. There are sectional loyalties. There is opposition to immigration. In short, there is a set of noneconomic issues—many racially tinged, all involving strong identities and strong emotions—that draw a sharp line between "us" and "them."

The question is not whether these cleavages will enter democratic politics. They will. Given their allegiance to economic elites, conservative parties are compelled to take this route. As Ziblatt notes, the question is subtler: in focusing attention on social and cultural cleavages rather than economic divisions, can conservatives generate sufficient voter support to compete in elections without destabilizing a country's politics? Or do they end up promoting conflicts that are increasingly divisive, dangerous, and uncontrollable? Do the alliances they create allow compromise and the accommodation of diverse interests? Or do they open a Pandora's box of divisive appeals that sharply split ordinary citizens from each other—even as the party continues to protect the priorities of elites?

The embrace of strategies of cultural division in turn introduces two great risks. First, conservative parties may become vulnerable to capture by outside organizations that specialize in generating outrage. Politicians and parties generally try to avoid making appeals that might alienate moderate voters. The most skilled politicians often invoke a kind of earnest ambiguity. They are capable of convincing you they are on your side while giving themselves enough room to build a broad coalition and adjust to changing circumstances. So too, as a rule, are successful parties. They are set up to compete in and win elections, to recruit and support candidates who can do that, and to organize members to govern in the aftermath. These goals generally push party insiders toward a moderating, brokering role that encourages compromise and the blurring of divisions.

What parties are not always equipped to do is generate intensity sufficient to motivate potential voters and convince them to put their economic concerns to the side. For these purposes, other kinds of organizations—single-issue groups, cultural institutions such as churches, and certain kinds of media outlets, for instance—are often more effective. These organizations can focus on building strong emotional bonds with citizens and tapping shared identities. Crucially, these organizations may feel much less need to moderate and equivocate. Unlike parties, they are not trying to gain the support of a majority, nor will they face the task of governing. They can thrive by appealing to a smaller but highly motivated subset of voters.

Parties may find these outside groups useful surrogates. This is particularly true of conservative parties, since they face the tricky challenge of broadening their mass appeal while maintaining their allegiance to economic elites. Depending on the nature of the alliance between the party and outside groups, these relationships may be limited and intermittent, or deep and lasting. Like all alliances, the terms depend on the balance of power between the allies—a balance that, along with the terms, remains subject to change.[9]

Surrogate groups may seem like a boon to the party, and in the short run they often are. Yet relying on outside organizations that have their own interests and ways of doing things can also create problems. If these surrogates develop a zealous following among voters, a frail party may become their servant rather than their master. In a worst-case scenario, the party falls into a spiral of weakening control over the most extreme elements of its coalition. Ultimately, conventional politicians who are cross-pressured by competing demands may be outflanked, supplanted by demagogues who are happy to work with such elements and know how to do so. Reliance on surrogates can thus lead a party down the path to extremism.

The second risk associated with the Conservative Dilemma is no less serious: the prospect of diminishing commitment to democracy. Parties that open Pandora's box don't just face the possibility of being overrun by extreme surrogate groups. If the party's appeals to voters are not enough, they may attempt to shift the electoral math more directly. If playing by the rules is ineffective, bending or breaking those rules may become an appealing alternative.

Political developments around the globe today, from Hungary to Turkey to the Philippines, remind us that those in power have tools to protect themselves from electoral backlash and other sources of political accountability. The incentives of leaders to use these tools increase if they and their allies doubt their ability to win on a level playing field and are so deeply committed to unpopular policies that they cannot afford to cede control. Party loyalists in power can engage in gerrymandering, transforming minorities into majorities. They can make it harder for their party's opponents to vote. In more extreme situations they can stuff ballot boxes, intimidate opposition voters, or engage in violence. Political power can be used to diminish democratic competition, weakening opponents and strengthening supporters through corruption (the purchasing of support), manipulation or intimidation of the media, and harassment of political rivals. Courts can be stacked with loyalists who use their power to shackle partisan opponents, metaphorically and at times literally.

Political scientists have a term for the systematic resort to such tactics: "democratic backsliding." As the image suggests, once a party in power loses confidence in its ability to win in fair and open contestation and starts down the path of rule-breaking, it may be hard to turn back. Investing in such efforts may have pulled resources away from the party's investments in broader outreach. Extreme appeals may have alienated major parts of the electorate. Rule-breaking may have exposed leaders to career or even legal risk that increases their desire to protect themselves and their allies no matter the cost. Shady or thuggish practices may have damaged the party's brand. All this can make reliance on narrow groups, extreme appeals, rule-breaking, and shady or thuggish practices even more necessary to stay in power.

The reality of an increasingly rigged political game may also discourage moderates within the ruling party, who find it harder to climb the ranks, or become fearful of the consequences of dissent. As the system slides toward authoritarianism or persistent minority rule, these trends may encourage ambitious types to choose career over democratic principles while the intimidated or disgusted retire to private life.

In short, the Conservative Dilemma can lead to very frightening outcomes. But those outcomes are not inevitable. In the late nineteenth and early twentieth centuries, some conservative parties in highly unequal societies endangered democracy by opening Pandora's box. But many others, facing the same challenges, found a successful resolution without doing so, surviving the transition from elite bastion to successful mass party. They managed to maintain elite attachments but also respond, at least partially, to the pressing economic concerns of a broader electorate. They managed to find noneconomic appeals that could attract the loyalty of voters of all classes, but also retained control over how these potentially explosive issues entered the political mainstream. Construction of a strong party apparatus helped party leaders remain ascendant over the more extremist elements within their coalition and encouraged them to play by the rules rather than flouting them.

The conservative parties that successfully managed this transformation were hardly pure—in the world of mass politics, no prominent parties, left or right, can plausibly claim to be. Yet they became robust competitors without handing over power to volatile surrogates or resorting to systematic rigging. In the process they played a vital role in stabilizing democracies. Few conservative parties managed the challenge more successfully than the oldest continuous major party in Europe, the Conservative Party of Britain.

BRITAIN WAS AMONG THE FIRST European powers to wrestle with the Conservative Dilemma. Lord Robert Cecil, later to be Conservative Party leader and prime minister, put the challenge bluntly in the mid-nineteenth century as he observed the growing popular clamor for political reform. Echoing John Adams, this member of the landed aristocracy predicted that expanding the electorate would mean "that the whole community shall be governed by an ignorant multitude, the creature of a vast and powerful organization, of which a few half-taught and cunning agitators are the head . . . in short, that the rich shall pay all the taxes, and the poor shall make all the laws."[10]

When Lord Cecil wrote these frightened words, Britain had already embarked on a long-term transformation from control by landed elites toward mass democracy. Facing popular pressure, Parliament expanded the suffrage in 1832, 1867, 1884, and 1918. The Conservative Party frequently resisted—equating political reform with the demise of the party, the nation, or both. In some instances, Tory leaders would come to support the extension of voting rights only under duress, or in search of short-term tactical advantages. Lord Cecil's observations explain the Tories' reticence: as defenders of established economic elites, they feared they would be unable to compete in the new political world.[11]

The fear was well-founded. As Conservatives embraced protectionist agricultural policies that propped up the incomes of landowners at the expense of workers and businesses, the party suffered at the polls. Between 1857 and 1886, they only once won a parliamentary majority, while on three other occasions they managed to cobble together weak and short-lived minority governments. The Liberals, who more rapidly embraced economic and political reform, became the nation's leading party.[12]

Yet these struggling Tories would overcome the Conservative Dilemma. Even as they suffered setbacks in national elections, British Conservatives were remaking their party and learning to compete effectively. In time, they would become the nation's dominant political force, a foundation stone for one of the world's most stable political systems, and the most durably successful conservative party in the history of democracy. In the twentieth century, Conservative prime ministers—Winston Churchill and Margaret Thatcher among them—governed for a total of fifty-seven years.[13]

Crafting a successful strategy took decades of experimentation and struggle, carried out under a succession of leaders of varying capacities and relying on the hidden labors of now-forgotten political operatives. Despite Lord Cecil's fears, British Conservatives fashioned a robust party organization that could appeal to the poor as well as the rich, and to everyone in between. Moreover, the Tories managed to do so while making only modest economic concessions, leaving the elite's privileges diminished but still considerable.

The foundation for this extraordinary feat is encapsulated in a line frequently attributed to Tory prime minister Benjamin Disraeli—that he saw working-class Britons as "angels in Marble." Just as Michelangelo could first discern and then release a sculpture from unformed stone, a skilled politician could summon forth the loyal working-class Tory. The actual phrase comes not from Disraeli but from the *Times* of London in 1883:

> What distinguished Lord Beaconsfield [Disraeli] from the ordinary Tory leaders was his readiness to trust the English people whom they did not trust, and his total indifference to the barriers of caste, which for them were the be-all and end-all of politics. In the inarticulate mass of the English populace

which they held at arm's length he discerned the Conservative working man, as the sculptor perceives the angel prisoned in a block of marble. He understood that the common Englishman, even when he personally has nothing to guard beyond a narrow income and a frugal home, has yet Conservative instincts as strong as those of the wealthiest peer.[14]

The writer does not specify what he meant by the "Conservative instincts" of the "common Englishman." But readers at the time surely understood well enough. In a democratizing but highly unequal country, ordinary voters did not have deeply "conservative instincts" about economic policy. British Conservatives did, when necessary, give ground on economic issues and political reform. At the heart of Tory success, however, was the articulation and promotion of another set of issues that would resonate with voters. Conservatives harnessed—and, for the most part, domesticated—the forces of nationalism (by supporting and expanding the Empire), religion (by maintaining the preeminence of the Anglican church), and tradition (by backing the monarchy).

Perhaps most important, these forces were simultaneously mobilized and contained. As we have already seen, such social divisions, once inflamed, can quickly engulf a nation's politics. According to Ziblatt, the Conservative Party's increasing organizational capacity helped Britain avoid this fate. Beginning in the mid-1800s, the Tories built robust networks that reached into local communities. In 1883, a small group of leading Tories, including Lord Randolph Churchill (Winston's father), founded and rapidly expanded the Primrose League, named for Disraeli's favorite flower; Queen Victoria had sent a wreath of primroses to the funeral of her beloved prime minister. A cross-class organization, the Primrose League mixed social activities with conservative themes ("to Uphold and support God, Queen and Country, and the Conservative cause").[15]

Over many decades, the Conservatives summoned these sentiments in electoral campaigns, building a mass following that eventually surpassed the Liberals'. After 1900, the Labour Party rose to challenge the Liberals from the left on economic issues, setting off a three-way struggle for political supremacy. Britain's first-past-the-post electoral system, however, was built for two. Eventually it would be the Conservatives, not the Liberals, who emerged as Labour's enduring rival.[16]

Only once during this political ascent, in the midst of the fierce struggle over Irish Home Rule, did the Tories threaten to open Pandora's box. Having lost in a landslide to the Liberals in 1906, many conservatives feared they had entered an irreversible political decline. Their confidence in democracy wavering, the Tories used the explosive issue of Irish Home Rule to go on the offensive, stoking anti-Catholic sentiment and nationalist loyalties and framing the issue as one of British survival. To a degree never before seen in modern British politics, Conservative leaders proved willing to challenge constitutional norms and political stability. In response to emerging Liberal plans for Home Rule, they made thinly veiled threats of violent resistance. Prominent conservatives signaled support for military insubordination to civilian authority.[17]

Existential fears about the future of the party helped drive Conservative politicians to take these dangerously destabilizing stances. Party leaders also faced intense pressure from activists, ambitious political rivals, and elements of the conservative media, who lobbied for confrontation. In the end, the forces of disruption were quelled. Tory leaders, drawing on the organizational resources and voter loyalty they had developed over two generations, were able to hold off extremists within the party ranks. They stayed within the confines of a democratic system and gradually regained political strength. In 1918, they would win a landslide victory over their long-time nemesis the Liberals, who never recovered.

The reactionary British aristocrat, struggling helplessly to hold back the rising tides of capitalism and democracy, is a standard cultural trope. In the television show *Downton Abbey*, it takes a mild and sympathetic form. Lord Grantham grumbles about the death of the old ways, but (encouraged by his modern and pragmatic American spouse) he faces the aristocracy's slow decline with a stiff upper lip. Unfortunately, a darker framing is more in line with the historical reality of the Conservative Dilemma. In Kazuo Ishiguro's *The*

Remains of the Day, the naïve and pompous Lord Darlington works to promote friendly relations with Hitler's Germany. The same occurs, this time rooted in fact, in Netflix's *The Crown*, in which the former king, the Duke of Windsor (a critic of "slip-shod democracy"), engages in dalliances with the Nazis that may have spilled over from sympathy to complicity.[18]

The crucial point, however, is that in British politics such reactionary figures were largely pushed to the side. After World War I, British Conservatives, working within democratic institutions, would emerge as the nation's dominant political power. They would hold this position, with intermittent interludes of Labour governance, for the next hundred years.

Eventually British conservatives tamed or marginalized the party's extremist elements. Across the channel, however, their cousins (sometimes literally so) chose a different way to deal with the Conservative Dilemma.

STUDENTS OF DEMOCRACY have long been fixated on the catastrophic experience of Germany's Weimar Republic and the rise of Hitler's Third Reich. Like the British Tories, German conservatives struggled to find their footing within an emerging and highly unequal democracy. Unlike the Tories, they never found it. A seemingly endless series of factional battles culminated in the defeat of moderate pragmatists at the hands of radicals. The crucial center-right space, so vital to the creation of stable democracy and weak from the beginning in Germany, emptied entirely. Hard-right conservatives amplified fierce social divisions. As Germany's leading conservative party moved further right, its actions strengthened still more radical forces. Attempting to simultaneously compete with and exploit a demagogue, conservative political elites accomplished neither. Instead, they ended up helping Hitler seize power.

When Germany made its first halting steps toward democracy in the last third of the nineteenth century, its conservative parties faced formidable competitors—especially Europe's strongest social democratic party, the SPD, but also the (Catholic) Center Party and, eventually, the Communists. These competitors were well positioned to win over an expanding working-class electorate with economic appeals (in the case of the Center Party, grounded in Catholic theology). Conservatives—tightly linked with the powerful landed aristocracy and, later, with German industrial barons—would have to hone an effective electoral message.[19]

In key respects, the German setting was starkly different from the British one. Prior to the First World War, Germany had universal male suffrage, but for the bulk of voters, the ballot didn't mean much. Not only was the power of the elected parliament restricted, but Prussia, the heartland of conservative strength, employed a "three-tier" voting system that radically underweighted working-class and middle-class voters. Prussian representatives in turn exercised an effective veto power in the national parliament, allowing them to protect their narrow interests in a manner somewhat akin to the role the Senate filibuster played in preserving white supremacy in the American South.[20]

As if this highly skewed system wasn't bad enough, it was propped up by systematic fraud. The social dominance of local elites meant that elections were held against a backdrop of coercion, especially in the countryside. There were no secret ballots, and local landlords often doubled as election officials. Supervisors could march tenants to the polls, where they might hand over a color-coded ballot to their landlord. At the same time, election intimidation and manipulation were more widespread in parts of Germany where employment was concentrated in a few large industrial firms.[21]

Nineteenth-century British elections were hardly fair. (Gerrymandering was often extreme, as the UK coinage "rotten boroughs" suggests.) Yet these contests gradually became more equitable through a series of incremental reforms. As we have seen, from early on the Tories labored to construct an organizational apparatus and persuasive appeals for voter mobilization, giving them confidence that they could compete with parties to their left. Fatefully, Germany's conservative elites failed to adapt, remaining disdainful of democracy and confident of their right to rule. In 1912, the party leader of the German Conservative Party (DKP) in the Prussian State Assembly decried universal suffrage as "an attack against the basic laws of nature, according to which the capable, the best and the worthiest contribute to a country's fate."[22]

Thus, German conservatives, protected by a state they viewed as their own and able to bolster that advantage by cheating, failed to equip themselves for robust electoral competition. When that competition intensified and ill-prepared German conservatives scrambled to catch up, they turned to already established pressure groups that knew how to reach voters. The reliance of German conservatives on surrogates would have dire consequences. It weakened the party's own efforts to build loyalties, made it harder for party leaders to craft more inclusive appeals, and eventually left the party vulnerable to an extremist takeover.

Though conservative politicians in office were generally preoccupied with winning elections and hence inclined toward compromise, pressure groups had different priorities. Above all, they needed to sustain their organization by keeping members riled up. Typically, the most intense and active members were prone to extremism. Unlike in Britain, the balance between these outside groups and professional politicians tilted toward the outsiders. Prominent right-wing groups that were brought into the conservative orbit included the ultra-nationalist and imperialist Pan-German Association, assorted networks of virulent anti-Semites, and the powerful Agrarian League—an organization of landowners and farmers that, around the turn of the century, boasted 160,000 members, a huge staff in Berlin, and top officials who occupied many important offices within the DKP. These and other groups would retain considerable autonomy and influence until the end of the Weimar Republic.[23]

In Britain, the transition to democracy had been a slow and gradual ascent. In Germany, it was a long-delayed and then dizzyingly rapid climb. When the monarchy, which had only the most minimal democratic features, collapsed at the end of World War I, it was replaced by the Weimar Republic, ushering in a full-fledged, if turbulent, democracy. Amid the upheaval, the main conservative forces coalesced within the German National People's Party (DNVP). It combined several precursor political factions, most importantly the extremely conservative DKP, from which much of the DNVP leadership would come.

The newly constituted DNVP sought to establish itself as the dominant conservative party within Germany's new multiparty system. Associated with the discredited pre-1918 regime, it called for the restoration of the monarchy and thus started out on the defensive. As the right gradually recovered, however, so did the DNVP. By the mid-1920s, it won around 20 percent of the national vote in two consecutive elections. In Germany's multiparty system, this made it the nation's second largest party after the SPD. Prominent figures within the party looked to the British conservatives as a possible model. They referred to the prospects of creating what one prominent historian called *Tory-Konservativen*—a conservatism capable of ruling and comfortable within the confines of parliamentary democracy. But while pragmatists saw this model as an aspiration, their radical opponents within the party treated it as an epithet. The radicals feared that the party's moderates would abandon core principles—support for Empire and monarchy, opposition to labor unions, hatred of the welfare state—and make their peace with the Weimar system they loathed.[24]

In fact, the party's moderates were trying to do just that, though reluctantly. In the mid-1920s, the DNVP twice entered government, accepting powerful ministries. A DNVP representative became president of the *Reichstag*, the German parliament. Party members provided crucial support for major initiatives to stabilize the fledgling Republic over the howls of the nationalist right. During this brief "golden age," the Weimar Republic seemed to be inching along the path toward stable democracy. A conservative but modernizing DNVP would have to be a central part of this emergent system.[25]

But the DNVP would abandon that path. Battered by economic crisis and repeated humiliations at the hands of other nations, Germany's weakly institutionalized democracy began to founder. What political scientists call "anti-system" parties, ones that refused to accept the Weimar Republic's legitimacy, grew on both the left and the right, waging street battles amid growing rumors of coups and fears of civil war. The already shrinking space for democratic politics contracted still further as leading conservatives, aristocrats, and military figures pursued their own narrow and personal agendas, their maneuvering undercutting parliament and mainstream parties. A shared commitment to reactionary politics and a pronounced (and justified) insecurity about their capacity to compete effectively in the electoral arena made these leading figures unwilling to cooperate with pro-Weimar parties to their left, even as the regime's crisis deepened. Instead, they encouraged Germany's aging president Paul von Hindenburg to turn his back on democratic politics, to rely on emergency power decrees and on shifting and narrowing political coalitions, and eventually to invite Adolf Hitler to form a government.

Though hardly the only cause of the Weimar Republic's tragic collapse, the suicidal radicalization of the DNVP represented a critical and revealing subplot. At the center of this story was Alfred Hugenberg, who personified much of what went wrong on the German right. Long a prominent figure in German politics, Hugenberg had been one of the founders of the hard-right nationalist Pan-German League in the 1890s. Originally a civil servant, he had moved into business and eventually rose to be a member of the board of Krupp Industries, the powerful armaments manufacturer.

From this perch, Hugenberg built a formidable political base. He drew on his industrial connections to found a communications empire, eventually owning a number of prominent newspapers, a major advertising firm, and, most important, the wire service employed by much of the nation's press. Hugenberg wielded his media power to push radically nationalist themes, relentlessly promoting the toxic idea that cooperating with the Weimar Republic constituted treason. His prodigious fundraising only reinforced his influence. He became the main conduit for political money from industrialists and thus a dominant financial power within the DNVP.

Hugenberg cultivated party activists as well as financing them. Power in the DNVP depended on the loyalties of regional associations, which played the critical role of selecting legislative candidates as well as the party's leader. The activists who ran the associations were often ideological extremists or fixated on protecting narrow interests. They reveled in Hugenberg's attacks on those who would compromise the right's cherished principles.[26]

While Hugenberg appealed to the party base, less extreme conservatives who advocated participation in government found themselves pressured from both sides. They depended on the expressions of outrage that attracted voters to the party, but the realities of coalition government also required them to compromise. Most notoriously (in the eyes of party radicals), DNVP legislators had provided the support necessary to pass the Dawes Plan for World War I reparations payments. Given the desperate state of the German economy, many industrialists supported the Dawes Plan, which helps to account for why some DNVP legislators backed the measure. Yet activists on the nationalist right regarded both the initiative and its supporters as traitorous.

Hugenberg seized the moment. When the DNVP suffered a serious setback in the May 1928 election, winning just under 15 percent of the national vote, he attacked the weakened moderates. Drawing on the support of the party's activist base, Hugenberg became the party's new leader in October 1928. Once there, he sought to purify the DNVP by forcing a series of confrontations with more moderate members of parliament. They responded with mass resignations, cutting the party's already diminished parliamentary representation in half.

Not only did moderates desert the party; so did more reactionary elements. In 1929, Hugenberg had tried to mobilize voters by pursuing a referendum for a "Law against the Enslavement of the German People" that would make it a crime for German government officials to sign or enforce the Young Plan (an international agreement that had been intended to soften some of the conditions of the Dawes Plan). In doing so, Hugenberg aligned himself with the Nazis and their extremist but captivating leader.

Yet sharing a stage with Hitler only legitimated him. As a peddler of mass outrage, the stuffy and uncharismatic Hugenberg was hopelessly outclassed. The party's remaining voters switched to the Nazis in droves. The infamous September 1930 election saw a huge surge for Hitler's party, while the DNVP received a feeble 7 percent of the vote. In just under two years, the party Hugenberg had captured was effectively destroyed as an electoral force.[27]

Still craving power but now lacking an electoral base, Hugenberg chose to form an "alliance" with Hitler. His prominence (and self-delusion) allowed him to believe that he could exploit the rising Nazis, even as his own political extremism and sabotage of the moderates within the DNVP had shattered the party and helped open the space for Hitler's rise. In the end, he and other overconfident reactionaries dug their own political graves along with that of the Weimar Republic.

In Germany, unlike Britain, right-wing elites and their political allies failed to manage the Conservative Dilemma. With a weak party organization and a reluctance to compromise with rising democratic forces, they struggled to compete in a transformed political context in which extreme inequality made their long-standing allegiance to elites a liability rather than an asset. Their choices helped unleash forces of extremism that first captured and then fractured their own party. From this weakened position, they foolishly partnered with a political outsider particularly skilled at stoking racism, tribalism, and fear. In doing so, they opened the door to Nazism and world war.

ALTHOUGH THE CONTRASTING historical experiences of Britain and Germany reveal that the choices of conservative parties are crucial, the Conservative Dilemma is a structural feature of any democracy in which economic elites and ordinary voters are pulling those parties in conflicting directions. In Latin America—the continent most familiar with the challenge of combining extreme inequality and mass democracy—scholars have identified the same basic dynamic. Successful conservative parties, in the words of one expert, manage the inherent conflict within their coalition by "weakening class-based solidarity [among voters] and replacing it with other sources of collective identity." As in Europe, where Latin American conservatives failed to create well-institutionalized and electorally competitive center-right parties, political systems were vulnerable to breakdown in the face of extreme inequality. As two leading scholars put it, unless the parties representing the privileged "can muster enough votes to stay in the game, they are likely to desert the electoral process in favor of antidemocratic conspiracy and destabilization." Argentina, Brazil, and Chile are just a few of the countries where democracy at some point collapsed under the weight of these pressures.[28]

Nor has the United States escaped the tensions that produce the Conservative Dilemma, even though there is no easy analogy to be made to Germany, Britain, or Latin American nations. At the time of the nation's founding, economic inequality was seen as a pressing matter (as John Adams noted), but income and wealth were in fact far more widely distributed than they were in the older nations of Europe with their aristocratic heritage. Property ownership was of course highly skewed, and slavery represented the most profound inequality of all. Yet everywhere democracy gets its start within a restricted circle, and among white men, wealth was much less concentrated in the United States than it was elsewhere. Compared with Europe at the time, the American economic divide was narrower, the imbalances of power smaller, and the threat to elites from the nation's still-tentative democracy weaker. On top of this, the country was riven by a sectional cleavage over slavery that subordinated other divides.[29]

American democracy began to take form earlier in the United States than in Europe, part of a wave of democratization that took place in relatively egalitarian settler societies (the United States, Australia, Canada, New Zealand). As the United States industrialized, however, inequality increased rapidly, approaching European levels. When it did, the Conservative Dilemma emerged as well.[30]

It did so, however, in a distinctive manner that reflected the deep legacies of both slavery and America's early democratization. In the aftermath of the Civil War, the economic elite was spread across the two major political parties. In the rapidly industrializing North, the commercial and financial elite came to dominate the Republican Party. In the still agrarian South, large landowners were Democrats, forming the bedrock of opposition to the Party of Lincoln.

In the 1890s, both North and South experienced growing class tensions. In both regions, elites had long used racial and ethnic enmities to divide the have-nots from the have-almost-nothings. With the rise of economic populists in the South and West, though, multiracial coalitions of the economically disadvantaged became plausible. When a "fusion" ticket of Populists and Republicans gained power in Wilmington, North Carolina, white Democrats staged a violent coup, and after regaining control stripped blacks and poor whites of access to the ballot box. The construction of Jim Crow and the restriction of the franchise, already well under way throughout the South, accelerated. Southern elites were responding to the Conservative Dilemma in the worst possible fashion: they stoked racism, and where that was insufficient, they starved democracy.[31]

In the North, the intensifying class conflict of the Gilded Age came to a head in 1896. Democratic presidential candidate William Jennings Bryan, backed by rising populist sentiment in the farm states, tried to unite those forces with a rapidly growing and frustrated industrial working class. Nervous business elites rallied around the Republican William McKinley. At a time of economic distress, it didn't help Bryan's chances that a Democrat, Grover Cleveland, was currently president. McKinley also made effective appeals to working-class voters in the industrial heartland, reached out to immigrants, insisted that protectionism was vital for industrial workers, and promoted fears of Bryan's monetary policies. In what is reported to have been the most expensive American election ever (as a share of the economy), McKinley vastly outspent Bryan and won a decisive victory.[32]

Yet while the elite-dominated Republicans won this key battle, they also began to make economic concessions as the progressive wing of their party grew. Especially after Theodore Roosevelt took office following McKinley's assassination in 1901, the GOP responded to the Conservative Dilemma by moderating on economic issues and embracing some democratizing reforms. They also relied on sectional, religious, and ethnic cleavages to sustain electoral support. Then, the Great Depression and World War II—and the egalitarian reforms associated with the New Deal—dramatically reduced

America's extreme inequality, ushering in a long period marked by middle-class prosperity. For a generation, the Republican Party settled into the moderate center-right position it was to abandon when the Conservative Dilemma reappeared.[33]

THE HISTORICAL RECORD REVEALS a clear pattern. Whenever economic elites have grossly disproportionate power and come to see their economic interests as opposed to those of ordinary citizens, they are likely to promote social divisions. They are also likely to come to fear a fair democratic process in which those citizens have significant clout. These elite responses to extreme inequality enter into politics mainly through conservative parties, which must navigate the tension between unequal influence and democratic competition. The Conservative Dilemma is not a problem of a particular moment. It is a problem inherent in democratic politics in contexts of extreme inequality.

Today many countries are experiencing rising inequality. Yet what's going on in the United States is distinctive. Not only has inequality grown spectacularly; it has grown in precisely the manner most likely to worsen the tensions at the heart of democracy. A tiny segment of Americans has catapulted to pinnacles of wealth and income never before seen in a democratic society. We're virtually alone in these respects. Among rich democracies, Israel keeps us company, and it is no coincidence that it has produced its own version of plutocratic populism, as a conservative coalition has pursued starkly inegalitarian policies while abetting and harnessing ethnic resentment and fear. Mostly, however, the countries that come closest to sharing our current distribution of income and wealth are autocracies, such as China and Russia.

There are good reasons to be skeptical of facile analogies to the past. A century separates most of the episodes recounted in this chapter from the troubles of our times. As we have noted, democracies in rich societies tend to be self-reinforcing. For all their imperfections, they tend not only to deliver broad prosperity, but also to encourage key groups in society to adapt to their rules and expectations. In the

United States, the world's oldest democracy, these rules and expectations are long-standing.

But the history chronicled in this chapter also reminds us that rapidly rising inequality creates tensions for democratic politics, and that these tensions are greatest when inequality takes the winner-take-all form it has taken in the United States. It also reminds us that these tensions—rooted in the growing divergence of power, interests, and commitment to democracy that extreme economic divisions produce—are greatest for a nation's conservative party.

As American inequality increased, America's conservative party confronted those tensions. Republicans had new incentives to deliver for the economy's biggest winners, especially as the influence of those winners grew. They also faced new challenges attracting support among the vast majority of Americans on the losing side of inequality's rise. Like conservatives of the past, Republicans had a choice. They could embrace a policy agenda more favorable to struggling families. They could welcome racial minorities and recent immigrants under their party's big tent. They could promote "conservative instincts" rooted in broad appeals—patriotism, celebrations of families and communities, private and civic problem-solving.

Or they could double down in support of America's emerging plutocracy.

Chapter 2

REPUBLICANS EMBRACE PLUTOCRACY

EXTREME INEQUALITY CREATES three fundamental threats to healthy democratic politics: divergent elite interests, disproportionate elite power, and diminished elite commitment to democracy itself. In the United States, all three of these threats increased as inequality rose after 1980, and all put growing pressure on America's two major parties. Yet, as in the early twentieth century, the most dramatic shifts occurred on the conservative side of the partisan divide. As the concentration of wealth and power at the top increased, the Democratic Party faced cross-pressures that muddied its message and moderated its stances on economic matters. The Republican Party, in stark contrast, radicalized. Starting as a standard-issue center-right party, it mutated into an ultraconservative insurgent force, one that cast its lot with plutocracy even as plutocracy's rise endangered the economic security and opportunity of many of its voters.

To see this, we need to step back from our present moment. Because inequality has increased gradually and seemingly inexorably, it is easy to miss just how profoundly it has transformed our society and our politics. A longer perspective reveals the scope of the change. It also shows how it has reignited the political dangers described in the previous chapter.

The place to start is with another Republican president who tried to forge an electoral majority by exploiting white working-class discontent, Richard M. Nixon. The ways Nixon's "Southern Strategy" helped seed the ground for Trump's brand of right-wing populism are now well recognized. Much less recognized, but equally revealing, are the ways it did not. In a far more equal political economy, Nixon's bid for white nonaffluent voters looked very different from the one that would be launched by an even more controversial Republican a generation on.

IN APRIL 1970, NIXON RECEIVED A MEMO from the Labor Department entitled "The Problem of the Blue-Collar Worker." Sixteen months earlier, Nixon had entered the Oval Office after a narrow electoral win—a victory that, like Trump's, ended eight years of Democratic control of the White House. Now, he was seeking to expand his unexpectedly strong margins among a group of voters long loyal to the Democratic Party, a demographic we would now call the white working class.

"Recent reports have identified the economic insecurity and alienation which whites in this group have felt," the memo began. It then catalogued a long list of problems: "educated workers . . . have been getting the biggest pay gains"; "blue-collar workers . . . feel most threatened by automation"; "the children of this group in our society are not 'making it' to the same degree as are children in the middle and upper-middle classes." Yet the conclusions that surely most interested Nixon concerned not workers' problems but their politics. "The blue-collar worker is more prone to transfer his economic and social frustrations to racial and ethnic prejudices," the memo noted. It also suggested that the resentment felt by white workers created opportunities for outreach: "They are overripe for a political response to the pressing needs they feel so keenly. . . . they feel like 'forgotten people'—those for whom the government and the society have limited, if any, direct concern and little visible action." After reading the memo, Nixon ordered his top aides to figure out how to get those forgotten people to vote for him in 1972.[1]

Long before the ascent of Donald Trump, in short, a Republican president tried to realign the electorate through appeals to white workers discomfited by racial and cultural change. Yet *how* Nixon appealed to these voters shows just how fundamentally the

American economic and political order has changed since his time. Nixon moved right on race and culture—though not nearly as far as the GOP would later go. Building on his 1968 Southern Strategy, his coded rhetoric signaled the Republican Party's sympathy for those who were unenthusiastic about the civil rights movement. Yet he pushed his party left on economic policy, cultivating labor leaders and largely ignoring business groups. In British politics, he might have been called a "red Tory," a conservative who embraced the welfare state to carve his own working-class angels out of marble.[2]

In historical memory, Nixon's economic policies have been overshadowed by his aggressive posture abroad and the Watergate scandal at home. But Nixon was a big spender who signed on to a huge expansion of Social Security and nationalized the Food Stamps program; a social policy innovator who supported a guaranteed family income and national health plan; a Keynesian pump-primer who imposed wage and price controls; and a command-and-control regulator who established a string of agencies protecting workers, consumers, and the environment—from the Environmental Protection Agency, to the Occupational Safety and Health Administration, to the Consumer Product Safety Commission. On racial and cultural issues, Nixon was the harbinger of a new kind of Republicanism in the White House. On economic policy, he was the last social democrat of the twentieth century.[3]

Nearly all of Nixon's red-Tory forays faced intense business opposition. But the president was untroubled. He believed the Republican Party's tilt toward corporate and economic elites was an electoral liability, especially with the less affluent white voters he was courting most aggressively. Nor did he think those elites were organized or powerful enough to push back effectively. When business leaders complained about his wage and price controls, for example, Nixon didn't back down; he sent his treasury secretary to the US Chamber of Commerce's annual convention to berate them for their own inability to deal with inflation.[4]

Meanwhile, Nixon aggressively courted organized labor, which was then, in the words of one historian, "the best-funded and most powerful interest group in Washington." Even as the corporate community lined up against many of his policies, Nixon wooed labor bosses with everything from policy proposals and pro-labor rhetoric to golf outings and invitations to the White House. When a top official in the Commerce Department urged "a more antagonistic stance toward organized labor," one of Nixon's top aides fired back: "This President, regardless of what the business community urges, what the polls show, or what Republican orthodoxy would dictate, is not going to do anything that undermines the working man's economic status."[5]

Nixon's combination of racialized appeals and lunch-pail economics took inspiration from Kevin Phillips's book, *The Emerging Republican Majority*—the publishing sensation that turned the unknown twenty-something, fresh out of law school and a stint on Nixon's 1968 campaign, into the party's top young strategist. Phillips believed the GOP would never get more than a tiny share of black votes. Yet the expansion of voting rights in the South was nonetheless an opportunity, because it would drive "negrophobe" white voters (Phillips's coinage) into the Republican fold. To reap these rewards, however, Nixon would not only have to signal his sympathies to resentful whites, Phillips argued. He would also have to dispel "[f]ears that a Republican administration would undermine Social Security, Medicare, collective bargaining and aid to education."[6]

In seeking his emerging majority, in other words, Nixon paired resentment and reassurance, employing "dog-whistle" racial appeals but also affirming the New Deal's commitments to a strong welfare state and federal support for organized labor. For a canny conservative seeking to realign American politics, this combination made sense. The business lobby and the wealthy were captured constituencies with limited power to insist on their demands. Organized labor and working-class voters, by contrast, had the clout not only to deliver electoral wins but also to challenge corporate priorities, in Washington as well as the workplace. At a time when wages were growing and unions strong, trust in government was high and inequality continuing to fall, Nixon faced an opportunity, not a dilemma. Because the party could take for granted its old economic backers, it could direct its policies toward new electoral blocs. As a result, Nixon envisioned a Republican Party that moved left on economics while moving right on race, appealing to the pocketbooks as well as the prejudices of "the forgotten Americans."[7]

THE NIXON MEMO NOW READS like the product of an archeological dig—a description of a society buried in the rubble of America's inequality explosion. In one passage, the memo reports that blue-collar workers "had increased their incomes by only 84 percent between 1949 and 1968." The "only" is a reminder that, despite the increasing economic turbulence of the early 1970s, the forty years after 1940 were a time of widely distributed affluence, as workers' productivity and pay increased rapidly and in tandem.[8]

Not so the last forty years. Statistics about America's extreme inequality have become so familiar that they have lost their power to shock. But consider Figure 1, which shows the changing distribution of national income from 1980 to 2016. During this period, the share of income accruing to the richest 1 percent of households doubled, increasing from just over 10 percent to more than 20 percent. Over the same period, the share of national income accruing to the bottom half of households declined by half, from (roughly) 20 percent to 10 percent. In other words, these two groups—the top 1 percent and the bottom 50 percent—switched places. The top now has what the (fifty times larger) bottom used to have.

The transformation charted in Figure 1 is arguably even greater than these two crossing trajectories suggest. For one, the top 1 percent is actually too broad a group to truly reveal the sharp tilt of the American economy toward the superrich. Most of the top 1 percent's rising share has in fact accrued to those in the top 0.1 percent (the richest 1 in 1,000 Americans). According to tax records, the majority of these big winners from the winner-take-all economy are not media stars or celebrity athletes, but corporate and financial executives—the main beneficiaries of regulatory and tax policies friendly to large corporations and Wall Street.[9]

For another, the story of America's inequality explosion is not

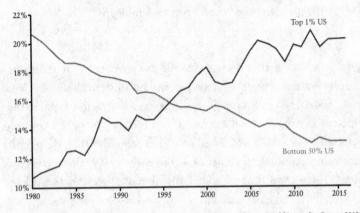

Figure 1

THE RISE OF THE TOP 1 PERCENT AND FALL OF THE BOTTOM 50 PERCENT, 1980–2016

Source: Facundo Alvaredo, Lucas Chancel, Thomas Piketty, and Emmanuel Saez, *World Inequality Report 2018* (Paris: World Inequality Lab, 2017). See https://wir2018.wid.world for data series and notes.

In 1980, 11 percent of national income was received by the top 1 percent in the United States, compared with 21 percent received by the bottom 50 percent. In 2016, 20 percent of national income was received by the top 1 percent in the United States, compared with 13 percent received by the bottom 50 percent.

the "trickle down" scenario so beloved by inequality's defenders, in which growth was rapid for all economic groups, just more rapid for the top group. In fact, there has been little or no growth for nearly everyone below the top. Meanwhile, growth at the top has been extraordinary—year after year, in all regions of the nation, during booms and recessions, and for more than a generation. We can see this most clearly in the steady disappearance of the kind of upward mobility that defined the American Dream. It used to be that almost all kids grew up to have higher incomes than their parents. Among the most recent generation to reach middle age, however, barely over half exceeded their parents' incomes. And the main reason for this collapse in mobility is that our economy now showers most of its rewards on the highest-income households.[10]

Nor are inequality's broader effects limited to mobility. A wide range of fundamental social outcomes track rising inequality, including disparities in health, gaps in college completion, and inequalities in access to affordable housing. According to many of these crucial measures, the gap between rich and poor is now at least as large as the gap between black and white—that is, at least as large as a social and economic divide so deep and pernicious that generations of thinkers have questioned the very capacity of our society to grapple with it.[11]

America's skyrocketing inequality also looks very different from the experience of rich nations across the Atlantic. Figure 2 shows the parallel trends of the top 1 percent and the bottom 50 percent in Western Europe. There is no comparison: the share of income going to the top 1 percent in Europe was relatively stable over the past generation, even while it was rising dramatically in the United States. Meanwhile, the relative standing of the middle and bottom has fallen much more in the United States than in other rich nations.[12]

American wealth inequality is also unusually high. Wealth—what

Figure 2
CONTRASTING TRENDS OF THE TOP 1 PERCENT AND THE BOTTOM 50 PERCENT IN WESTERN EUROPE

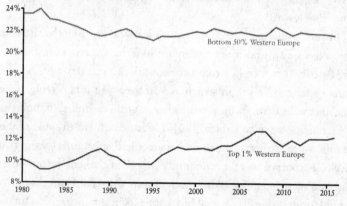

Source: *World Inequality Report.* See https://wir2018.wid.world for data series and notes.

In 1980, 10 percent of national income was received by the top 1 percent in Western Europe, compared with 24 percent received by the bottom 50 percent. In 2016, 12 percent of national income was received by the top 1 percent in Western Europe, compared with 22 percent received by the bottom 50 percent.

households own, such as real estate and financial assets—is critical to both economic opportunity and political influence, and the United States once stood out for its broad distribution. In *Capital in the Twenty-First Century*, Thomas Piketty shows that as late as the early twentieth century, American levels of wealth inequality were lower than in Europe. But wealth inequality in the United States is now higher than in Europe. And unlike in Europe, it's rising toward its historical peak—levels that, when reached in the past, were seen as preludes to political upheaval or even social revolution.[13]

And while inequality in the United States is advancing toward historical highs, the organized power of workers is retreating toward historical lows. Today, despite polls showing widespread interest in joining a union, the share of the private workforce that belongs to one is barely over 6 percent, a level not seen since the 1920s. The rise of inequality and fall of unions are closely linked. Not only do unions raise worker pay. They are also one of the few organized interests that have consistently advocated on behalf of less affluent Americans. Compared to the private unionization rates of Western European democracies—countries in which, on average, a third or so of private workers are represented by unions (and an even larger share benefit from union contracts)—America's rate is essentially a rounding error.[14]

In sum, American inequality looks less and less like the situation of Nixon's day, and more and more like the situation confronting the British Tories and German conservatives a century ago. Nixon's career spanned an era in which almost everyone was getting richer and inequality was falling—the classic positive-sum dynamic that makes democracy so robust. It also spanned an era in which labor unions were strong and ordinary voters had substantial sway relative to corporations and economic elites. Thus, when Nixon moved right on race and culture, his motives were different from those that would animate similar Republican appeals in the future. He turned to strategies of outrage-stoking not to make up for conservative economic policies—in fact, he embraced the popular legacies of the New Deal—but to augment his reelection margins and accelerate a Republican realignment.[15]

Within a few decades, however, the growing resource and power gap between the rich and the rest—and the divergent interests and commitments that came with it—would put the GOP in a tightening vise. To build and maintain power in a transformed economic world, Republicans would have to confront the Conservative Dilemma.

In 1995, *Washington Post* columnist Steven Pearlstein observed that "the income gap between rich and poor has become the central issue in American politics, and the party that figures out what to do about it—or makes the right noises about it—will dominate American politics."[16]

Pearlstein did not elaborate on why the "income gap" had become so pressing. Had he done so, he might have concluded that it had been "the central issue" in American politics for some time, just an issue that many in power didn't want to talk about. During the Reagan years, Republicans and conservative Democrats—responding to more aggressive business lobbying as well as the popular tax revolts of the late 1970s—put in place a range of policies that fostered winner-take-all inequality. These included weakened labor laws, lower corporate and income tax rates, and reduced constraints on corporate pay and high-risk financial engineering. Broad economic pressures, such as globalization of trade and finance and technological change, contributed to rising inequality as well. Yet it was how American political leaders responded (or failed to respond) to these pressures that was decisive in sending the United States down its distinctive path toward the stark divisions to which Pearlstein called attention in 1995.

Still, Pearlstein's words remind us that both parties had to grapple with inequality as it became more salient—and both had options for doing so. Although the Republican Party was unmistakably a center-right party in the early 1990s, it was by no means monolithically committed to the contemporary GOP program of tax cuts for the rich, hostility to the welfare state, and rollback of labor, environmental, financial, and consumer protections. In fact, President George H. W. Bush—the Republican who would lose his bid for reelection to Bill Clinton in 1992—raised taxes on high earners in 1990 and backed the Americans with Disabilities Act and a major expansion of the Clean Air Act. Nor was he a singular figure within his party: he represented a sizable, if shrinking, Republican wing that still prized bipartisanship and believed in fiscal restraint, progressive taxation, and active regulation of the economy.[17]

Yet, by the end of the 1990s, this economically moderate wing was in rapid decline. In the space of just a few election cycles, a new Republican Party emerged. Between Bush's loss in 1992 and his son's controversial victory in 2000, Republican leaders wrestled with the reemerging Conservative Dilemma. On the one side, American voters were losing ground and losing faith in a political system they saw as catering to economic elites. (Pearlstein's 1995 article cited Kevin Phillips, the author of *The Emerging Republican Majority*, who reported that this majority was now threatened by "the reluctance of Republicans to face up to the inequality issue"—which was "costing them the support of one-third of their natural base of voters.") On the other side, American elites were gaining ground and gaining organizational and financial resources they could use to encourage that system to cater to them. Caught in the middle, Republican leaders were forced to reassess their political and electoral prospects in a world transformed by the economic forces, power shifts, and policy choices driving up incomes at the top. They decided to accelerate those forces, exploit those shifts, and reinforce those choices.[18]

The Republican Party's embrace of plutocracy emerged in two stages—the first centering on Congress, the second on the presidency. In 1994, Newt Gingrich led his revolutionaries to a decisive victory not just over Democrats, but also the old Republican guard, and refashioned the party into a vehicle for advancing plutocratic priorities that focused its electoral efforts on stoking voter outrage. In 2000, George W. Bush carried these plutocratic priorities into the White House after using that outrage to beat back a primary challenge from his left. In both fights, the question was what kind of party the GOP would be: a party that was relatively moderate on economics or one firmly allied with America's rising plutocracy. In both fights, the plutocrats won.

NEWT GINGRICH, THE GEORGIA CONGRESSMAN who became Speaker of the House after engineering his party's first House majority in forty years, is now regarded as something of a founding father of our current political dysfunction. As the *Atlantic Monthly*'s McKay Coppins put it in 2018, "[F]ew figures in modern history have done more than Gingrich to lay the groundwork for Trump's rise. During his two decades in Congress, he pioneered a style of partisan combat—replete with name-calling, conspiracy theories, and strategic obstructionism—that poisoned America's political culture and plunged Washington into permanent dysfunction."[19]

Though accurate enough, accounts of this sort imply that Gingrich's revolution was mostly about tactics. It was not. It was mostly about building more aggressive organizations and pushing more radical policies. The organizations enabled the tactics, and both in turn advanced the policies. Gingrich built a coalition within the GOP that went to war not just with Democrats but also with Republicans willing to compromise with them. And he built that coalition to pursue reactionary economic policies that allied the Republican Party with America's rising plutocracy.

Gingrich's insight that influence required organization actually came from Nixon. In 1982, the young congressman traveled to New York City to meet with the former president, a man he disagreed with on policy but admired as a strategic thinker. Nixon warned Gingrich to expect a long struggle and urged the Georgia backbencher to form his own faction to fight it. Gingrich ended up calling his House guerilla army the "Conservative Opportunity Society."[20]

The Conservative Opportunity Society reached a decisive juncture in 1990. Gingrich had sought out Nixon's advice in 1982 because moderate Republicans had reversed some of Reagan's tax cuts, convincing the president to support higher taxes. Gingrich had not had the power to respond then, but he did have the power in 1990 when George H. W. Bush did the same. In agreeing to raise taxes in return for spending cuts, Bush not only broke his "Read my lips: no new taxes" pledge. He also broke with America's emergent plutocracy. The tax increases he and congressional Democrats agreed to were laser-targeted on the superrich: an increase in the top marginal tax rate, a strengthened alternative minimum tax on affluent taxpayers, new excise taxes on luxury items like furs, yachts, and private planes. Although these were exactly the kinds of taxes for which voters expressed the most support, Gingrich and his allies in Congress revolted, pledging to take down any Republican who supported new taxes—even if those taxes were popular with swing voters and even if that Republican was in the White House. "The number one thing we had to prove in the fall of '90," Gingrich would later say, "was that, if you explicitly decided to govern from the center, we could make it so unbelievably expensive you couldn't sustain it."[21]

Bush couldn't, and neither could Clinton. When Bush went down to defeat in 1992, the ascendant Gingrich faction welcomed his loss. A year later, not a single Republican supported Clinton's 1993 budget plan, which looked a lot like Bush's 1990 deal. Clinton had thought he might peel off a few Republicans by focusing his tax hike on the affluent. He was wrong. By defending the class they called "job creators," Republicans insisted they were defending "the working people in this country who are going to get the penalties from people who don't want to invest more, take any more risks," as one Gingrich stalwart put it. Republicans' opposition to a centrist deficit-reduction package was of a piece with their scorched-earth rejection of bipartisanship. Amidst rising acrimony, they rode a wave of discontent into a House majority, running on what they called their "Contract with America."[22]

The "Contract" offered vague promises to clean up government, in the form of sharp cuts in congressional staff and term limits on committee chairs. It also promised to pass "The Job Creation and Wage Enhancement Act," which was very explicit about what House Republicans thought would create jobs and enhance wages: halving the capital gains tax. Once Republicans took control of the House, business-friendly conservatives such as House majority whip Tom DeLay pushed GOP policy even further toward plutocratic priorities, embracing a broad program of tax cuts on corporations and the rich and deregulation of large swaths of the economy. By 1997, congressional Republicans had pressured Clinton into backing a budget and tax deal—ostensibly aimed at balancing the budget—that included huge new tax cuts for the affluent, including a near-doubling of the amount rich Americans could pass to their heirs tax-free.[23]

The new GOP majority also pursued a goal they hadn't featured in their 1994 campaign: scaling back programs for the middle class and poor that had become increasingly vital to Americans' economic security. Clinton ultimately won that fight—after a three-week government shutdown that was, until the early-2019 impasse over Trump's border wall, the longest in US history. But Gingrich had won the war within his party. Republicans no longer stood for fiscal constraint or moderate economic and regulatory policies. They stood for aggressive tax cuts, spending cuts, and deregulation. Launched in the name of Reagan, the Gingrich agenda went beyond what Reagan ever tried to achieve. Pondering his transformed party, Reagan's former budget director, David Stockman, would conclude, "They're on an anti-tax jihad—one that benefits the prosperous classes."[24]

"THE PROSPEROUS CLASSES" were indeed central to Gingrich's vision. He understood that Republicans' ability to outspend Democrats and build supportive organizations rested on the backing of America's rising plutocracy. In their 1996 book on the Gingrich revolution, veteran journalists David Maraniss and Michael Weisskopf wrote, "With the new alignment of ideological allies in the business and political worlds, there were unparalleled opportunities for both the people who [gave] the money and the people who [received] it." Gingrich—and the GOP's plutocratic allies—were quick to seize these opportunities.[25]

From the day he entered politics, Gingrich embraced the growing role of money in the American political system. He and his team cultivated deep ties with narrow economic groups, ushering lobbyists into the inner sanctums of lawmaking. He cheered as a more conservative Supreme Court unraveled campaign finance rules. He welcomed the growing reliance of campaigns on costly TV advertising (most of it fiercely negative), convinced that Republicans would win the resulting arms race. And when Republicans took power, he sent a clear message: if plutocrats wanted Republican policies—and increasingly, they did—they would have to invest in Republican politicians.

The role of enforcer was given to the man known as "The Hammer," Tom DeLay. As majority whip, DeLay seized on the work of a rising conservative activist named Grover Norquist, a self-declared "market Leninist" who headed the anti-tax group Americans for Tax Reform. Norquist had a list of the DC lobbyists who gave money to Democrats or were themselves registered Democrats. Wielding it, DeLay told lobbying firms and big donors, "If you're going to play in our revolution, you've got to live by our rules."[26]

The Gingrich team also put intense pressure on business-allied groups to take more conservative positions. The US Chamber of Commerce, for example, reversed its stance on Clinton's health care proposal after fierce "reverse lobbying" by House Republicans. Republican leaders, including future House Speaker John Boehner, threatened to punish the group legislatively and encouraged its corporate members to defect to hard-right business organizations. Emboldening conservatives within the Chamber, the episode marked the beginning of the organization's transformation from a broadly right-leaning group into a much more conservative one tightly aligned with the GOP.[27]

Once in the majority, DeLay launched what House Republicans called "Project Relief," a major program of consumer, environmental, and labor-market deregulation. Project Relief was jointly run by DeLay's team and lobbyists for industries willing to pony up. It segued seamlessly into the "K Street Project"—so named because so many lobbying firms set up shop on DC's K Street—another concerted effort by Republican leaders to entice corporate lobbies to back their agenda and hire GOP loyalists. By the early 2000s, journalists were marveling that DeLay's "huge fundraising machine . . . seems capable of extracting money and servicing its clients like nothing ever seen in Washington."[28]

In time, rueful conservatives would argue that a "true" revolution was hijacked by the "K Street Gang," as the journalist Matthew Continetti termed DeLay and his circle. In a lament that would soon become a trope, Continetti argued that Republicans had betrayed their professed principles "by giving corporations unprecedented access to a governing majority's internal operations." Yet a powerful logic of mutual dependence explained why an already strongly pro-business party would move toward an ever more blatantly plutocratic agenda as inequality increased. Republicans' electoral fortunes, their ability to recruit candidates, their activist cadre, their party organizations—all required escalating sums of money and the efforts of savvy institution-builders. As inequality grew rapidly, business groups and the donor class had these in abundance. In turn, Republicans had the power to deliver favorable policies— and to demand in return that those who benefited operate as team players rather than free agents. Thus, Republicans and conservative plutocrats each encouraged the other to become more extreme, accelerating the party's march toward plutocratic populism.

AMERICA'S CORPORATE AND FINANCIAL ELITES have always defended their priorities and privileges. And a segment of these elites—larger or smaller, depending on the times—has always invested heavily in politics to do so. What has changed is that this segment has become much bigger, much richer, much better organized—and hence much more powerful. Its goals, moreover, have become much more at odds with what most Americans say they want. The result is an intensifying cycle in which democracy weakens and plutocracy strengthens. As those at the top gain economic and political power, they become more extreme and less interested in the give-and-take of democratic politics. As they do so, they also become more able and willing to exercise their power to further shift political and economic resources in their favor.

By the time Gingrich took power, that cycle was well under way. Responding to the wave of new federal regulations that crested under Nixon, American corporations and executives greatly expanded their political capacities in the 1970s and 1980s. Deploying the now-familiar tools of professionalized advocacy—think tanks, political action committees, DC lobbying houses—they out-muscled their organized opponents and helped reset the agenda of Washington, pulling both parties toward their newly aggressive stances. Part of their agenda entailed reversing Nixon-era environmental and consumer regulations. Part of it was about shifting the tax burden away from capital. Part of it was aimed at crippling organized labor. And part of it was about deregulating the financial economy so that corporations could restructure their practices in ways that increased their ability to direct profits to executives and large shareholders.[29]

A revolt was brewing among *individual* millionaires and billionaires, too. In contrast with organized business, these anti-government investors focused less on immediate influence and more on shifting the agenda of Washington toward plutocrats' long-term priorities. Some of the most persistent and ideologically extreme think tanks and intellectual networks of our day entered the scene in the 1970s and early 1980s—the Heritage Foundation (1973), the Cato Institute (1977), the Federalist Society (1982)—while already existing ones, such as the American Enterprise Institute, grew dramatically. Funding this juggernaut of plutocrat-friendly organizations was a long list of extremely wealthy individuals, along with corporations looking for intellectual cover for business-friendly policies. In short order, these new influence machines blanketed Washington with thinly sourced white papers and self-styled experts proclaiming the virtues of hard-right policies previously seen as well outside the mainstream, such as rolling back environmental protections, getting rid of progressive taxation, and turning Social Security into a system of individually managed accounts.[30]

The growing influence of corporate and economic elites reflected two fundamental shifts in the American political economy. First, the balance between capital and labor was tilting in capital's favor, as labor rapidly lost ground and corporations shifted their operations (or threatened to shift their operations) to low-tax regions with weak unions, both within the United States and overseas.[31]

Organized labor's weakening and capital's unshackling, in turn, had a lot to do with a second basic shift: the growing inequality of the wealth holdings that empowered economic elites in American politics. Over the four decades between 1979 and 2016, the share of national wealth held by the richest 0.1 percent of Americans increased from 7 percent to roughly 20 percent. To put this staggering figure in perspective, the top 0.1 percent (fewer than 200,000 families) now holds almost as much wealth as the bottom 90 percent of Americans combined (about 110 million households). Again, these are levels of wealth inequality much higher than seen in the United States since the late 1920s, or than seen in other affluent nations: the wealthiest households in the United Kingdom (one of our main competitors for the title of most unequal democracy) own only around half as large a share of national wealth as the wealthiest households in the United States do. We should not be surprised these extraordinary trends have coincided with widening opportunities for the very rich to shape politics and policy, nor that these widening opportunities have resulted in political and policy trends that make the wealth gap even larger.[32]

Not all of those who took advantage of these trends were on the ideological right, of course. But the most influential and organized of them certainly were. The public prominence of a small number of liberal billionaires makes it possible to see America's plutocratic class as left-leaning—or at least more or less evenly divided between the parties. But this common perception is mistaken. The very rich invest most heavily in the Republican Party: its politicians, its party organizations, its allied groups, and its causes. Of the 100 richest Americans on *Forbes*'s famous wealth list, according to a recent study, roughly two-thirds contributed mainly or exclusively to Republicans or conservative causes, and their spending outweighed the spending of those in the top 100 who gave to Democrats or liberal causes by a ratio of three to one.[33]

This conservative tilt is even more pronounced when one considers the most organized segments of the plutocracy, including influential networks of donors and powerful business groups. And it's even *more* pronounced when one considers the many nonpublic ways the superrich and corporations can support politicians and lobby for their causes—not just so-called dark money (unreported campaign and lobbying expenditures) but also hidden flows to interest groups and advocacy spending laundered through nonprofits.[34]

Everything we know about the economic preferences and priorities of America's plutocracy, moreover, indicate that they are far to the right of those of the American public. There is ideological diversity within the top decimal places of the American economic distribution, and the views of the superrich do not always align with their material self-interest. Still, we now have plenty of evidence that those at the very top of the economic ladder tend to hold much more conservative positions on economic issues than those lower on it, and to place higher priority on causes associated with those conservative positions, such as cutting popular spending programs. We have evidence, too, that the wealthiest and most politically active plutocrats are farthest to the right—that aforementioned study of the richest 100 Americans found more than a dozen actively working to cut taxes and not one actively seeking to raise them. In short, the evidence reveals a truth that would be unsurprising if it weren't so often denied: the superrich are a lot more likely to be conservative Republicans.[35]

Perhaps most telling, we now have evidence that when the affluent hold policy opinions that differ from those of middle-income and poor citizens, the views of those lower on the economic ladder seem to have no measurable influence on actual policymaking. Whether we look at the positions of elected representatives or the likelihood of policy changes, there seems to be little clear association between the opinions of nonaffluent Americans and what happens in Washington. By contrast, there are comparatively strong relationships between the attitudes of the well off and the positions of elected officials and the policy changes they support.[36]

Not surprisingly, the sharpest opinion differences between the rich and the rest are over precisely the kinds of issues that activate the Conservative Dilemma: taxes, regulation, labor unions, and the relative importance of fiscal restraint versus spending to safeguard economic security. The wealthy are much more conservative on average: more anti-tax, more anti-regulation, more opposed to unions, more concerned about deficits, and less supportive of programs like Social Security. Indeed, many of these conservative positions are surprisingly prevalent even among the most "liberal" plutocrats. A recent survey of big donors in Silicon Valley, for example, finds that even executives in the generally liberal tech sector are more opposed to government regulation and organized labor, on average, than are *Republican* voters.[37]

Consider just a few of the starker differences between voters and plutocrats, which come to us thanks to an intensive effort by a team of political scientists to get a sizable sample of rich Americans to respond to a set of standard survey questions. (Given how narrow the group of big economic winners are and how hard it is to reach those within that group, most surveys reach only a handful of truly rich Americans at best.) The survey asked whether government had a responsibility to reduce income differences between rich and poor. In prior surveys, 46 percent of Americans had said government had that responsibility. In the focused survey of the wealthy, just 13 percent of respondents did. What about national health insurance? Sixty-one percent of citizens were supportive; only 32 percent of the wealthy were. An even bigger gap separated the rich and the rest on the question of whether government should make sure all Americans could go to college: 78 percent of Americans said yes; just 28 percent of the wealthy agreed.[38]

While plutocrats are generally to the right of voters on economic issues, they are generally *not* to their right on social and cultural issues—though, judging by how they spend their political dollars, the economic issues are the issues that really matter to most among the superrich. Liberalism on cultural matters is particularly evident among those who donate to Democrats: that survey of tech entrepreneurs that shows they harbor conservative economic attitudes also finds them to be extremely liberal on social issues, such as gay marriage. This pattern helps explain why, over the 1990s and 2000s, Democrats simultaneously became more liberal on many social issues and more conservative with regard to some of the party's traditional economic commitments, including the regulation of Wall Street, defense of labor unions, and increased taxation to fund new or expanded social programs. Yet these ideological changes within the Democratic Party were much less drastic than those within the Republican Party. As conservative plutocrats gained greater power, what had been a relatively mainstream conservative party came to embrace positions far to the right of both its historical stances and the positions of conservative parties abroad.[39]

Nowhere is this clearer than in economic policy. Political scientists have developed rigorous measures of the ideological position of elected officials based on roll-call votes in Congress. According to these indicators, the cleavage between the parties centers on economic issues, such as tax policy, regulation, and the size of government. These indicators show that Republicans became sharply more conservative in the 1990s, 2000s, and 2010s. Over this same period, no comparable leftward movement can be seen among Democrats.

Polarization, in other words, has been "asymmetric." According to one widely used measure, for example, about one in five congressional Republicans and a similar share of congressional Democrats were "ideologically extreme" according to their left–right voting patterns in 1990. By 2000, three in five Republican members of Congress were, with no change in the Democratic share. A decade on, more than four in five Republicans in Congress were—again, without any parallel movement among Democrats in Congress.[40]

Tax and budget policies offer a representative (and highly consequential) example. Republicans have become much more conservative over time, and much more friendly to plutocrats. George H. W. Bush's budget plan was, in fact, the last time that a single Republican in Congress voted for anything more than a trivial or technical tax increase. Since then, Republicans have instead pushed for tax cuts whenever they've had scope to do so: in 1997, in the early 2000s, and in 2017. Each of these cuts, moreover, has been more skewed toward corporations and the rich than the last. The tax cuts that Republicans pushed for under Gingrich were tilted toward the top. But the "Contract" also contained a child tax credit favored by evangelical leaders, and many of the signature GOP initiatives of the era, such as expanded retirement savings plans, were focused on upper middle-class voters (whom Republicans not only were courting electorally but also hoped to wean off Social Security). The Republican tax cuts to come, however, would be more and more narrowly focused on estate, gift, dividend, and capital gains taxes and cuts in the top corporate and income tax rates.

After 1992, Republicans also united in opposition to every proposed tax increase, no matter how minimal or focused—starting with the modest Clinton tax increase of 1993. Despite the tax cuts of the 2000s (not to mention the continuing growth of inequality), Republicans were even more insistent that taxes should never go up when faced with President Obama after 2008. In their budget battles with him, they even shunned a possible "grand bargain" because it included modest tax hikes on the affluent alongside large spending cuts. On the campaign trail in 2012, every Republican candidate vowed to reject a hypothetical budget deal that contained one dollar in tax increases for every ten dollars in spending cuts. Such cuts were a growing Republican priority, too, particularly if that spending went to safety net programs for the poor and insecure. Apparently, though, it was not a priority that outweighed the imperative of cutting taxes for the richest Americans.[41]

NO CHANGE WITHIN THE REPUBLICAN PARTY better signaled its plutocratic turn than the generational handoff from George H. W. Bush to his son, George W. The Gingrich revolution transformed the congressional GOP, and Republicans discovered they could do much without the presidency. Nonetheless, the bitter struggles of the Clinton years—culminating in the unsuccessful effort to impeach and convict the president for lying under oath about an affair with a White House intern—revealed the limits as well as the benefits of a congressionally based party. For those hoping to deliver on the party's biggest aims, the presidency was the ultimate prize. And they knew who they wanted to seize that prize: the Texas governor whose folksy style cloaked his close ties to the plutocracy.

In 1998, Grover Norquist made a pilgrimage to Austin, Texas, to meet with the rising Republican star who carried the Bush family name. He returned with soothing words for his fellow anti-tax warriors. He later recalled, "I was one of the few people who could stand up and say to the movement, 'This guy is not a real Bush. He's adopted. He's no relation to that jerk who raised your taxes in 1990.'" During the campaign, the Texas governor made slashing taxes the centerpiece of his agenda. Once in office, he would cut taxes again and again, upholding the pledge that the man he fondly called "41" had fatefully broken. He would also embrace the plutocracy like no modern president before him.[42]

Because Bush's fealty to the plutocrats is now standard Republican procedure, it's difficult to recapture just how ecstatic corporations and big donors were about his candidacy. As the *New York Times* reported in 2000, Bush and his VP pick Dick Cheney—the former hard-right member of Congress who headed the oil-services giant Halliburton—"excited the corporate world" as no modern presidential ticket had. By the time of the election, Bush's fundraising haul was the largest ever for a presidential candidate. The campaign dubbed Bush's strongest backers "the Pioneers." Nearly 250 strong, these business executives and wealthy conservatives were anything but hard-scrabble frontiersmen, given that each had to raise over $100,000 in individual contributions. After the election, 104 of the Pioneers ended up with federal appointments.[43]

Much of the money channeled to Bush ran through the Republican Party as "soft money" that was not subject to contribution limits. The soon-to-be bankrupt energy firm Enron, for instance, gave close to $2 million—an almost unheard-of sum at the time. The Republican convention in Philadelphia was "really two conventions," according to the *Times*, "one for the delegates in the hall and another for the party's biggest contributors, who will be treated to a panoply of perks, from yacht rides to skyboxes high above the convention floor." As the *Times* summed up the implication of the GOP's two-tier celebration, "A core group of business donors now . . . form the financial backbone of the modern Republican Party."[44]

The joy in the skyboxes was understandable. Bush's business-backed candidacy promised to bring to the White House what the Gingrich speakership had brought to the House: a mutually beneficial bargain between the extremely conservative and the extremely rich. But the plutocrats would not win the presidency without a fight.

IN POLITICS, THE BALANCE OF POWER is usually most visible when it faces a significant challenge. Under Bush's father, that challenge played out over several years, and it pitted Gingrich Republicans against the moderate wing of their party. With Bush the younger, it played out over several months, and it pitted the plutocrats' candidate against Arizona Republican John McCain. Like the first fight, it too revealed where the balance of power lay.

The substance of McCain's 2000 campaign is now mostly forgotten. Yet more than any other viable Republican bid for the presidency in the last quarter century, it directly challenged the party's turn toward the economic right. Relying on small-dollar contributions, a novel approach at the time, McCain criticized both the centrality of tax cuts to the GOP program and the party's coziness with corporate lobbies and big donors. And he looked to be a serious challenger to Bush—until, that is, the party of the plutocrats weighed in.[45]

The two central planks of McCain's insurgent campaign—the renovation of crumbling campaign finance rules and a moderate 1990-style budget plan—directly confronted the GOP's plutocratic priorities. McCain's tax plan in particular was fundamentally at odds with the Bush-Cheney program: it would have set aside a sizable chunk of then-anticipated budget surpluses to shore up Social Security. It also would have closed a variety of corporate tax loopholes to fund a tax cut for the middle class. Bush's tax plan promised to deliver nearly 40 percent of its benefits to the top 1 percent. Independent estimates suggested that the McCain plan would deliver less than 2 percent of its benefits to the top 1 percent. In introducing his plan, McCain declared, "Let the warning go out to the army of lobbyists who so stoutly resist our campaign. Every tax dollar now wasted on special breaks for oil companies, ethanol giants, insurance companies and the multitude of other powerful special interests with their armies of lobbyists are now at risk." Judged by what happened to his campaign, the "warning" got through.[46]

The ambush came in South Carolina. Using surrogates in the conservative evangelical movement, Bush's allies spread racially charged accusations, including that McCain had fathered a black child out of wedlock. (The child in question was their daughter, a dark-skinned Bangladeshi orphan they had adopted at the request of one of Mother Teresa's nuns.) Today, George W. Bush is seen as a moderate on race and immigration, and thus by the Trump-supporting right as an utter failure. But when his campaign was faltering, he didn't abandon plutocracy; he abandoned racial moderation. (His father, notoriously, had also dabbled in racial division when elections were at stake, agreeing to use the racist "Willie Horton" ad against Michael Dukakis in his successful 1988 presidential campaign.) It was a preview of the much uglier combination of right-wing populism and conservative plutocracy to come.[47]

In time, McCain would surrender to the logic of plutocratic populism himself. When a path to the Oval Office reopened for him in 2008, the former anti-plutocrat embraced huge tax cuts heavily skewed toward the rich and ran a campaign aligned with the party's now entrenched ultra-conservative orthodoxy. To shore up support with social conservatives, he picked as his running mate the underqualified governor of Alaska, Sarah Palin—the base-boosting right-winger who would later be seen as a harbinger of Trump's even more bombastic style. Though an ailing McCain would cast one of his final votes against Republican efforts to dismantle the Affordable Care Act in 2017, he would never return to the full-throated critique of his party's plutocratic turn that characterized his 2000 run.

Bush had learned the same lesson long before. He liked to call it "Lesson 101 in politics": "never forget your base." Bush and his top adviser, Karl Rove, knew his support among conservative donors and business groups rested on his repudiation of his father's politics. When his Democratic opponent Al Gore correctly predicted that Bush's tax plan would plunge the budget back into the red and disproportionately benefit the rich, Bush derided the argument as "fuzzy math." A more honest admission came at the annual Al Smith dinner a month before the election. Looking out at his well-heeled audience, Bush joked, "Some people call you the elite; I call you my base."[48]

When Bush won, he did not forget his base, nor his pledge to Norquist. Even as budget surpluses were replaced with deficits and the nation entered into costly wars in the Middle East, he and Republicans in Congress just kept cutting taxes. They focused on those most hated by the superrich: the capital gains tax, the gift tax, the dividend tax, the top tax rate, the estate tax (which Republicans skillfully relabeled the "death tax"). By the time they were done, they had racked up a ten-year tax loss of $4 trillion. Projecting forward, the revenues lost each year because of the tax cuts would amount to roughly three times the annual cost required to permanently fund Social Security.[49]

When Nixon was in office, the richer you were the higher the tax rate you paid. Thirty-three tax brackets and a top marginal tax rate of 70 percent ensured that the superrich paid a higher rate than the run-of-the-mill affluent. By the end of the Bush presidency, thirty-three brackets had become six, the top tax rate was 35 percent, and many billionaires were paying a lower share of their income in taxes than families with six-figure incomes. For the richest 400 households, local, state, and federal taxes were over 70 percent of income at the end of World War II and still more than 50 percent as late as 1970. They fell to 40 percent by 1995 and again to 30 percent by 2005. (By 2018, the effective tax rate of the top 400 families was 23 percent.[50])

These changes clearly signaled that Republican priorities were not the public's. A relatively slim majority of Americans expressed support for tax cuts in general, but much larger majorities said they preferred other uses for the budget surplus, especially shoring up Social Security. Large majorities also felt the cuts should target the middle class, not the rich, and wanted some kind of "trigger" that would scale back the tax cuts if the deficit spiked. In most cases, Republicans as well as Democrats held these reservations. For years, in fact, the biggest complaint about the tax code reported in surveys was that it was too favorable toward corporations and the superrich. But Republicans in Congress were undeterred, aggressively peddling misleading and false claims about the tax cuts' distribution and using budgetary smoke and mirrors to obscure their huge fiscal drain.[51]

Perhaps the most revealing case of plutocrats thumbing their noses at the public came in 2005, after Bush won reelection. The president who had escaped the fate of his father declared he had "political capital" to spend. Though the 2004 race had focused on the ongoing response to the terrorist attacks of 9/11—a focus favorable to the president, since the Iraq War was not yet the highly unpopular action it would soon become—Bush suggested he had a mandate to pursue the great policy ambition of anti-government conservatives: Social Security privatization.

Bush knew his "base." No other policy aspiration so cleanly divided those at the top from the rest of Americans. Wall Street saw the prospect of managing millions of new retirement accounts, conservative think tanks believed that their prize was finally within reach, and budget hawks in the donor class soberly declared that the nation was finally facing its fiscal problems, notwithstanding the reality that creating private accounts would involve massive borrowing alongside its benefit cuts. But the public was so opposed to the idea that even conservative GOP members of Congress balked. Facing a midterm in which Republicans' House majority was in jeopardy, party leaders in Congress told Bush that while they agreed with him in principle, his plan was political suicide.[52]

It was a major setback, and it was followed by two others: the party's loss of the House in 2006 and McCain's defeat in 2008. But those whose wealth and power had risen sharply under Bush did not see the 2008 outcome as a cause for retreat. They saw it as a call to arms.

IN 2009, MUCH OF THE NATION was celebrating the election of the first African-American president and welcoming a more aggressive response to the worsening financial crisis. At a secretive private gathering outside of Palm Springs, the mood was very different. As described by the *New Yorker*'s Jane Mayer, "The guests . . . included many of the biggest winners during the eight years of George W. Bush's presidency." Vanguards of the conservative plutocracy, this select group of superrich donors called themselves "investors," according to Mayer—investors "whose checkbooks would be sorely needed for the project at hand."[53]

The man who assembled this advance guard was Charles Koch, the head of Koch Industries. Charles and his brother David (who died in 2019) had long supported conservative think tanks and public intellectuals. In the 2000s, however, they emerged as the nation's leading benefactors and coordinators of organizations and donors espousing a hard-right philosophy. Their unprecedented investments flowed from spectacular wealth: in 2014, the two Koch brothers tied with each other for sixth on a list of the world's richest individuals, with $42 billion each. The Kochs did not start out closely aligned with the GOP, despite its continuing rightward shift. With George W. Bush at the helm, in fact, they viewed the party as far too moderate. Thus, they took it upon themselves to construct a parallel set of organizations that would, in short order, command resources comparable to the GOP itself.[54]

These efforts had two key goals: ramping up political spending by the conservative wealthy and building organizations to push the GOP further to the right (and, after 2008, to fight President Obama). Even in the age of big-money politics, the amount of money raised at Koch meetings was astonishing. Under Nixon, Americans had been scandalized by a prominent businessman's $2-million contribution (around $10 million today) to the president's reelection campaign. A single Koch event in 2011 resulted in $70 million in commitments from attending donors. Five years later, the brothers were vowing to raise nearly a billion dollars to defeat Hillary Clinton, roughly the same amount the entire Republican Party raised in the 2015–2016 election cycle.[55]

We have become accustomed to numbers like these. But we shouldn't minimize the transformation they represent. Not only has the amount spent on elections exploded; more and more of that rising total is coming from the superrich. In 1982, less than 10 percent of campaign dollars came from the top 0.1 percent of donors. By 2018, nearly half (46 percent) did, with almost a quarter (22 percent) coming from just 400 mega-donors. In the run-up to the 2018 midterm, one Koch-allied billionaire, casino magnate Sheldon Adelson, made a single contribution of $30 million to the House GOP's "Super PAC" on his way to spending roughly $100 million in total.[56]

Much of this growing spending is channeled through nonprofits labeled "trade" or "social welfare" associations—tax-exempt organizations empowered by the conservative majority on the Supreme Court in the 2010 *Citizens United* decision. These groups are not required to disclose their donors, and most don't. But sometimes tax records, corporate filings, and court cases allow a glimpse into their opaque finances, though usually long after the money gets spent. In 2019, for example, the pleasingly named Americans for Job Security—which mostly tried to stop President Obama from keeping his job—lost a federal legal battle to keep its donors private. Some of their names had come out in 2013 when the group ran afoul of California law. But the full list showed just how much dark money organizations relied on a handful of mega-donors. The brokerage titan Charles Schwab gave $9 million over three months. The Fisher family—made rich by the Gap clothing empire—gave $9 million, too. The roster of smaller donations ($2 million on down) reads like an invitation list to a dinner party for conservative billionaires: Richard and Helen DeVos (in-laws of education secretary Betsy DeVos), Steve and Elaine Wynn (of Wynn Resorts), Vince and Linda McMahon (the WWE chief executive and future head of the Small Business Administration); tech investor (and soon-to-be Trump supporter) Peter Thiel. All turned out to be contributors to a group that participated in what California officials called the largest political money-laundering case in the state's history.[57]

Even more remarkable, these seven-to-nine-figure donations aren't the primary avenue of plutocratic influence. The primary avenue is organization-building, and organization-building on the economic right is a boom business. We have already discussed some of the groups that make up the well-funded infrastructure of the hard right. Many of them dramatically increased their resources and activities in the 2000s. Even among these powerful players, however, the Koch brothers stand out. One recent study comparing the Koch Network with a similar effort on the left (the Democracy Alliance) finds that the Koch Network is much larger and more influential, fueling "a tightly integrated political machine capable of drawing national and state Republican officeholders and candidates toward the ultra-free-market right."[58]

Given the standard ideological profile of the conservative superrich—hard right on economics, more moderate on social issues—most of this private activity is devoted to pursuing the goals of extreme economic conservatism: tax cuts, deregulation, union-busting, and so on. Most, but not all: as we shall see in the next chapter, the Christian right, National Rifle Association, and other groups that focus on cultural backlash have their own wealthy benefactors, not to mention their own sources of revenue. They also have much larger and more active memberships than conservative economic groups do, which makes them important allies for the plutocrats. In battles like the struggle to remake the nation's courts, the groups with members and the groups with money have distinctive strengths that permit mutually beneficial bargains.

Yet while conservative plutocrats appreciate the role of these ground-level GOP surrogates, rarely do they devote major resources directly to their causes. (The most striking exception is financial-industry billionaire Robert Mercer. He and his daughter Rebekah showered tens of millions of dollars on key architects of American ethnonationalism in the mid-2010s, especially Steve Bannon and the Breitbart News Network.) Much more typical is the tacit alliance between corporate interests and conservative groups embodied in the American Legislative Exchange Council, or ALEC—a long-standing group focused on the states that works to put Republicans in office and rewrite state laws to favor corporations and the rich.[59]

ALEC briefly appeared in headlines in 2012 after the killing of Trayvon Martin, when it was discovered to be a major source of "stand your ground" laws. These laws were a boon not only to the NRA but also to weapons manufacturers who bankrolled ALEC. Most of the policies that ALEC pursues, however, are more typical anti-tax, anti-labor, and anti-regulatory fare. ALEC has recruited thousands of state legislators, overwhelmingly Republican, to its ranks, and it provides them with so-called model bills on issues ranging from collective bargaining (read: union-busting) to electoral procedures (read: voter restrictions). ALEC's priorities are highly conservative and highly favorable to the GOP. For example, ALEC has been central to efforts to curtail public-sector unions in Wisconsin and other states, and it's also been an advocate of voter identification requirements that disproportionately affect minority and low-income voters.[60]

A younger but arguably stronger plutocratic group, particularly at the national level, is the centerpiece of the Kochs' organized efforts, Americans for Prosperity (AFP). Featuring an annual budget of more than $150 million, AFP has more than 500 paid directors and nearly 3 million activists. For its volunteers, AFP initially drew heavily on local Tea Parties, although AFP became entrenched even as many of the Tea Party organizations lost steam.[61]

Whereas ALEC focuses on individual politicians, the AFP focuses more on state and national GOP organizations, particularly through the work of its paid directors. In the fifteen states where AFP established operations by 2007, nearly 70 percent of those who served as directors previously worked within the Republican Party, either on election campaigns or as staff to legislators or executives. Moreover, close to a third of directors who left AFP before 2007 joined Republican campaigns or staffs, frequently in top positions. Many others moved to lobbying or advocacy groups serving GOP clients.[62]

Nor is AFP the only influential group pushing for plutocratic policies at the national level. The US Chamber of Commerce has steadily expanded its operations while steadily shifting right under the aggressive leadership of long-serving head Tom Donahue. Since its startling about-face on health care in 1993, the Chamber has become the most powerful business group in Washington, with the Kochs' organization its only real rival, albeit one with which it shares many goals. Like AFP, the group is deeply integrated into the fundraising infrastructure of the GOP and employs many former Republican operatives.[63]

The Chamber makes little pretense of bipartisanship. Once known for supporting at least a handful of moderate or pivotal Democrats, virtually all its election spending now goes to helping

Republicans in general elections, with most of the rest focused on GOP primary elections, where the group has tried to ensure that more electable and business-friendly candidates win.

Campaign spending is just one aspect of the Chamber's formidable political power. Its reported spending on lobbyists, for instance, dwarfs that of any other DC organization. Indeed, it has effectively become a lobbyist-for-hire for industries—health insurance, finance, some parts of the energy industry—that want plausible deniability as they fight popular bills or try to pass unpopular ones. The Chamber has also spent enormous sums on influencing the federal courts, where, in an era of legislative gridlock, more and more of the policies affecting business are made. It plays an active role in placing pro-business judges on the courts and in advancing pro-business litigation, and has even started devoting a chunk of its considerable resources to state-level legal activities, especially the election of state attorneys general.

Parsing the precise influence of these plutocratic ventures is not always easy. Yet there's considerable evidence that the organized forces of plutocracy have pulled the Republican Party toward them. The clearest example is climate change, where the party has become militantly opposed to regulation or taxation to address carbon emissions. From a global perspective, the GOP is an outlier among conservative parties in the depth and breadth of its rejection of established science, and this was true well before Trump's presidency. As the world's temperature has steadily risen, the party's commitment to addressing, or even acknowledging, the perils of climate change has steadily declined.[64]

This is now so numbingly familiar that we need to remember it was not always true, either among Republican elites or the party's voters. Richard Nixon founded the EPA. George H. W. Bush upgraded the Clean Air Act. John McCain championed a national "cap-and-trade" program that had substantial GOP support. In the 2000s, however, Republican elites tacked sharply right as the energy industry mobilized to ward off the growing threat of national action—a campaign in which the Koch Network, Chamber of Commerce, and key fossil-fuel companies were highly active and effective. Republican voters, swayed by conservative media's now decades-long effort to discredit climate science, largely followed suit, though even today the GOP electorate is far more concerned about climate change than are its ostensible representatives.[65]

The Republican Party has moved toward the outer fringes not just on climate policies, but on virtually every economic issue. Again, this is true not only when you compare the party with its own past positions, but also when you compare it with conservative parties in other rich democracies. As Figure 3 shows (based on a systematic analysis of the campaign platforms of leading parties), the Republican Party is an outlier relative not just to center-right parties in other nations, but in some cases to right-wing parties that place themselves well to the right of mainstream conservatives.[66]

Republican politicians are not just to the right of conservative parties elsewhere. They are now to the right of their own voters on

Figure 3

IDEOLOGICAL POSITIONING OF POLITICAL PARTIES IN WESTERN EUROPE, CANADA, AND THE UNITED STATES

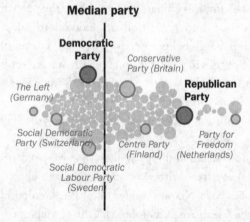

Source: Sahil Chinoy, "What Happened to America's Political Center of Gravity," *New York Times*, June 26, 2019, https://www.nytimes.com/interactive/2019/06/26/opinion/sunday/republican-platform-far-right.html.

Circles sized by the percentage of the vote won by the party in the latest election in this data. Only parties that won more than 1 percent of the vote and are still in existence are shown. Analysis is based on party campaign platforms, as coded by the Manifestos Project (https://manifesto-project.wzb.eu/), and includes a selection of parties in Western European countries, Canada, and the United States.

many issues—not just on climate change and taxes. Medicaid, for example, has strong public support in every state, including among Republicans. Yet after the Supreme Court ruled that states did not have to expand the insurance program to moderate-income Americans under the 2010 Affordable Care Act, state after state controlled by Republicans refused to pursue a popular policy that was essentially costless. At the center of the fight (and later at the center of the struggle to "repeal and replace" the entire law) was Americans for Prosperity. The Koch-directed group pushed Republican legislators to hold the line, often in the face of local business pressure and lobbying from medical providers eager for more paying patients. In this case, Republicans—encouraged by an ultra-conservative, billionaire-funded group—shifted to the right not just of the voters they ostensibly represented, but of many in the local business community and health care industry as well.[67]

PERHAPS NO POLITICAL LEADER of the last decade better encapsulates the embrace of plutocratic priorities among party elites than former Wisconsin representative Paul Ryan. A self-styled policy wonk, Ryan became chair of the Budget Committee after Republicans re-took the House in 2010, halfway through Obama's first term. He was Mitt Romney's 2012 running mate and, in 2015, he became Speaker of the House. Throughout, the press and fellow Republicans hailed Ryan as the party's most serious tax and budget expert. Ryan claimed his inspiration was Jack Kemp, the New York Republican who had been George H. W. Bush's secretary of housing and urban development and was said to be the party's conscience on issues of poverty and exclusion.

But Ryan's conservative positions consistently belied his Kempian rhetoric. Kemp had, according to a sympathetic 2015 biography, "focused obsessively on the subjects of race and inequality" in the run-up to the 1996 presidential campaign. (He initially decided to sit out the race, telling his son he felt "somewhat alienated from the current party," but then agreed to be Bob Dole's running mate.) Ryan's policies had a consistent focus on inequality too—only they were designed to make inequality worse. He proposed a string of budget plans that cut taxes on corporations and the rich so much that, even with patently unrealistic assumptions, they required savage cuts in programs for the poor. In an infamous explanation of his views, Ryan warned, "We don't want to turn the safety net into a hammock that lulls able-bodied people to lives of dependency and complacency." Kemp called himself a "bleeding-heart conservative." Ryan was more like a "no-heart" one.[68]

But Ryan did have a place in his heart for the plutocrats. More well-mannered than Gingrich, he was also more conservative. According to the roll-call indicators cited earlier, each of the three Republican Speakers since Gingrich was to the right of the last. But since the whole party was shifting right, too, these very conservative men all ended their tenures tussling with an even more conservative party. More revealing than their voting records, however, were the priorities they set as House leaders. Ryan, in his 2015 book, *The Way Forward*, had promised an agenda that would "address what families face in their lives" and, in doing so, show that "the rich, comfortable, cold-hearted Republican who cares about protecting his own wealth from taxes and about little else, indifferent to the hardships of poor people who live in the same country but a different world, is mostly a figure of caricature."[69]

What that agenda ended up looking like could be summarized in two numbers: $90 million and $3 trillion. The first was what his famed fundraising arm raised in 2016, his first year as Speaker, with most of this impressive haul coming from donors and PACs contributing more than $50,000. (Charles Koch and his wife gave $488,000 in just the first quarter of 2016, with an additional $71,000 contributed by Koch Industries' PAC.) The second was the approximate ten-year cost of the tax cuts that Ryan introduced that same year. More than three-quarters of this total would go to the richest 1 percent. In the more rarified company of the top 0.1 percent, the average tax cut would be $1.3 million—for every household, every year.[70]

As the party headed in Ryan's direction, the politician Ryan claimed as inspiration drifted further from it. Kemp recognized the Conservative Dilemma, but as with McCain in 2000, his proposed answer—to offer a serious conservative-minded response to the widening income gap, while embracing America's growing diversity—was not the answer of his party. His last policy foray before his death in 2009 came during the 2007 debate over immigration reform, when he backed a bipartisan bill crafted by McCain and Democratic senator Ted Kennedy. The bill went down to defeat in the face of a right-wing rebellion, led by conservative talk radio and the growing ranks of anti-immigration Republicans. After Obama's election, in one of his last public statements, Kemp called on his party "to rethink and revisit its historic roots as a party of emancipation, liberation, civil rights and equality of opportunity for all."[71]

Most of the GOP had already done that rethinking—and long since decided to open Pandora's box.

Chapter 3

ORGANIZING THROUGH OUTRAGE

THE CONSERVATIVE DILEMMA FIRST AROSE as democracy struggled to take root in societies marked by huge divides between the
rich and the rest. It has reappeared in our day as America's new
superrich have pulled away from everyone else. Then and now, the
basic question for conservative leaders was the same: how to reconcile their allegiance to wealth and power with the need to attract the
electoral support of voters without much of either. Their answer,
then and now, carried profound implications—for their party's survival and, in our era, for the well-being of American society.

The modern Republican Party's choice to side emphatically with
those at the top narrowed its options. With plutocratic priorities
dictating the party's economic agenda, its electoral appeals shifted
toward cultural issues. In the next chapter we will explore why and
how racial appeals took center stage. Before doing so, we need to
understand how the party developed a political infrastructure that
could mobilize mass support, even as its alliance with the wealthy
constrained the form that infrastructure could take.

The party's embrace of the plutocrats had two major consequences for that mobilization strategy. First, it reduced the range of
issues on which the party could compete and thus the range of voters it could reach. Without broad or deep popular backing, Republicans' pocketbook agenda was increasingly insufficient. Second,
it made maximizing engagement and emotion among the party's
core voters—while finding ways to recruit new voters who could

be similarly stirred—even more essential. The party needed groups that could rile voters up and reach deep into communities, and they needed groups willing to do so on terms compatible with the party's embrace of the plutocrats. As that embrace strengthened, Republicans cast about for willing and capable allies.

They found them in a set of organizations that came to form the backbone of white electoral backlash. Following the 2016 election, journalists would rush to the bars and diners of "flyover country" to interview voters who had sided with Trump. Yet the explanations that these aggrieved voters offered did not suddenly emerge out of a single campaign, much less from a single voter's mind. Just as the transformation from a reasonably moderate party into one dedicated to plutocracy required decades of organization-building on the economic right, the rise of a party built on the kinds of incendiary appeals that Donald Trump would employ required decades of organization-building on the social right. The process wasn't planned in advance, much less fully orchestrated from above. It involved trial and error, internal disputes, accommodations, and course corrections. Yet over a generation, it not only changed the priorities of the Republican Party's base; it changed the party itself.

If finding groups Republicans could rely on to navigate the Conservative Dilemma took time, it was time well spent. For the groups that aligned with the GOP proved unusually skilled at creating durable shared identities that motivated citizens, and then getting those citizens to show up, not just on election day, but whenever big shows of strength were needed. These were groups, in short, that could rally their troops, creating sharp lines between friend and foe and instilling a sense of threat. And what best rallied those troops, they discovered, was outrage.

The early specialists in outrage-stoking were the Christian right and the NRA. Racial backlash helped propel both movements: white resistance to desegregation fueled the defense of Christian schools; white fear of black city dwellers motivated the case for unregulated gun ownership. Yet Republican outrage-stoking came to encompass a constantly renewable set of threats. Pioneers in the politics of resentment, the Christian right and the NRA scaled up new technologies of outreach (Christian broadcasting, direct mail) and new strategies of recruitment and certification (church-based mobilization, candidate loyalty "scores") that proved highly effective at generating intense, albeit narrow, support. Soon they would be joined by another powerful set of organizations: the rapidly growing "outrage industry" of right-wing media.

These groups had little interest in the conventional approach to party-building. Parties generally seek to reach out to the uncommitted or weakly committed, the swing voters who decide close elections. Parties generally thrive on ambiguity that allows many factions to gather under one big tent. Outrage groups care first and foremost about survival (or, as social scientists put it, "organizational maintenance"). They gain the members and money they need to survive by building ranks of passionate followers and ramping up those followers' sense of threat. They disdain swing voters and ambiguity. They seek to tear down big tents.

Thus, like some ill-fated conservative parties in the past, Republicans came to depend on extreme factions that provided valued resources but also pulled the party further toward the fringe. Each new ally offered the party an inroad into precincts of the electorate it might otherwise lose. But each new ally came at a price. By contracting out the task of persuasion, the GOP increasingly lost the capacity to shape its own agenda and fight elections on its own terms. Indeed, the Republican Party itself eventually became a weaker part of the Republican coalition, spending less than powerful private interests allied with the party and doing less to mobilize voters. Surrogates and their extreme agendas came to permeate the GOP so completely that it became increasingly difficult for party leaders to chart a moderate course. By the time a true master of outrage came along, a party that had outsourced identity-building would be easy prey.

THE FERVENT SUPPORT OF WHITE EVANGELICALS is the bedrock of the modern Republican electoral coalition. In recent campaigns, white evangelicals have made up roughly a quarter of the nation's electorate. Almost four out of every five of those votes have gone to the GOP. Without strong backing from this community, no Republican presidential candidate can win the party's nomination, let alone the presidency. No recent Republican candidate has been able to pick a running mate—or, if elected, a Supreme Court nominee—who doesn't garner evangelical backing too.

That a disproportionately conservative, rural, and Southern demographic would find a comfortable home in today's GOP may appear to have been inevitable. Yet while prescient observers envisioned the coalition-to-come in the early 1970s, the picture didn't come into sharp focus until the mid-1990s. What's more, the alliance had to be repeatedly reconstructed, because the modern history of the Christian right has been marked by personal scandals, financial implosions, and the rise, fall, and reinvention of a dizzying array of organizations and leaders.

This turmoil can obscure a basic truth about the GOP-evangelical alliance. To work for both sides as inequality skyrocketed, it had to be built along particular lines. Many of the regions of greatest evangelical strength are also those that are most rapidly falling behind—regions characterized by increasing social dislocation and decreasing opportunities for economic mobility. Against this backdrop of deep economic stress, the basis for the alliance between party and movement nonetheless needed to lie elsewhere, ideally with an emphasis on threats depicted as existential.

In a secularizing culture, conservative Christians had reason to see their cultural commitments as endangered. Yet the history of the alliance makes clear that racial antagonism was the primary catalyst for the mass mobilization of evangelicals and, eventually, for their tight alignment with the GOP. Racial resentment has continued to act as a binding agent, leading to rhetoric and policies that work for plutocrats and religious conservatives alike. But at the same time, racial resentment had to be tamed and redirected to serve as a foundation for the Christian right's comfortable GOP home.

While the contours of what would become the Christian right were hazy in the early 1970s, the cornerstone of the movement was already in place: tens of thousands of churches, including almost 35,000 within the Southern Baptist Convention (SBC) alone. From abolitionism to prohibition to the civil rights movement, churches have been central to grass-roots politics. They offer a roof under which the like-minded and similarly situated can gather, build solidarity, and deepen conviction. These trusted and rooted local institutions offer a potent mix of face-to-face activities, while a loose, clergy-based network makes it possible to aggregate these local energies into national action.[1]

If churches provided the initial sites for evangelical organizing, by the mid-1970s new technologies amplified the influence of religious voices, bringing them beyond the walls of churches into families' living rooms. Cable television had opened the possibilities for religious broadcasting on an international scale, and "televangelists" were beginning to attract huge audiences. By one estimate, roughly 20 million American households watched religious programming in the 1980s.[2]

The organizational resources that sustained the religious right's push into politics were of unparalleled scale. These resources supported a sequence of powerful leaders, including Jerry Falwell, Pat Robertson, and James Dobson. By the late 1970s, Falwell's Lynchburg, Virginia, church filled its 4,000 seats every service and had a membership of 17,000, while his *Old-Time Gospel Hour* had a weekly audience in the millions.[3]

As Falwell's organization faded in the late 1980s, Pat Robertson's savvier Christian Coalition would emerge. It was run on a daily basis by the skilled operative Ralph Reed, who had ties to Republican elites (despite an impressive trail of scandals, Reed is now the head of the Faith and Freedom Coalition). Robertson's TV empire was far larger than Falwell's. By the 1980s, his satellite network was the third largest in the country after HBO and the Turner Broadcasting Network, extending to Latin America and Asia and reaching 30 million households. In time it would make Robertson a very wealthy man, as it purchased rights to a collection of wholesome shows that were eventually spun off, taken public, and sold for nearly $2 billion.[4]

In turn, as the Christian Coalition faded in the mid-1990s, James

Dobson would become the leading figure on the religious right. Though not a pastor, he had extraordinary reach among conservative Protestants. His radio show had a domestic audience of over five million families; his books sold over sixteen million copies. Focus on the Family, the organization Dobson headed, had a staff of more than a thousand at its peak, and its magazines a combined circulation of three million. Each year, 200,000 people visited its huge campus in Colorado Springs, which had its own zip code and freeway exit.[5]

In the mid-1970s, much of this lay in the future, but political operatives could see the vast potential. As Gary Garmin, lobbyist for one of the early conservative evangelical organizations, Christian Voice, put it: "The beauty of it is that we don't have to organize these voters. They already have their own television networks, publications, schools, meeting places and respected leaders who are sympathetic to our goals."[6]

The initial challenge, in fact, was mobilizing those sympathetic leaders. A striking feature of the Christian right's early history was the crucial role that movement conservatives from outside the evangelical community played in bringing this powerful force into partisan politics. Two of the central figures were Richard Viguerie and Paul Weyrich, both experienced conservative activists with strong linkages to the Republican Party. Viguerie was a campaign specialist and innovator of direct mail fundraising. Weyrich, who called himself a "political mechanic," was wired into the formidable network of emerging groups pushing a radically conservative agenda. He had worked as a Republican staffer in the Senate, then used funding from hard-right beer magnate Joseph Coors and other benefactors to establish the first major right-wing think tank, the Heritage Foundation. He was also a cofounder of ALEC.

Both Viguerie and Weyrich were Catholic, but they recognized the opportunities for movement-building among evangelicals. In 1976, Viguerie prophesied that "the next major area of growth for the conservative ideology and philosophy is among Evangelical people." Focusing on those who led those people, he and his allies worked to translate this potential into a broad and emphatically conservative movement.[7]

Viguerie and Weyrich lobbied Falwell in particular—it was Weyrich who suggested the name "Moral Majority." Falwell had a mailing list of two million and, by 1980, his organization's annual revenues were $50 million and its staff nearly 1,000 people. And he was ready to fight. "The local church," he proclaimed, "is an organized army equipped for battle, ready to charge the enemy." It was Falwell, Frances FitzGerald concludes in *The Evangelicals*, who "introduced the fundamentalist sense of perpetual crisis, and of war between the forces of good and evil, into national politics, where the rhetoric has remained ever since." In 1979, Falwell launched the Moral Majority to fight what in one sermon he had called a "war . . . between those who love Jesus Christ and those who hate Him."[8]

Reading this history backward, it is easy to imagine that the Christian right emerged as a backlash against the secular and sexual revolutions of the sixties (in part because this is the story Falwell and other key figures told). Yet historians have thoroughly debunked this account. For most prominent evangelicals in the mid-1970s, abortion was not a central concern. Their positions on the issue, when offered, tended to recognize the case for allowing abortion under limited circumstances. Robertson, in 1975, called it "purely a theological matter." Falwell did not give a full sermon on abortion until 1978. The SBC reacted mildly to *Roe v. Wade*, rejected anti-abortion resolutions in 1976, and did not adopt a strong anti-abortion stance until 1980.[9]

Race was far more central. The Southern Baptist Convention had been founded in 1845, separating from northern Baptists over the question of whether missionaries could own slaves. A century later, fundamentalists and many evangelicals, including Jerry Falwell, had defended segregation. Bob Jones Jr., the second president of the conservative Christian university that bore his father's name, gave George Wallace an honorary degree.

Race became a catalyst for political mobilization in 1978, five years after *Roe*. That year, the IRS issued a ruling that put the tax-exempt status of segregated Christian schools in jeopardy. The "Seg Academies"—private and nearly or completely segregated— had proliferated as the desegregation of public education progressed.

Many churches, including those associated with prominent figures such as Falwell and Tim LaHaye, maintained such schools. The case that led to the IRS ruling concerned Bob Jones University, which had been entirely segregated. Falwell's own Lynchburg Christian Academy counted just five African Americans among its 1,147 students.[10]

For many evangelical churches, the IRS ruling represented a profound threat, and it pulled them into politics. Weyrich later acknowledged as much, while erroneously attributing it to "Jimmy Carter's intervention": "What galvanized the Christian community was not abortion, school prayer, or the ERA. I am living witness to that because I was trying to get those people interested in those issues and I utterly failed. What changed their mind was Jimmy Carter's intervention against the Christian schools." In the 1960s, Falwell had chastised pastors such as Martin Luther King Jr. for their civil rights leadership; as he put it, "preachers are not called to be politicians but to be soul winners." Now he declared that the "idea of 'religion and politics don't mix' was invented by the devil to keep Christians from running their own country."[11]

The entry of white evangelicals into organized politics coincided with the migration of white southerners from the Democratic Party to the Republican Party. It was the goal of Weyrich, Viguerie, and other activists to make sure these two transformations converged. George Wallace had hired Viguerie to help him pay off his 1976 campaign debt. Having noticed that roughly half of the letters Wallace received invoked religious themes, he accepted Wallace's mailing list as part of his compensation. He and others searched for ways of framing the political contest that would mobilize evangelicals but were compatible with the GOP's existing constituencies and aspirations.

Explicit appeals to race would no longer work. They alienated white moderates and foreclosed the possibility of modest but useful inroads among nonwhite voters. Hostility to the power of the federal government, by contrast, was a natural rallying cry. So was abortion, soon enough. Due in part to the teachings of the popular theologian Francis Schaeffer, abortion, once a "Catholic issue," was becoming a principal focus among evangelicals. Doctrinal squabbles had often prevented cooperation even among conservative Protestants, but Schaeffer argued that evangelicals should find common cause with "co-belligerents" who shared their hostility to abortion. The ambition to build bridges to other denominations and faiths proved crucial. It not only brought together Catholics and Protestants, but also—especially for many otherwise liberal Catholics—provided a compelling entryway into the broader world of conservative politics. By the early 1980s, abortion was a focal point for organizing on the Christian right.

The GOP needed to catch up. In the late 1970s, the two major parties' positions on abortion were hardly distinct. Gerald Ford was a moderate on the issue, and his wife Betty had hailed *Roe v. Wade* as well as the Equal Rights Amendment. Ronald Reagan had moved to a strong anti-abortion stance, but he had once signed liberalizing abortion legislation as the governor of California, and his 1980 running mate, George H. W. Bush, had battled him for the GOP nomination as a pro-choice candidate. The party's voters were divided, too; in fact, it was not until 1988 that Republican voters were, on average, more hostile to abortion rights than Democratic voters.[12]

The terms of the alliance emerged primarily from the top down, especially as the Christian right's focus on abortion intensified. In 1979, conservatives defeated moderates to take the SBC presidency. They soon launched a successful takeover of the broader organization, including its seminaries, service agencies, and organized representation in Washington. Reagan's about-face on abortion (Bush followed suit when he joined the ticket) delivered a clear message about the direction the GOP was heading.

Christian right leaders got the message. According to one survey, the percentage of SBC ministers identifying with or leaning toward the Republican Party skyrocketed: from 27 percent in 1980 to 66 percent in 1984 to 80 percent in 1996. The most conservative clergy, and those who described themselves as more conservative than their congregations, were the most likely to become politically active. As FitzGerald concludes, "The conservative SBC clergy did not simply ride the groundswell of popular reaction to the social revolutions of the 1960s; they helped create it."[13]

The challenge was to identify a set of positions that would work for both the Republican Party and evangelicals. Abortion motivated and unified social conservatives. By contrast, school prayer—a major evangelical concern—antagonized "co-belligerents" fearful of Protestant hegemony. Although some prominent evangelicals angrily rejected a "big tent" alliance, the majority accepted demographic and political realities. To maximize their clout, religious conservatives needed to stick together. By 2012, four-fifths of evangelical voters could support the Mormon Mitt Romney's candidacy; by 2018, four of the five Republican-appointed Supreme Court justices would be Catholics.

The increasing focus on issues related to sexuality had an additional advantage: it was compatible with a court-led policy agenda. If Christian conservatives saw themselves as a besieged minority, Republican politicians understandably feared associating themselves too closely with a social agenda the majority of voters rejected. (The exception, for many years, was the issue of gay rights—and gay marriage in particular—which did not attract popular support until well into the new millennium.) The cross-pressures could be significant. In his insurgent 2000 campaign, John McCain distanced himself from prominent figures on the Christian right. He described Robertson and Falwell as "agents of intolerance" and chastised George W. Bush for "pandering to the outer reaches of American politics" when Republicans should be building "a party as big as the country we serve." McCain, of course, lost. To capture the nomination in 2008, he made amends by doing a lot of pandering himself. No leading Republican candidate has tried a similar move to the center since. Instead, the GOP has found itself increasingly whipsawed between the Christian right's clout within the party and the unpopularity of its agenda.[14]

A consistent theme in the Christian right's short history is its frustration with the GOP's unwillingness to get behind conservative social legislation. It is a chronicle of deflection, delay, and half-hearted symbolic measures. For good reason: In 2005, the spectacle around Terri Schiavo, a Florida woman who had been brain-dead for fifteen years, revealed the political danger for

Republican officials. Egged on by Dobson and other religious activists, leading Republican figures—including President George W. Bush and his brother, Florida governor Jeb Bush—aggressively intervened in the heartbreaking case to overrule the decisions of Florida's courts. Senate Majority Leader Bill Frist, a doctor, chimed in with an optimistic diagnosis of Schiavo's health gleaned from video. The backlash was immediate. An overwhelming majority of the public saw the intervention as politically motivated; in one poll, 82 percent said Congress and the president should not have intervened. Even evangelical voters strongly disapproved.[15]

Focusing on the courts was a safer course. While of intense interest to activists, judicial politics generally receives little notice from voters. Yet, as Dobson recognized, "religious liberty and the institution of the family [and] every other issue we care about is linked in one way or another to the courts." After 1980, Republican Party platforms dramatically increased their emphasis on the constitution and the courts, reflecting and reinforcing the growing emphasis of the Christian right on judicial nominations. By the time of George W. Bush's election in 2000, social conservatives could claim an effective veto over GOP court appointments. In 2005, Bush's surprise nomination of White House counsel Harriet Miers hung in the balance while he attempted to rally leading social conservatives. Many, including Dobson, were reassured—until a speech surfaced that suggested she had once expressed sympathy for abortion rights. Support for her nomination instantly collapsed.[16]

The evolution of Republican judicial appointments demonstrates the carefully crafted terms of the solidifying alliance between the party and the Christian right. There were to be no more mistakes, no David Souters or Anthony Kennedys, Republican nominees who proved lukewarm (at best) about evangelical priorities. An increasingly coordinated and extremely well-financed network of culturally and economically conservative groups, led by Leonard Leo, the Federalist Society's executive vice president, now vets judicial nominations. Leo has connections to both the plutocratic and social conservative wings of the coalition—neither of which felt it had to give much ground to accommodate the other.

A judicial philosophy that combines a retreat of the state on economics and the advancement of the state to protect and sometimes enforce the views of religious conservatives was the logical endpoint of the long effort to merge the agendas of the Christian right and the GOP's plutocratic paymasters. Nominees needed enthusiastic backing from both social conservatives and the party's plutocratic allies. A focus on the courts gave each side ample opportunity to pursue coveted yet unpopular policies in the venue least accountable to public opinion and best able to accommodate both agendas simultaneously.

The flip side of this development was the Christian right's abandonment of its earlier interest in economic issues. Conservative activists of the 1970s had argued, along the broader "forgotten man" lines sketched by Nixon and his aides, that supporting working people should be part of the GOP's platform. In the early 1990s, the Christian Coalition's Ralph Reed—the politically savviest of the movement's leaders—stressed that "people care about their pocketbook. Jobs, taxes, educational issues are important to them." Reed warned against being "ghettoized by a narrow band of issues like abortion, homosexual rights, and prayer in school." He argued that to extend their "limited appeal," social conservatives be more inclusive and pursue "specific policies designed to benefit families and children," including an expansion of IRAs for homemakers and a tax credit for children.[17]

Few of these proposals made much progress, however, especially if they carried a substantial price tag. The inclusion of a child tax credit in the GOP's 1994 Contract with America was the main exception, and it proved a lonely one. As the political scientist Daniel Schlozman puts it, "The Christian Right offered social conservatism in a form maximally acceptable to big and small business alike." Evangelical leaders themselves placed less and less emphasis on demands for lunch-pail initiatives. In the run-up to the 2004 campaign, the SBC's Richard Land led an "I Vote Values" registration and education drive, featuring an eighteen-wheel tractor trailer driving from church to church. "We want people to vote their values and convictions over economic issues," Land insisted. David Barton, a long-time Bush associate from Texas hired by the Republican National Committee as a consultant, gave three hundred briefings to pastors around the country. The capital gains tax, the estate tax, the progressive income tax, and the minimum wage—all were affronts to Christian values against which the Bible, Barton explained, "takes a very clear position. All these are economic issues that we should be able to shape citizens' thinking on because of what the Bible says."[18]

For his part, James Dobson was comfortable with the GOP's economic agenda. He was fixated on social issues, especially the perceived threat of gay marriage, which was, in his words, "poised to deliver a devastating and potentially fatal blow to the traditional family." ("With its demise," Dobson warned, "will come chaos such as the world has never seen.") Revealingly, Dobson's proposed solution was a constitutional amendment prohibiting gay marriage, and he made support for this idea a prerequisite for any politician who desired the backing of his empire. After an initially hesitant George W. Bush acceded to this demand, Dobson reciprocated, offering his first explicit endorsement of a presidential candidate.[19]

Over the course of Bush's presidency, the Christian right began to lose some of its organizational coherence. After evangelical turnout disappointed in the 2000 election, Karl Rove hired Ralph Reed to work directly on the president's reelection campaign. In 2004, evangelical voters heard political appeals primarily from the Bush campaign itself. The year before, Dobson had stepped down from the presidency of Focus on the Family (he resigned as chairman of the board in 2009). No clear successors emerged, leaving the Christian right more fractured than in decades. Even more alarming for GOP and Christian leaders was the demographic decline of Christian conservatives. Just as mainline Protestantism had declined in earlier decades, white evangelicals were now experiencing the same slow but steady fall in numbers. From 2008 to 2016, white evangelicals fell from 21 percent to 17 percent of the US population. SBC officials estimated that, if the trend continued, membership would fall by half by 2050.[20]

These developments only strengthened the Christian right's perception of threat and its identification with the GOP. While an organized movement had ushered evangelical voters into Republican politics, they could now take their cues from local church communities, which have become overwhelmingly Republican, as well as from right-wing and religious media. Eager to squeeze every vote out of a declining but fiercely loyal demographic, Republican elites have increased both the stridency and intensity of their outreach. Between 1996 and 2016, references to religion in GOP platforms increased nearly five-fold. According to surveys, the share of Republican activists who come from evangelical traditions has risen from around 20 percent in the early 1960s to 47 percent in 2008. The share of Republican convention delegates with such commitments increased slowly into the early 1990s, but then jumped from 15 percent to over 30 percent by 2012.[21]

Evangelicals' sense of grievance has also grown. Just before the 2016 election, two-thirds of white evangelicals said the growing number of immigrants in the nation threatened American values. Almost as many (63 percent) said discrimination against whites was as big a problem as discrimination against blacks and other minorities. And three-quarters—more than any other demographic—said that things had changed for the worse in the United States since the 1950s. Devout evangelicals are now far more conservative than other Republican activists. They are prone to depicting politics as a struggle between good and evil and to denigrate compromise. They are now a powerful radicalizing force within the party in their own right.[22]

The same is true of another influential GOP-aligned group, one that brings an essentially religious fervor to an ostensibly secular issue.

THE MODERN HISTORY of the National Rifle Association has been almost as tumultuous as that of the Christian right, involving mass firings, coups, financial crises, and credible accusations of conflicts of interest and widespread graft. Yet for all the turmoil, there is a clear narrative: after the NRA reinvented itself as a social movement organization in 1977, it rapidly expanded its organizational strength and political capacity. As it did so, it built a formidable and fateful alliance with the Republican Party.

It would be easy to mistake this alliance for a straightforward transactional pact between a political party and a single-issue group. The GOP would toe the NRA line on guns; the NRA would deliver votes for the party. But the relationship intensified over time, gradually changing both the GOP and the NRA. An ever-tighter alliance with Republican elites was an essential part of the NRA's remarkably successful (and lucrative) effort to make gun rights a symbol and cornerstone—the "first freedom"—of a broader social identity. That identity dovetailed perfectly with the GOP's hardening stance on cultural and social issues. Leaving behind its sporting club roots, the NRA became a vehicle for the party's rebranding of itself as the defender of embattled nonurban whites—and especially white men—against the malign forces of government, liberal media, metropolitan elites, and racial minorities. As with the emerging Christian right, the shrill anti-government cultural agenda of the NRA proved an ideal match for the shrill anti-government economic agenda of reactionary plutocrats.

It was not always so. The first century of the NRA's history reveals little hint of the radicalized political juggernaut it would become. Formed in the aftermath of the Civil War by former Union officers dismayed by the poor marksmanship of their troops, the organization focused on sporting and hunting. It forged ties with the federal government, which sponsored shooting competitions and provided cheap access to surplus military weapons. It displayed its motto— "Firearms Safety Education, Marksmanship Training, Shooting for Recreation"—outside its headquarters in Washington, DC. The NRA periodically involved itself in national politics, such as during the debates over the National Firearms Act of 1934, but gun regulation was rarely much of a concern. When it was, the NRA showed a willingness to countenance moderate regulation of firearms as an appropriate responsibility of government.

Like so much else in American politics, things changed rapidly in the 1960s and 1970s. Rising crime rates and urban unrest, along with the assassinations of Martin Luther King Jr. and Robert Kennedy as

well as two unsuccessful attempts on the life of President Gerald
Ford in just over two weeks in 1975, led to calls for gun control.
There was little partisan division over the issue. California gover-
nor Ronald Reagan signed major gun control legislation; Richard
Nixon and other leading Republicans generally equivocated. George
McGovern was an opponent of stronger gun laws.[23]

However, the prospect of substantial gun regulation did unsettle
the NRA's leadership. In 1975, it responded by establishing the Institute for Legislative Action to act as a lobbying wing. What followed
should have been a warning signal for a generation of moderate conservatives. The new organization-within-an-organization quickly
became home to a more aggressive cadre who clashed with the established leadership. The conflict came to a head in the "weekend massa-
cre." Hoping to put down the internal challenge, the NRA's leadership
fired eighty employees in October of 1976, including the entire staff of
the Institute for Legislative Action. It made plans to move the NRA
headquarters from Washington, DC, to Colorado, in the hopes of
recommitting the organization to recreation rather than politics.

The leadership wanted a decisive break, and they got one. The
rebels who had been sacked reorganized. At the next national NRA
convention in 1977, they bused in supporters to stage the "Revolt at
Cincinnati." In less than twenty-four hours, the old guard had been
voted out; the militants were now in charge. One of the first orders
of business was to reverse the planned move to Colorado. The NRA
would stay in Washington, and it would fight. The entry to the DC
headquarters would carry a new message: "The Right of the People
to Keep and Bear Arms Shall Not be Infringed." (Unsurprisingly, it
left out the Second Amendment's immediately prior reference to a
"well-regulated militia.")[24]

The NRA's reinvention was an immediate and spectacular success. Now conceived as an organization committed to beating back
threats to gun ownership, it tripled its membership, from 1 million
to 3 million, between 1977 and 1984. With ebbs and flows it would
increase to 4 or 5 million in the decades to follow. Revenues grew
(in 2018 dollars) from $36 million in 1964 to $183 million in 1986 to
$284 million in 2001.[25]

In 1991, the NRA lobbyist Wayne LaPierre, who had once vol-
unteered for McGovern's presidential campaign and been offered a
job on the staff of rising congressional Democrat Tip O'Neill, was
named executive vice president, a position he still held in 2019. LaPierre oversaw much of the organization's impressive growth, its savvy
marketing (including the famous "I am the NRA" campaign), its
growing stridency—and its fervent embrace of the GOP. An admin-
istratively skilled if uncharismatic figure, LaPierre was not an obvious public face for a gun group celebrating the frontier spirit. This
was true even before recent scandals, which revealed he had supple-
mented his generous salary with five-star European vacations and
over $200,000 worth of suits.

LaPierre's reign has not always been smooth. In the mid-1990s, he
faced a serious factional challenge during a time of financial tumult.
He beat back the upstarts and allied with the actor Charlton Heston, who would soon become NRA president. Heston was that obvious public face, a symbol of rugged individualism and moral clarity.
At the NRA's 2000 convention he made a famous, flintlock-wielding
declaration that the government would have to rip that gun from his
"cold, dead hands."

Heston effectively delivered the core message of the new NRA:
in a time of existential threat, it was an organization dedicated to
the protection of freedom itself. Since the 1977 revolt, the NRA
had moved toward ever more sweeping portrayals of the stakes in
the fight over gun regulation, first by making a highly contentious
reading of the Second Amendment central to its mission, and later
by emphasizing that the right to bear arms was not just one right
among many but the decisive issue in a struggle between good and
evil. Heston observed that "the gun itself is just a symbol. It's individual freedom we're fighting for." As he insisted, "The right to keep
and bear arms is the one right that permits 'rights' to exist at all."[26]

Heston employed the most incendiary analogies, including
comparisons between Jews in Nazi Germany and gun owners in
America. His rhetoric was typical of the organization. Most notoriously, LaPierre in a 1995 fundraising letter referred to government
officials as "jack-booted thugs" and insisted that in Bill "Clinton's

administration, if you have a badge, you have the government's go-ahead to harass, intimidate, even murder law-abiding citizens." Kayne Robinson, Heston's successor as president, argued that "We're at war today, against disguised, deceitful, stealthy, all-but-invisible enemies of freedom. We're at war at home and abroad. We're at war for no less than our very freedom as Americans." And the war was to be waged on a broad front. Proposals for campaign finance reform were treated as an attack on the NRA's free speech rights: a "senatorial jihad against the NRA."[27]

For the NRA—and, increasingly, the Republican Party—this kind of incendiary rhetoric was a feature, not a bug. The NRA's formidable clout is sometimes attributed to its political spending. But while the organization's wealth has made it an influential player in federal elections, the NRA's greatest impact comes from its ability to motivate voters.

Like the Christian right, a key source of the NRA's capacity to mobilize is its reach into local communities. The NRA buttressed its political messaging with a grassroots infrastructure built on recreation and gun safety education. Every year, 750,000 Americans receive firearms training from NRA-affiliated instructors. The spread of concealed carry laws in GOP-controlled states furthered these efforts, as the laws generally mandated training— training typically conducted by NRA-certified instructors, using NRA-designed curricula. Sociologist Jennifer Carlson, who joined the NRA and closely observed its training practices, noted that the course design includes an entire unit "dedicated to explaining the NRA's unique role in fighting for Americans' right to self-defense." Through these courses, "the NRA shapes the political rights and moral responsibilities that gun carriers attach to their firearms." Many instructors include NRA memberships in the cost of the course or offer memberships at discount. Estimates suggest there are now between 8 and 11 million concealed carry licenses in the United States.[28]

The NRA's organizational imperative is to translate support among ordinary citizens into political action. Kayne Robinson has described the NRA as a "motivational organization" that tries to get "free-riders" to join the "gun movement." Mobilization depends on intensity; intensity often depends on a perception of threat. As LaPierre puts it: "People respond when there's a threat." And if there is one thing the NRA excels at, it's generating that threat response. Though the high point of efforts to pass gun regulation was in the early 1970s, the NRA has kept the rhetoric of imminent crisis going for a generation. The warnings increased even as the Supreme Court broke with long-standing precedent to confer constitutional protections on individual gun owners in its 2008 *District of Columbia v. Heller* decision. They increased even as Democrats retreated to weaker and weaker proposals. And they increased even as the NRA over the past quarter century won consistently in statehouses as well as Congress. Most states have enacted "shall-issue" laws permitting concealed carry, and a majority have passed stand-your-ground laws as well.[29]

Fearmongering has gone hand in hand with alliance-building with the GOP. As late as 1992 more than a third of NRA campaign contributions went to congressional Democrats; today, virtually all its spending goes to Republicans. Democratic presidents, however, became the NRA's best recruiting and fundraising vehicle. The NRA seized on Bill Clinton's modest initiatives, including his signing of the (extremely popular) Brady Bill for expanded background checks and the banning of some assault weapons. "Clinton," LaPierre observed, "is mobilizing gun owners at record rates." When the forty-year-old Democratic majority in the House came to an end in 1994, Clinton called the NRA's mobilizing efforts the single biggest factor in his defeat.[30]

As the GOP drew closer to the plutocrats in the 1990s, the NRA became a vital organization within the new, more radical Republican coalition. Its fiercely anti-government posture reinforced the rhetoric of reactionary plutocrats, while its policy demands were entirely compatible. A feedback loop emerged: the NRA fed off of and reinforced a kind of apocalyptic partisanship, in which freedom was at stake every election and every day in between.[31]

Advocates of gun control often note, correctly, that when asked most Republican voters still support basic regulations like universal background checks. But more revealing are questions that ask voters to choose between protecting gun rights and gun regulation. Here, views have become starkly more polarized since 2000, with the big change taking place on the Republican side. Roughly 75 percent of Democrats have said consistently that effective regulation is the more important aim. But while a slight majority of Republicans agreed with that statement in 2000, 80 percent said protecting gun rights was the higher priority by 2017. Most of the increase took place during the Obama presidency, as the NRA hyped the threat from the administration's very modest policy proposals.[32]

The NRA's rhetoric has occasionally become so extreme that it has provoked a reaction among conservatives. Reagan (along with other former presidents Nixon and Ford) broke with the organization to back the Brady Bill. George H. W. Bush wrote a very public letter of resignation in reaction to LaPierre's "jack-booted thugs" comment, terming it "a vicious slander against good people." (Just days after LaPierre's fund-raising letter went out, Timothy McVeigh, who signed letters with an "I am the NRA" stamp and linked his actions to his views on gun rights, blew up a federal building that housed an ATF office in Oklahoma City, killing 168 people, including nineteen children.)[33]

Yet Reagan and Bush broke from the NRA only after they were no longer running for office. GOP leaders grew wary of too public an embrace—after Reagan's 1983 appearance, no sitting Republican president would address an NRA convention until Donald Trump did so in each of the first three years of his presidency. Yet the private alliance became ever closer. Appearing before a gathering of NRA members during the 2000 campaign, Kayne Robinson announced that "gun rights advocates would have 'unbelievably friendly relations' with a Bush White House . . . if we win, we'll have a Supreme Court that will back us to the hilt. If we win, we'll have a president . . . where we work out of their office.' " NRA membership rates among 2008 Republican National Committee delegates were almost 50 percent higher than in 2000. The NRA not only poured more and more dollars into federal elections. It shifted from supporting sympathetic legislators in both parties to concentrating its donations on the few pivotal races that might give the GOP control in the closely divided Senate.[34]

In 2015, even before he launched his campaign, Donald Trump brokered a visit to the NRA's annual meeting. The urban real estate developer who had once supported a waiting period for gun purchases and a ban on assault weapons declared, "I promise you one thing, If I run for president, and I win, the Second Amendment will be totally protected, that I can tell you." Just as evangelical leaders would concern themselves more with Trump's political reliability than his personal values, LaPierre and his team liked what they heard. In May 2016, the NRA embraced Trump, the earliest endorsement of a presidential candidate in the organization's history.[35]

IN DECEMBER 1994, the huge cohort of newly elected Republican members of Congress gathered in Washington for the first time. Their party had won an astonishing victory, sweeping away the Democrats' seemingly impregnable House majority. Billed as an orientation, the gathering was essentially a rally to celebrate the birth of a new, aggressive, and much more conservative Republican Party.

The capstone event, held in luxury boxes at the Baltimore Orioles' Camden Yards, featured red meat and apple pie against a baseball backdrop. But the new House members weren't there just to bask in Americana. They were cheering their champion: not Newt Gingrich, but radio shock-jock Rush Limbaugh. They declared their "majority maker" an honorary member of the freshman class. Vin Weber, one of Gingrich's top advisers but now retired from Congress and embarking on a second career as a lobbyist, introduced him: "Rush Limbaugh is really as responsible for what has happened as any individual in America. Talk radio, with you in the lead, is what turned the tide." Limbaugh's response to this lovefest was in character. He suggested that after remaking the country, House Republicans might want to "leave some liberals alive" so "you will never forget what these people were like."[36]

Twenty years later, Weber's tone would be less celebratory. He lamented that Republican politicians had become so terrified of attacks from their right that they could scarcely govern. He and some others who had been part of that Republican surge now saw right-wing media very differently. "Conservative media has become . . . much more powerful than John Boehner and Mitch McConnell," explained Matthew Dowd, a strategist for George W. Bush's campaigns. Prior generations of leaders, he noted, did not have to "confront them every time they took a turn." Former Senate majority leader Trent Lott, another veteran of the Gingrich revolution, now complained that "if you stray the slightest from the far right . . . you get hit by the conservative media."[37]

Recent social science research has corroborated these assessments. Right-wing media has moved voters to the right. It has moved members of Congress to the right, too, and likely encouraged them to think their constituents are more conservative than they are. Efforts to isolate the impact just of Fox News—a single, albeit powerful, outlet—indicate that it has had a notable impact on the electorate, bolstering the GOP. As Fox's audience has grown and the network has moved even further right, its impact has increased.[38]

Yet the true effect of right-wing media goes deeper. In fact, of the groups that have carried the GOP toward extremism and tribalism, arguably none has been more significant. The world of conservative media is its own ecosystem, with its own rules. And it is something new in the United States, and perhaps in modern democracies. Fox and other major outlets are closer to being a new kind of social movement, albeit one geared for profits, than a set of traditional news organizations. Conservative media hasn't just become a vital source of GOP persuasion and electoral strength. It has changed the Republican Party, inflaming tribalism and extremism among both its audience and the politicians who compete for its favor.

The conventional question is whether people are more conservative because they consume right-wing media. They are, but this effect is secondary. The biggest consequence of Limbaugh, Sean Hannity, and other conservative media stars is their profound impact on the kind of "news" this audience consumes—and the kinds of news it no longer consumes. Republican voters increasingly trust only a handful of movement outlets, rejecting any dissonant information coming from the "lame-stream" media. As conservative outlets ramp up intensity and shut out competing voices or inconvenient facts, previously unthinkable actions—including personal corruption, abusive or authoritarian moves, and abject fealty to plutocrats—all become possible, so long as the new conservative kingmakers provide a cover story.

The development of this distinctive ecosystem began on the AM radio dial. Talk radio emerged from the confluence of deregulation and the shift of music from AM to FM radio. In the late 1980s, AM stations desperate for marketable content began airing Rush Limbaugh's show. Four years later, it was heard by 14 million listeners a week, and Limbaugh's audience would eventually grow to 20 million. Few outside forces have so rapidly altered politics. By 1993 a *National Review* cover would crown Limbaugh "the leader of the opposition." The year after that, the party's traditional leaders would be giving him the hero treatment at Camden Yards.[39]

Talk radio was divided, essentially, between voices of the hard right and those of the harder right. Limbaugh was just the loudest of the many loud voices who would quickly join him, including Glenn Beck, Sean Hannity, Hugh Hewitt, Laura Ingraham, Mark Levin, and Michael Savage. All of them took similar approaches—a man-of-the-people (or, rarely, woman-of-the-people) persona, flattery of listeners, a tendency toward outrage, attacks on elites, ridicule of the opposition, and scorn for the mainstream media. At least 90 percent of the market for political talk radio was and is conservative, an ideological imbalance reflecting the demographics of AM radio audiences (older white men), the greater cultural diversity on the left, liberals' greater comfort with mainstream media, and the greater appetite on the right for the distinctive style of shock jocks. Liberals in time would develop a taste for left-leaning comedy news, but they never fell into anything like the tight media orbit of a few favored outlets that took hold on the right.

Fox News brought the conservative media model to TV in 1996. Like talk radio, Fox (along with the televangelists) was the beneficiary of a technological shift, in this case the spread of cable. The rapid proliferation of television options shattered the cozy world of three virtually identical mainstream TV networks. Australian billionaire Rupert Murdoch recognized that in this shattered world a network could profitably pursue a less mainstream audience and that conservatives represented the largest underserved market.

Right-wing media efforts had faltered in the past not only because establishment gatekeepers and regulatory constraints marginalized the far right, but because they had failed to make money. Following Limbaugh's lead, Fox president (and long-time Republican operative) Roger Ailes changed that. With the right technology, the right format, and a favorable political climate, it turned out you could build an organization that would make you rich *and* help construct an arch-conservative movement. The same formula that could drive profits—isolation, loyalty, emotion—could change American politics. Ailes would build a media juggernaut that would play a critical role in pushing the GOP both rightward and toward a particular resolution of the Conservative Dilemma.[40]

Isolation was essential. From the start, a striking feature of right-wing media was the immense energy devoted to attacking alternative sources of information and expertise, especially traditional media. Whatever one's view of organizations such as PBS, CNN, and the *New York Times*, the sheer volume of vitriol directed toward them seems like a strange priority for a news network. Yet it was the foundation for all that followed. It allowed right-wing media, especially Fox, to build an extraordinarily loyal following and to wield formidable influence over conservative political discourse.[41]

Creating a loyal and insular audience has powerful effects. In the modern world, we are all overwhelmed by complexity and flooded with information of highly uneven quality. Figuring out what is happening and why is a constant struggle. We cannot develop anything resembling expertise on more than a small slice of reality, and thus we depend on others for guidance. Another psychological limitation compounds the problem: we are prone to "motivated reasoning"—that is, to believe what we want to or already believe. The more our views are tied to our identity, the more skilled we are at sucking in information that confirms our views and shutting out information that doesn't.

Alongside other key institutions such as universities and scientific bodies, news organizations play an essential role in helping us cope with complexity and our vulnerability to bias. At their best, they help us separate what is known from what is not, what requires attention and what does not, what is true and what is not. They encourage us to wrestle with uncertainty, with uncomfortable facts, and with a range of plausible interpretations of those facts. Even at their best, news organizations are far from perfect: they too are prone to bias, conflicts of interest, and error. Yet they try. More important, they operate within competitive systems that generally reward accuracy and punish mistakes. Reputation depends on demonstrating that you are striving to illuminate the truth and that when you make a mistake, you will acknowledge it and attempt to correct course.

From the beginning, right-wing media turned all this on its head. Motivated reasoning wasn't a limitation to be overcome; it was a vulnerability to be exploited. Biases weren't just confirmed; they were cultivated. Viewers were told that their loyalty was a sign of their independence: "We Report, You Decide." Posing as a clear-eyed teller of "tough truths" became the defining persona of right-wing media stars, even though these "truths" were wholly palatable and typically flattering to their audience—and often not true at all.

This approach has been astonishingly successful. Attitudes toward the media and patterns of media consumption are now very different on the left and right. Among Democrats, general trust in the media has fallen moderately over the past few decades (it has risen again since 2016, presumably in response to Donald Trump's attack on mainstream outlets). Among Republicans, trust in mainstream media has simply disappeared. The collapse did not come gradually, but in two revealing plunges. In the post-9/11 period leading up to the Iraq War, as Fox took off and George W. Bush began to face questioning from mainstream sources, the share of Republicans expressing trust in the media fell from 49 percent to 31 percent. The second wave came during Donald Trump's campaign. By election day 2016, just 14 percent of Republicans said they generally trusted the media.[42]

Not coincidentally, as conservatives lost trust in most of the media, they became highly trusting of a very small number of sources. Moderates and liberals interested in public affairs generally trust and consume news from sources spread across the spectrum from center to left. Conservatives are far more concentrated on the right side of the spectrum, and especially around Fox. In 2014, 88 percent of consistent conservatives reported trusting Fox News, and 47 percent of those conservative respondents said Fox was their main source of news about government and politics. Right-wing outlets, and Fox in particular, have captured their audiences.[43]

The crowding of conservative audiences into a narrow, extreme, and exclusive media space is not only a departure from the past; it is also highly unusual in cross-national perspective. Researchers looking at a wide range of countries have found that American conservatives distinctively combine intense loyalty to their chosen sources and disdain for all others. They found a similar "trust gap" only among supporters of the right in Hungary and Israel. This is not the most reassuring company. In Israel, Benjamin Netanyahu has been a pioneer in scapegoating the mainstream media, fueling a culture of intense tribalism. Hungary's right-wing populist leader Viktor Orbán has led a stunning process of democratic backsliding. His governing party has gradually captured the press (now loved by his supporters and rightly distrusted by others), as well as packing the courts and gerrymandering parliament.[44]

As in these nations, the "trust gap" among conservative audiences in the United States has undercut the incentives for right-wing media to provide reasonably accurate information and correct mistakes. Instead, sources on the right are quick to disseminate thinly sourced but sensational claims that, as Stephen Colbert's fictional right-wing pundit once put it, "feel true." Fox and talk radio have peddled an endless list of conspiracy theories, and conservative audiences have proved highly vulnerable to such messages. Research shows that in general citizens with basic political knowledge (Who's your member of Congress? How many justices are on the Supreme Court?) are less likely to believe conspiracy theories than the sizable share of Americans who cannot answer these questions. Yet this is not true among conservatives with low levels of trust in the political system. Among distrustful conservatives, those with basic political knowledge—which likely means those who consume a lot of conservative news—are more likely to believe conspiracy theories.[45]

The false narratives boosted by right-wing media generally have two characteristics: they incite tribalism and they escalate a sense of threat. Audience capture provides an ideal foundation for both. Right-wing audiences hear about a litany of horrors linked to the right's enemies. Information that would cast doubt on these narratives is dismissed or goes unheard. The emphasis on tribalism and threat parallels the movement-style efforts of the NRA and the Christian right—groups very different from right-wing media but just as eager to stir up mobilizing emotions. Like conservative media, these groups have unusual power and reach on the American right. Not only do they attract and mobilize a devoted audience that overlaps considerably with the right-wing media audience. They also use their resources to promote virtually identical themes.

As with other GOP surrogate groups, right-wing media is also a formidable ally of the plutocrats. Much as is true of the Christian right, the alliance is practical, not doctrinal, and rarely made explicit—for good reason. Recall that the Conservative Dilemma involves a profound tension between the GOP's economic agenda and its mass electoral base. One of right-wing media's most vital contributions is its ability to direct the attention of that base toward certain subjects and away from others. Prominent (and typically quite wealthy) media figures often adopt a working-class persona, but it is a cultural rather than economic one. In centering the agenda on racial and cultural themes, fear of criminals and terrorists, and opposition to immigration, conservative media sources direct attention away from the stark economic realities associated with rapidly increasing inequality. Conservative media features plenty of attacks on "elites." But despite including the occasional liberal billionaire in the category, the focus is on figures conservatives can condemn without acknowledging plutocracy, let alone questioning it: public workers, left-leaning media types, community organizers, politically correct college administrators, and, of course, Democratic politicians, however inconsequential they may be.

But the focus of right-wing demonization goes well beyond "elites." The conservative media ecosystem has long been a critical conduit for the injection of racialized language and appeals into national politics. As within the Republican Party, these efforts have become more overt and frequent. Fox, of course, gave Trump's political aspirations a vital boost. Beginning in 2011, it provided the bellicose billionaire a weekly platform from which he could lie about President Obama's citizenship—a lie that Roger Ailes actually believed, according to John Boehner. Long before Birtherism and accusations that Obama was a closet Muslim, the kinds of highly racialized themes that Trump now promotes figured openly and prominently in right-wing media, from the portrayal of America's cities as hotbeds of black crime, to the notion that voter fraud committed by nonwhite citizens is a major threat to American democracy, to the blanket association of one of the world's great faiths with terrorism, to the fear-mongering about immigrants "invading" across the Southern border. Many of these racialized images and claims directed ire not just at minorities, but also at government, linking political leadership on the left with the right's two great bugbears: handouts to the poor and coddling of the lawless—shady groups that were seen (and meant to be seen) as threats to "real America."[46]

Indeed, media outlets on the right have begun to replace coded racial appeals with explicit efforts to galvanize white identity. The "dog whistle" invoking racialized themes has given way to the bullhorn. The conservative outrage industry has been perfectly positioned to facilitate this transformation. The use of images allows cable TV to racialize narratives without relying on explicit language—producers need only focus viewers' eyes on dark faces. Because they do not need to build a majority electoral coalition, niche media have far more room than politicians typically do to experiment with racism. If they go "too far"—for example, alienating advertisers—they can pull back or reprimand the particular host involved, without any serious long-term damage. The impact of all this is difficult to measure, but one recent study reports a striking pattern: controlling for other factors, in areas with higher viewership of Fox, elected judges issue harsher sentences, especially on drug crimes and especially for black defendants. These same communities also feature a disproportionate number of racist Google searches.[47]

The growing role of new media outlets like Breitbart, along with social media, has further reduced restraints on incendiary and conspiratorial content. Studies of traffic on Twitter and Facebook reveal that in 2016 Breitbart played a central role in shaping discussions on the right, seriously threatening the dominant position of Fox.[48] Some of that traffic moved directly from white-supremacist sites onto Breitbart, before getting picked up by other conservative outlets. And some of it was directed by provocateurs who would go on to play a central role in promoting the Trump candidacy; one of the most prominent, Stephen Miller, would become Trump's main adviser on immigration policy after the election.

Over the course of a generation, right-wing media became a formidable tool of conservative political elites. Long before Trump, conservative sources coordinated closely with Republican leaders to win victories and energize voters, with the two sides often sharing talking points and action plans in advance. In 2010, Fox News would play an explicit role in mobilizing backlash to Barack Obama, urging viewers to attend Tea Party rallies. Fox did not just report the events (as mainstream outlets did); it touted them in advance while noting that Fox News hosts would attend. Fox operated, in the words of two sociologists, as "a kind of social movement orchestrator, during what is always a dicey early period for any new protest effort—the period when potential participants have to hear about the effort and decide that it is likely to prove powerful."[49]

Yet, if Republican elites used right-wing media, right-wing media also used Republican elites. And as right-wing media grew more powerful, one of the great dangers associated with the Conservative Dilemma re-emerged. Outsourcing mobilization strengthens voter intensity, but it also weakens gatekeepers, shifts power toward extremists, and pulls power away from party leaders. Today, conservative outlets offer Republicans free airtime and fired-up voters; they also discipline and punish conservative politicians who fail their tests of purity.

In a classic "be careful what you wish for" story, ambitious Republicans spent years feeding the right-wing media beast. Doing so raised their profile among the GOP faithful and gave them greater leverage over their colleagues. It also validated extreme sources and gave these sources the power to portray these very same Republicans as traitors when, inevitably, they could not deliver on their promises. As the GOP's new inquisitors gained influence, the interplay between movement media and politicians became a one-way ratchet, increasing the hold of extremist voices and forces on the party. Former George W. Bush speechwriter David Frum pithily summarized the new reality: "Republicans originally thought Fox News worked for us and now we are discovering we work for Fox."[50]

That this dynamic is now widely recognized—and, among Republicans who've suffered from it, widely lamented—doesn't make it any less extraordinary. Repeatedly, top Republicans have found themselves caught in the squeeze, until they were yanked from their positions or quit in disgust. Virginia Republican Eric Cantor had a very conservative record, was second in command in the House, and was poised to rise further when he committed the sin of signaling openness to compromise on immigration. In 2014, he became the first sitting House majority leader to ever lose a primary (the position was created in 1889), falling to an unknown Tea Party candidate with strong talk-radio support who accused him of favoring "open borders." The next year John Boehner—a conservative lieutenant in the Gingrich revolution—faced similar unrelenting attacks from the extreme right. On September 23, 2015, Fox News released a poll indicating that 60 percent of Republicans felt betrayed by their leaders. The next day the Speaker announced he would retire at the end of his term. Two years later, following a similar onslaught, it would be his successor Paul Ryan's turn to announce he was quitting.[51]

By 2016, the ratchet had tightened sufficiently to squeeze Fox News. The network faced a growing challenge from upstarts. By far the most important was the Mercer-family-financed Breitbart News, which was even more sensationalist and played a growing role in driving conservative discourse. Fox had given Donald Trump a platform, but like many figures within the GOP orbit, leaders at

Fox were skeptical of his prospects and fearful he would drag the party down. When Fox hosts—most prominently Megyn Kelly—confronted Trump, Fox viewers, urged on by Breitbart, rebelled. Ultimately Fox would recover (and Breitbart would fade), but only when Fox had followed its viewers, fully embracing the GOP's new standard bearer.[52]

To HOLD POWER WHILE PURSUING an increasingly plutocratic agenda, Republicans needed to gain the backing of voters who had little interest in that agenda. Their response was not to take up positions or seek out allies who would help them respond to these voters' economic concerns. It was to turn to groups that could bring those voters into the GOP electoral coalition with incendiary non-economic appeals.

These groups proved highly skilled. They found that building strong, locally grounded networks elicited trust and loyalty. They found that this trust and loyalty provided a platform for effective messaging. And they found that their most effective messaging combined tribalized invitations to outrage with a clear sense of threat. They delivered what Republicans wanted: intense and committed voters willing to go along with the party's plutocratic turn.

But they also delivered more than Republicans bargained for, which is why we've invoked Pandora's box. Most of the time, parties try to balance the demands of their most intense believers with the more moderate views of the rest of the electorate. Movement organizations, focused on gaining and holding a loyal following, do not face the same constraints. Nor do the strange hybrids of movement-building and profit-seeking that have emerged in the conservative media ecosystem. For both types of conservative groups, success has entailed building an extremely loyal following—and for both, that has meant stoking anger and fear.

Yet anger and fear are hard to control. It is easy to turn the dial up. It is much harder to turn it down. Republican elites thought they were harnessing conservative groups to resolve the Conservative Dilemma. More and more, however, they found the groups were harnessing them. As John Boehner's chief of staff put it, "We fed the beast that ate us."[53]

The right-wing beast increasingly looks like the monster plant in *Little Shop of Horrors* that kept demanding "Feed me!" Unfortunately for its victims, the more the plant ate the more it grew, and the more it grew the more it needed to eat. As fans of the 1986 film version all know, its (sort of) happy ending was not the one originally filmed. In the first cut, the monster plant wasn't vanquished; it spread and destroyed the earth. Test audiences hated it, and the filmmakers rewrote and reshot the final scenes.

American voters have had their own mixed reactions to the growing extremism of the Republican Party. GOP leaders, however, have mostly ignored the unfavorable reviews and instead relied even more on the mobilizing energy of negative emotions. These tactics facilitated the construction of a voting base that could support plutocratic populism. They were unlikely to produce a happy ending.

Chapter 4

IDENTITY AND PLUTOCRACY

THE LAST TWO CHAPTERS HAVE EXAMINED how the Republican Party confronted the Conservative Dilemma and opened Pandora's box. That story is not one of omniscient leaders designing a winning strategy once and for all. Rather, it is a story of trial and error, in which elites groped for, and often fought over, ways of reconciling extreme inequality and electoral imperatives. In the process, Republicans simultaneously narrowed and widened their appeals—narrowed them to ensure they were consistent with an increasingly plutocratic agenda and widened them to move from specific policy stances to generalized forms of group identity: from "this policy versus that policy" to "us versus them."

This chapter is about how and why these strategies succeeded with so many voters. Our journey starts in the South, where modern GOP campaigning began. It then moves North and West, for these strategies would not remain confined to a single region, nor would they remain focused on the black-white divide that cleaved Southern politics. Race was always front and center, but the GOP strategy was adaptable: division on cultural or social issues was the consistent goal; the specific issues and the enemy "other" at the heart of this divide were multiple and changed over time. Throughout, however, the strategies that Republicans adopted were designed to be consistent with the party's plutocratic turn.

The endpoint may now seem inevitable: an electorate split sharply along racial lines, in which racially resentful Republicans with relatively liberal economic views back a party dedicated to American plutocracy while economically conservative Republicans who are more racially progressive appear untroubled by their party's efforts to exploit ethnic, racial, religious, and anti-immigrant backlash. But plutocratic populism was not inevitable. Other roads were possible, as the struggle within the party over how to respond to America's growing Latino population reveals. The path Republicans ended up taking emerged from a long series of choices by plutocrats, politicians, and the party's surrogates. Over time, that path narrowed, and many within the party ceased to see real alternatives to radicalizing their white voting base or rigging the electoral process. But other paths could have diminished resort to these dangerous temptations.

If Republicans had weakened their embrace of plutocracy, they could have adopted economic priorities closer to those of less affluent GOP voters and diminished their reliance on divisive appeals. And if they had moderated their economic stances and softened their cultural appeals, they could have brought more nonwhite voters into the fold. That they did neither—that they cultivated voter identities that were so intense, exclusive, and divisive; that they ramped up white backlash even as American society as a whole was becoming more tolerant—wasn't because voters gave them no other options. Ultimately, it was because they chose plutocrats over everyone else.

Making this fateful choice did limit their future options, for the receivers of their apocalyptic messages would become the arbiters of their candidates' prospects. By intensifying the politics of identity to protect the priorities of the plutocracy, Republicans won over voters who might otherwise have rejected a party with a hard-right economic agenda. But having invested in division, GOP elites found they had to keep on investing—not only to attract more voters, but also to respond to those voters' radicalizing views; not only to identify new scapegoats, but also to keep those they were scapegoating from exercising their growing electoral power. Republican leaders eventually discovered that the extremism they had unleashed to tackle the Conservative Dilemma was not theirs alone to control.

IF THERE IS A SINGLE REPUBLICAN STRATEGIST most closely associated with the party's exploitation of white identity, it's probably Lee Atwater. The South Carolinian operative would become notorious in 1988 for the racially incendiary Willie Horton ad. In 1983, however, he was mostly unknown, even within the Reagan White House where he worked. So it was an audacious move when the young Atwater sent a sixty-three-page memo to Reagan's top political advisers explaining how the Republican Party could build a solid majority in the traditionally Democratic South.[1]

Atwater's core message was that a party associated with business, Wall Street, and the country-club set wasn't going to build that majority. "The South is not conservative," he explained. "If one label had to be ascribed to the whole South, that label should be 'populist.' . . . Populists are not laissez-faire free-marketers. . . . They believe the government should solve their problems for them. They believe in candidates who promise to shake up the establishment—leaders who promise bold, decisive action. This profile fits the Democratic mold."[2]

Yet these voters could be poached, Atwater argued: "Populists have always been liberal on economics. So long as the crucial issues were generally confined to economics—as during the New Deal—the liberal candidate could expect to get most of the populist vote. But populists are conservative on most social issues, including abortion, gun control, and ERA [Equal Rights Amendment]. . . . Thus, when Republicans are successful in getting certain social issues to the forefront, the populist vote is lost to liberal causes and the Democrats."[3]

Whom these white voters should unite against was obvious, though Atwater didn't hesitate to spell it out: "We must stave off Democratic attempts to forge a strong coalition of populists and blacks." In the North, many working-class whites—guided, in part, by strong unions—voted with African Americans to support progressive economic policies. That alliance had no chance in the South so long as African Americans were disenfranchised. But now they could actually vote, and they were voting Democratic. "To win in the South," Atwater concluded, "Republicans must win up to 70% of the white vote to offset the phenomenal black majorities for the opposition."[4]

In his memo, Atwater didn't elaborate much on *how* Republicans could do this. In a now infamous interview recorded around the same time, he was explicit. Politicians appealing to the white vote, he told the interviewer, had to employ rhetoric that was, in his words, "a lot more abstract" than using the n-word. (Atwater's unsettling comments were recorded by a political scientist who initially treated the young politico as an anonymous source but revealed his identity after Atwater died of brain cancer at age forty in 1991.) Even Republicans "talking about cutting taxes," Atwater argued, could ensure "race [was] coming in on the back burner." The key was to find ways to speak about policies generous to affluent white voters using language that resonated with poorer white voters. (Atwater gave an example: " 'we want to cut this,' " which was understood to mean "blacks get hurt worse than whites.") Republicans could repackage regressive economic policies to make them resonate with whites fearful of the new racial order.[5]

We now take for granted that Republicans would come to own the South. Yet as Atwater's warning about a potential "coalition of populists and blacks" suggests, Republicans did not. In 1970, Kevin Phillips—the author of *The Emerging Republican Majority* who helped inspire Nixon's Southern Strategy—shared his own racial realpolitik with a writer at the *New Yorker*: "Republicans would be shortsighted if they weakened the Voting Rights Act. The more Negroes who register as Democrats in the South, the sooner the Negrophobe whites will quit the Democrats and become Republicans. . . . Without that prodding from the blacks, the whites will backslide into their old comfortable arrangement with the local Democrats."

Republicans made sure they didn't backslide, developing messages, themes, and tactics that not only united the Southern white electorate despite growing inequality, but also played well in the North as the parties continued to nationalize and polarize. The Southern Strategy would become a template for Republican efforts in what journalists came to call "flyover country," the vast swathes of the Midwest and Interior West where economic decline, racial backlash, and anti-government animus created a toxic stew of resentment. In Atwater's confident prediction that Republicans would be the party of white "populists," we can see the roots of the tribalized, us-versus-them politics that would come to define the party's response to the Conservative Dilemma.[6]

TODAY, IT'S MORE OR LESS ASSUMED that downscale white voters will stick with the Republican Party no matter how openly it shovels benefits to corporations and the rich. We no longer find it remarkable when majorities of elected officials in states struggling with public health crises reject what is effectively free federal money for expanded health insurance (paid for by taxpayers in richer, predominantly Democratic states)—and then get reelected with the support of a large chunk of voters who suffer the most from their choices.

We should find it remarkable. Both folk wisdom and social science research suggest that voters harmed by rising inequality should gravitate to the party that vows to tackle it. Of course, voters' choices are limited, and both parties may be deterred from tackling inequality by the power of wealth. But two-party elections are all about comparative stances. If one party shows greater concern for the large majority of citizens who are losing relative ground—even if the influence of donors and lobbies diminishes that concern—that party should be advantaged. Over time, the other party will need to respond, or risk consigning itself to permanent minority status.

Indeed, this is the essence of the Conservative Dilemma. Conservative parties want to stand up for the rich when writing laws, even as the rich are increasingly outnumbered when votes are cast. If conservatives are not willing to make policy concessions to these realities, then they need to find other ways to maintain their strength. Not all these responses require opening Pandora's box. Conservative parties can gain a reputation for sound public finance or good stewardship of the economy. (For example, Republicans long benefited from the association of the "stagflation" of the 1970s with Jimmy Carter and the mid-1980s recovery with Ronald Reagan, even though economists downplay presidents' effects on the economy.) Or they can change the subject in benign ways, emphasizing particular qualities of leadership or choosing particularly charismatic leaders. Yet these strategies have their limits, especially as economic rewards tilt ever more to the top, and they're unlikely to work without the party moving at least modestly left on economic issues.

This is not just a US story. Across contemporary democracies, there is a pronounced tendency for conservative parties to emphasize noneconomic divides when inequality spikes. A recent study looked at 450 parties in forty-one electoral democracies between 1945 and 2010. When inequality was higher, parties on the right ramped up their emphasis on divisive noneconomic issues, especially those surrounding race, ethnicity, religion, and immigration. Perhaps more troubling, they did so most when increasing inequality coincided with high levels of social division. The right didn't seek to exploit values debates to shift the focus from inequality when societies were ethnically or racially homogenous, or weakly religious, or lacked a large population of immigrants. But when these cleavages could be deepened, when the social fabric was most vulnerable to tearing, stark economic inequality and sharp cultural appeals went hand in hand.[7]

The United States certainly has such cleavages. Among rich democracies, it stands out not only for its history of chattel slavery, but also for the demographic transition it is currently experiencing. Although immigration is changing many rich democracies—even today the foreign-born share of the population in the United States is not unusually high—immigrants to the United States are more likely to be nonwhite (and especially nonwhite Hispanic) than immigrants to most other rich nations. When Atwater wrote his 1983 memo, the central racial divide was black versus white. In time, backlash against the nation's growing immigrant population would become another essential ingredient in the GOP formula.[8]

Before we examine why this formula worked, we must remember why it was necessary. As inequality exploded after 1980, Republicans embraced the plutocrats and moved sharply right on economic issues. This was not a vote-maximizing shift. Plutocrats tend to be conservative on economic issues. Most voters do not. Indeed, the largest group of voters holds preferences that are almost completely inverse of the plutocratic norm. Recall that the richest Americans generally hold conservative positions on economic issues and liberal positions on social and cultural issues. By contrast, the typical voter leans *left* on economic issues and *right* on social and cultural issues. Voters are scattered all over the ideological map, but there are strikingly few that thrill to the plutocratic combination of economic conservatism and social liberalism.

If you map voters based on their answers to questions about economic issues and social issues, you get the basic picture shown in Figure 4. The figure displays the ideological placement of 8,000 nationally representative voters at the time of the 2016 election. The solid dots are Trump voters; the light gray dots, Clinton voters; the slightly darker ones, independents.

The figure has two axes, based on two sets of survey questions. The first set of questions—the horizontal axis—measures the familiar left–right divide on economics, pitting bigger, more generous government against smaller government and greater reliance on markets. The second set of questions—the vertical axis—measures social and cultural divisions, including differing perceptions of racial identity. The first set is where the conservative plutocrats put their emphasis; the second is where the Christian right, NRA, and anti-immigrant forces do.

Politicians are usually on the same side on both divides—that is, they're either liberal on both economic and social issues (bottom left) or conservative on both (top right). If you know whether members of Congress have an R or a D after their names, you know where they fall on almost all issues, economic or social. A good chunk of voters have similarly consistent views, and these voters, not surprisingly, closely align with the party that fits their liberal (Democratic) or conservative (Republican) profile.

But there are many voters who aren't so consistent: economic liberals with conservative views on social issues (upper left), and economic conservatives with liberal views on social issues (bottom right). As noted, there aren't many of the second group outside moneyed circles (and they seem pretty frustrated: notice that many of them are independents). Instead, it's the remaining bloc, economic liberals who are socially conservative, that is the more pivotal up-for-grabs faction. These are Atwater's "populists," they make up something like a third of the electorate, and they are split between

Figure 4

IDEOLOGICAL POSITIONING OF VOTERS IN 2016 ON ECONOMIC AND SOCIAL ISSUES

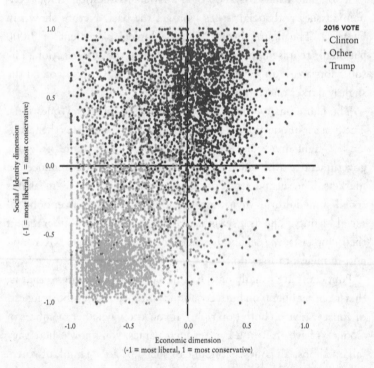

Source: Lee Drutman, "Political Divisions in 2016 and Beyond: Tensions Between and Within the Two Parties," Figure 2, Democracy Fund Voter Study Group, June 2017.

Circles represent individual voters from a nationally representative random sample. Black circles are Republicans; light gray circles Democrats; and dark gray circles, independents. The "economic dimension" is an index scaled from -1 (most liberal) to 1 (most conservative) based on reported attitudes toward the social safety net, trade, inequality, and active government; the "social/identity dimension" (y axis) is an index scaled from -1 (most liberal) to 1 (most conservative) based on reported attitudes toward moral issues, as well as views toward African-Americans, immigrants, and Muslims.

the parties. If Republicans want to hold onto power, they have to win this group. And they're not going to win them by explicitly touting hard-right positions on economics.

Or, perhaps, by touting issues at all. What Republicans learned as they refined their strategies for reaching these voters is that issues, whether economic or social, are much less powerful than *identities*. Issue positions can inform identities, but it is identities—perceptions of shared allegiance and shared threat—that really mobilize. As Republicans grappled with the Conservative Dilemma, they became increasingly reliant on such identity claims to motivate voters, and on surrogate groups that knew how to weaponize them. This fateful turn toward tribalism, with its reliance on racial animus and continual ratcheting up of fear, greatly expanded the opportunities to serve the plutocrats. Republican voters would stick with their team, even when their team was handing tax dollars to the rich, cutting programs they supported, or failing to respond to obvious opportunities to make their lives better. They would also become a much more radicalized and unpredictable force, turning their ire not just on Democrats but also on those within the party viewed as insufficiently protective of us-versus-them boundaries.

THE SOUTH WAS WHERE REPUBLICANS perfected the politics of identity, racking up larger and larger margins among white voters on their way to capturing the region. These margins would eventually reach levels comparable to those enjoyed by Democrats before 1965. In 2012, roughly 90 percent of white voters in Mississippi cast their ballot against the nation's first black president. Yet, even in the South, loyalty to the GOP had to be generated, solidified, reproduced, and broadened over time. And it had to be repeatedly intensified even as overt racial prejudice became harder for many voters to swallow and the plutocratic commitments of the party harder for many leaders to deny.

The South was where that prejudice was most embedded, of course. From Strom Thurmond's third-party run in 1948 to George Wallace's in 1968, election-night tallies consistently revealed that if given the choice between a Democrat seen as sympathetic to civil rights and a candidate who championed Jim Crow, the majority of white Democrats would defect. Between 1958 and 1980, the share of white voters who said they were Democrats fell by roughly twenty percentage points, with most of the decline occurring amid the civil rights struggles of the 1960s. Essentially all of that twenty-point decline occurred among voters who were resistant to black political equality. No other factor accounts for the shift—not Southern voters' Cold War hawkishness, not their fattening wallets, and certainly not their stances on economic issues (which were actually more liberal, on average, than those of voters in the North).[9]

Still, the transformation of the South into a Republican stronghold took much longer than is commonly appreciated. It was not until 1994, for instance, that a majority of white Southern voters backed Republican congressional candidates, allowing Newt Gingrich to consolidate his party's deepening alliance with plutocracy. Nor was 1994 the highwater mark of the party's emphasis on social issues and racial resentment. A decade later, the head of the Republican National Committee, Ken Mehlman, spoke with unusual frankness when he admitted that "into the eighties and nineties . . . Republicans gave up on winning the African American vote, looking the other way or trying to benefit politically from racial polarization." Even then, the process was still unfolding. That initial twenty-point drop in the share of white Southerners who identified with the Democrats was more than matched by an *additional* decline of more than twenty points between 1980 and 2016.[10]

This second drop was not steady; it accelerated after the mid-1990s. The share of Southern white voters identifying with the Democrats was 42.6 percent in 1996, 34.8 percent in 2008, and 27 percent in 2016. During this second drop, moreover, white identification with the Democratic Party fell sharply *outside* the South, too.[11]

Behind this precipitous drop was a set of strategies that emerged out of the distinctive Southern context but became more and more essential to GOP success nationwide. Call them the three Rs of Republican base-building: resentment, racialization, and rigging.

Resentment is the most important R, the one that ultimately

keeps voters in the fold even when their economic interests conflict with their party's priorities. It reflects deep perceptions of unfairness—but not the unfairness that comes with plutocracy. Instead, as Katherine Cramer explains in her study of rural consciousness in Wisconsin, voters' indignation is directed at fellow citizens "who they think are eating their share of the pie." In his 2004 book, *What's the Matter with Kansas?*, Thomas Frank speaks of "backlash" rather than "resentment," but he too shows how the GOP mobilizes working-class whites using cultural outrage, "which it then marries to pro-business economic policies." Whatever the chosen label, resentment is a way of seeing the world that replaces one way of defining us versus them—the way that might seem obvious given runaway inequality—with another. Nor do these interpretations simply bubble up from below; they are, in Cramer's words, "encouraged, perhaps fomented, by political leaders who exploit these divisions for political gain."[12]

Resentment has a who and a what: a shared sense of group membership and a shared dislike, even hatred, of those outside this circle. Social groups are ubiquitous, especially in complex modern societies. Not all groups, however, feed feelings of resentment. Social psychologists have found that even trivial group differences can be made consequential by heightening inter-group competition, but the most intense resentment emerges from the most salient divides. What has made resentment such an asset for the GOP is that, more and more, partisanship has mapped onto these divides, creating a self-reinforcing loop that aligns and magnifies both.

Voters have always identified with parties. Over the past generation, though, partisan identities have become more strongly held, more uniform across the nation, and more powerful determinants of how people vote. In short, voters have become more tribal. Voters don't just express affection for their own party; increasingly, they harbor deep antipathy for their perceived opponents—the "affective" or "negative" polarization that defines American politics today.

This sense of antipathy is particularly strong on the Republican side (though Donald Trump now seems to be creating similar levels of grievance among Democrats). Voters are not nearly as polarized as their representatives, but their attitudes and activities display some of the same asymmetries seen among elites. As the parties diverged after 1980, Republican voters expressed greater hostility toward Democratic officeholders than did Democratic voters toward Republican officeholders. They also expressed much less enthusiasm for the notion that their party's politicians should seek compromise. Moreover, extreme conservative positions were most prevalent among the most active Republican voters, whereas a sizable chunk of the most active Democrats remained relatively moderate. In the race toward affective polarization, Republicans led the way.[13]

Republican antipathy reached a new high after Barack Obama's election. In the first two years of the Obama presidency, Republican voters expressed levels of distrust in government never before recorded in US polls: in one survey that gave voters the option of saying they "never" trusted government, half of Republicans chose that option. As late as August 2016, only around a quarter of Republican voters were confident that President Obama had been born in the United States; the most informed GOP voters were no more likely to acknowledge the truth. This intense hostility is all the more notable because Republican politicians have moved further from the center than have their Democratic counterparts: GOP voters may have decried President Obama as a foreign-born socialist, but, according to the best political science measures, he was far closer to the political middle than was George W. Bush.[14]

There is one way in which Republican voters look less extreme. Despite a steady diet of anti-government rhetoric, many still hold relatively liberal views on economic issues, as the map of voters' attitudes in Figure 4 suggests. Figure 5 provides another revealing picture of the stark divide between GOP elites and the party's voting base. Based on a 2012 survey designed by academic researchers, it shows what proportion of various segments of the electorate supported two central GOP policy aims of the period: the extension of the early-2000s Bush tax cuts, even for the richest Americans; and Paul Ryan's ultra-conservative budget. (In both cases, the basic features of each bill were neutrally described.) Among all voters, the complete extension of the Bush tax cuts had just 25 percent support, while the Ryan budget commanded an even more dismal 19 percent support. Among Republican voters, the results were better but still bad: 42 percent and 32 percent, respectively. In other words, the two central planks of the GOP tax and fiscal agenda in 2012 each fell well short of majority support among the party's own voters—in the case of the Ryan budget, spectacularly short. The only group within the electorate for which support topped a majority for both proposals was GOP donors with incomes in excess of $250,000 a year.

Figure 5

THE STARK DIVIDE BETWEEN GOP ELITES AND THE PARTY'S VOTING BASE

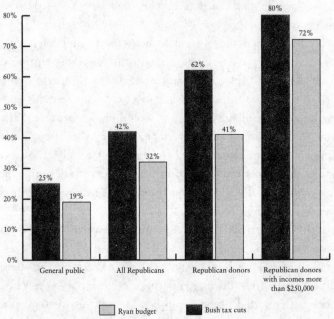

Ryan budget   Bush tax cuts

Source: Center for American Progress analysis of the Cooperative Congressional Election Survey, https://www.americanprogress.org/issues/economy/news/2016/03/15/133350/how-the-house-budget-sides -with-the-wealthy-over-everyone-else-even-republican-voters/. Data available at "CCES Common Content, 2012," Harvard Dataverse, V8, available at http://hdl.handle.net/1902.1/21447. See also Didi Kuo and Nolan McCarty, "Democracy in America, 2015," *Global Policy* 6 (2015).

Share of the public, Republicans, Republican donors, and wealthy Republican donors (more than $250,000 annual income) supporting the Ryan budget (gray) and extending the Bush tax cuts even for the rich (black). Only among wealthy Republican donors do majorities support both policies.

No wonder Republican elites attempted to root partisanship in the kind of intensely held allegiances associated with surrogate groups such as the NRA. These leaders intuited what a burgeoning body of research would soon quantify: If you can align partisanship with resentment, voters will largely ignore your retreat from even strongly held positions. In fact, they might even bring their own positions in line with those of the party claiming to defend their way of life, even when that party is doing them material harm. This is how the particularly intense form of negative polarization on the right has enabled Republicans' tightening embrace of plutocracy. If voters are already in your camp and will remain there almost no matter what you do, you can do things that directly hurt them without facing the consequences that politicians usually confront for such betrayals.

In short, Republicans tried to both purify and intensify their base, creating a party electorate with as few cross-cutting commitments as possible. Racial resentment was the party's entering wedge, so to speak, because white identity was potentially so powerful. But white identity was so powerful in part because it aligned with so many other identities emphasized by the party: Christian conservative, gun owner, rural and small-town resident, believer in traditional gender roles. (By contrast, the Democratic voting base is much more racially and religiously diverse.) The important thing, as revealed by the narrowing approach of the party's surrogates, was to reinforce partisan allegiance in ways consistent with the party's plutocratic turn.

The process can be seen most clearly in the changing character of party primaries. Beginning in the South, primary voters became much better sorted: Republicans were more consistently conservative; Democrats more liberal. Yet moderates continued to run in, and win, Democratic primaries. Republican primaries, by contrast, increasingly pitted candidates of the right against candidates of the far right—first in the South and then nationwide. The difference between the two parties reflected contrasting patterns of candidate recruitment (according to surveys of local party leaders, there is much greater emphasis on ideological purity on the Republican side), as well as the distinctive role of extreme groups on the right (Republicans who turn out for primary elections are much more extreme than their party's typical voter; Democratic primary voters are not). But it also reflected GOP voters' greater affective polarization, which made it much easier to win general elections with extreme Republican candidates because voter defections from the party were so rare.[15]

At the same time, the defections that occurred from the Democratic Party over this period—captured in that long-term slide in Democratic identification—do not seem to have been driven mainly by economic issues. Rather, they occurred first among voters who held conservative views on racial issues. After the 1990s, views on religion, gun ownership, gender roles, abortion, gay rights, immigration, and crime seem to have loomed large in driving defections. The result was a tightening alignment of partisanship and strongly held social identities, especially identities associated with the politics of resentment. But resentment did not do its work alone. There was another powerful weapon in the GOP arsenal that helped it serve the rich while rhetorically championing the working class.[16]

THE SECOND R of Republican base-building is racialization. The term is unwieldy, but no other denotes so accurately the alchemical process by which racial stereotypes can be carried along by seemingly race-free rhetoric. Social psychologists have spent decades showing just how powerful white Americans' implicit biases are. Political scientists have spent almost as much time showing how politicians use coded "dog-whistle" language and imagery to inflame these biases. Today, Donald Trump sees no reason to euphemize. But it is the hidden ways in which racism gets voiced—developed over decades—that paved the way for Trump's more overt rhetoric to become acceptable to so many.[17]

The reasons for speaking in code may seem obvious, but they're worth itemizing. For one, Americans have grown more racially tolerant over time, including in the South. Or at least they profess greater tolerance when asked by pollsters, which is why canny politicians prefer to whisper, rather than shout. Consider a simple measure of racial resentment: whether voters say they would support a candidate of their own party who was black. In the late 1950s, less than half of white voters in the North and just one in ten in the South said yes. By 1980, the share was three-quarters in the North and six in ten in the South. By 2000, the South and North had converged, with almost all voters in both regions saying they would support a black candidate.[18]

When open racism is seen as retrograde, coded appeals make sense. They might not have as visceral an impact, but they still do their dirty work and they're far more effective among voters who may not even recognize their own racial biases—voters who respond with genuine anger when told that the ostensibly race-neutral positions they take have roots in highly race-laden assumptions and associations. Moreover, coded appeals are less likely to elicit pushback from trusted sources in the media or politics. In 1988, for example, Atwater's Willie Horton ad produced an immediate shift toward Bush, but some of these gains were reversed when journalists (responding to black opinion leaders and Dukakis's campaign) began to decry Bush's attack. This pushback effect also helps explain why the increasingly exclusive reliance of GOP voters on conservative media is so important: not only are they much less likely to be exposed to such counter-narratives, but even when they are, their trusted sources encourage them to see it as yet another insult to their character rather than a reason to question their leaders' intentions.[19]

Finally, coded bias can become campaign boilerplate, repeated over and over in the way that studies suggest is necessary to form enduring associations. Old-fashioned racism is much less likely to make this transition from message to meme.

The memes that trigger racial bias are many and varied: crime, law and order, radical Islamic terrorism, anchor babies, chain migration. Yet the racialization of government spending may be the biggest coding success of all. The collapse of trust in government in the 1960s and 1970s had many causes. But it was not just a response to objective events; it was a product of unrelenting efforts—mostly by Republicans and particularly by Southern

Republicans—to demonize and delegitimize the federal government. From Reagan's claim that "government *is* the problem" to Newt Gingrich's denunciation of a "bureaucratic, corrupt, liberal welfare state," Republicans attacked government in order to win control of government. In the process, they devised a language of resentment that's now so familiar it's virtually impossible to banish from our minds—one in which public spending supports the idle and criminal (read: blacks), taxes are essentially theft from hardworking families (read: whites), and the brokers of this corrupt transfer are Washington politicians on the take (read: Democrats) who look down on "real America."[20]

The legacies of this rhetorical sleight of hand are everywhere. No decoder ring is necessary when Bill O'Reilly tells Fox viewers, "I don't believe that my money and everybody's money who's worked for a living should be going to people who are on crack. . . . Yet it continues and continues into trillions of entitlement money that goes right down the rat hole."[21]

Notice the word "entitlement." Technically, federal programs are entitlements when they guarantee benefits to all who are eligible. The largest such programs are Social Security and Medicare. These programs also happen to be overwhelmingly popular, particularly among the older white voters so crucial to Republican electoral prospects. Most programs for the poor, by contrast, aren't entitlements in the strict sense. But conservative elites use "entitlement" not because of what it denotes, but because of what it connotes: people who feel "entitled" to the hard-earned tax dollars of those who "worked for a living." (What distinguished Mitt Romney's infamous assertion in 2012 that 47 percent of people "believe that they are entitled to health care, to food, to housing, to you-name-it" wasn't its coded use of "entitlement" but its insinuation that half of Americans were "takers." Usually Republicans let their listeners come up with their own image of whose entitlement they should be resentful of.) By using the term, conservatives are also able to talk about cutting "entitlements"—by which they actually mean Social Security, Medicare, and Medicaid—and many of those who listen to them think they are talking about eliminating giveaways for freeloaders who don't look like them. Atwater couldn't have come up with a better way of turning "cutting" into "blacks get hurt more than whites."

But the most potent racialized descriptor is unquestionably "welfare." Public opposition to antipoverty assistance is closely associated with racial prejudice: white Americans who are most hostile to "welfare" overstate how much it costs, overestimate how much of it goes to African Americans, and draw on negative stereotypes about black people—often subconsciously—in forming their views. In the South, these racially rooted attitudes are particularly prevalent and powerful. But the conflation of federal spending and aid to the poor is a feature of public opinion nationwide. Whether using national polls or conducting in-depth interviews with right-leaning voters, social scientists have found the same basic patterns. Most of the things that government does to aid the rich, such as tax breaks for vacation homes, aren't seen as public benefits at all. Big programs for the middle class are seen as distinct from "big government" and as "earned" (even though, for most who receive them, benefits considerably exceed contributions). Meanwhile, small programs for the poor get labeled "welfare," take on outsized importance, and elicit strong racial resentment.[22]

This distorted view of government is now so ingrained that it can be deployed in almost any context. In places that experience a large influx of immigrants, the roots of resistance are often culturally grounded—"they're not like us"—but the most common complaints that get voiced concern fiscal burdens. Expert after expert has debunked these arguments: immigrants pay taxes, they're less likely to be involved in criminal activity, and they're often not eligible for public benefits. Yet racialized perceptions work not because they're true, but because they "feel true." Furthermore, they can do that work among resentful voters who might recoil at overt nativism, enabling these voters to see their opposition to immigration or distrust of Hispanic citizens as opposition to lawbreaking and freeloading, not to people with darker skin.

Resentment and racialization thus shifted over time to encompass a wider and wider range of targets. In the 1970s and 1980s, Southern politicians led the way in the development of language and issues that could reliably activate resentment against African Americans. In the 1990s and especially after 2000, they also played a major role in shaping the party's response to immigration. For as the South absorbed increasing flows of Hispanic immigrants, the racial balance shifted dramatically in places where racial divisions had always been at the center of partisan struggle. Republicans had to respond, and they did—although not, for the most part, with welcoming arms. With strategies of resentment and racialization already well established, they would have had to reverse course to compete more effectively for Hispanic voters. Republicans did not reverse course. Facing a new demographic challenge, they reached for the third R: rigging.

Now that Republican efforts to suppress voting and gerrymander districts are at the center of national debate, rigging is the element of the GOP formula least in need of elaboration. Vote rigging has a very long and very ugly history in the South, and its resurgence in recent decades has also had a strong Southern accent. Yet vote rigging has become deeply ingrained within GOP strategy in all parts of the nation where Republicans have had sufficient power and incentive to pursue it, especially over the last decade. We will look at these affronts to the integrity and fairness of the electoral process at length in Chapter 6. For now, let's briefly consider how they fit into Republicans' response to their Conservative Dilemma.

Resentment and racialization are about keeping white voters loyal, even as rising inequality and the GOP's embrace of plutocracy place that loyalty at risk. Rigging is about keeping voters who are not so loyal—and especially those who are not white—from challenging the electoral sway of those white voters. Virtually without exception, every form of vote rigging used by Republicans is designed to weaken the electoral influence of nonwhite voters (and the areas in which they live) and to heighten the influence of white Republicans (and the areas in which they live). If you doubt this, look at any state in which Republicans have had unified power and superimpose the state's legislative map onto a map of where racial minorities live, or tally the racial mix of those most likely to run afoul of voting restrictions. Rigging was just as focused on race as resentment and racialization.

In effect, the party's Conservative Dilemma played out in two overlapping phases. In the first, which began as the rising share of income going to the rich became unmistakable, Republicans had to find an electoral strategy that worked alongside their embrace of plutocracy. In the second, which began as the rising share of the US population made up of non-white Hispanics became undeniable, they had to do this *and* grapple with a demographic transformation that collided with that strategy. Kevin Phillips welcomed the Voting Rights Act because he knew whites fleeing to the GOP would bring with them electoral majorities in the South. But the demographic changes resulting from immigration destroyed such confidence— both in the South and outside it. Fortunately for Republicans, but not American democracy, their solid majorities built on resentment and racialization made rigging a viable means of tackling this challenge.

As with the embrace of plutocracy, there were divisions within the GOP over whether to moderate their rhetoric and policies to attract nonwhite voters. Well into the Obama presidency, in fact, key Republican figures argued for building a bridge to Hispanics—a strategy that could have slowed or even reversed the party's slide toward plutocratic populism. Ultimately, however, they received little tangible support for their efforts from their plutocratic allies. Nor were their efforts adequate to defuse the resentment and racialization they had already unleashed, the surrogate groups they had empowered, or the skilled practitioners of social division with whom they shared a party label. These forces didn't want to build a bridge; they wanted to build power (and, some of them, a wall). And they were more than willing to exploit white backlash to do so.

PICTURE A CROWDED COMMUTER TRAIN station at rush hour in a typical suburb. Two young men walk onto the platform and start speaking to each other. They're good-looking, cheery, and well-dressed; people who see pictures of them describe them as "friendly." They also look Hispanic—like "immigrants," according to those same photo-viewers—and they're speaking in Spanish. Virtually everyone else at the station is white.

Within a few days, the white passengers—commuting from the overwhelmingly Democratic suburbs of Boston—offer substantially more conservative responses to questions about immigration than they had before the arrival of the two men. They are more likely to say immigration from Mexico should be reduced and less likely to say the children of undocumented immigrants should be allowed to stay in the United States. Two people among hundreds encountered for a short time—that is, signals that might seem pretty subtle—are enough to create backlash among citizens inclined to support immigration.[23]

The signals sent by American immigration over the last generation have been anything but subtle. Between 1990 and 2016, the share of the US population self-identifying as Hispanic doubled from 9 percent to 18 percent. Immigrants and their immediate descendants now represent one in four Americans. More than half of children under age five are nonwhite. Births now contribute more to the growing Hispanic population than immigration. More than 90 percent of Latinos younger than eighteen are citizens. Within Latino America, a group larger than San Francisco's entire population becomes eligible to vote each year.[24]

Against this backdrop, the story of those Boston commuters—an actual experiment carried out by a Harvard political scientist in 2012—looks more ominous. When outsiders breach the boundaries of established social groups, those within them often react with resentment, even revulsion. "In-groups" don't just feel threatened by "out-groups"; they may seek to exclude them and deny them the benefits of community membership, with the force of law if necessary. According to decades of research, the outs don't even need to be numerous relative to the ins for resentment to set in, certainly not numerous enough to pose any real threat. Even small changes in their numbers, if visible and proximate enough, can create a visceral response.[25]

Demographic changes in America since the 1990s have not been small. By the midpoint of this century, the United States is expected to become a majority-minority nation. In truth, this well-known forecast is misleading. For one, the voting-eligible population greatly lags the national population aggregates, both because many of America's minority residents aren't citizens and because recent immigrant populations vote at lower rates than either blacks or native-born whites. For another, much of the change will be driven by mixed families—especially Asian-white and Hispanic-white families—and children in these families often identify as white. But the shift is still dramatic. More important, today's native-born whites see it as dramatic.[26]

In a series of clever experiments, the psychologists Jennifer Richeson and Maureen Craig have shown that simply sharing population projections predicting that whites will become a minority produces big reactions, including anger, fear, greater identity with whites, and greater resentment toward nonwhites. At the same time, it produces a significant shift to the right on a range of issues, from those related to race (affirmative action, immigration), to those not about race but clearly racialized (health care, taxes), to those with no obvious racial connection (oil and gas drilling). Telling white people that they're losing their dominant status produces a large and broad-based conservative response.[27]

The conclusion seems unmistakable: white backlash is inevitable, and it invariably helps Republicans. Yet that's not the only possible conclusion. Although the perception that out-groups are gaining ground does trigger in-group fear and anxiety, social scientists have found that the response of elites—those with the power to shape how these changes are understood and how politics and policy get reoriented around them—is crucial in determining the consequences. In Richeson's experiments, simply telling white Americans that their social status wasn't likely to change because of increased racial diversity wiped out all the effects of the demographic forecasts. Just reframing the projections that showed whites would become a minority—without changing those projections in any way—seemed to reassure white Americans that their initial feeling of threat was unwarranted.

Consider a real-world example: white voters who backed the nation's first black president in 2008. It turns out that there's a widely neglected factor that powerfully shapes whether middle-income whites—the voters with whom Trump did particularly well in

2016—back Democratic candidates. That factor is whether a voter lives in a household with at least one union member. In 2008, middle-income whites in union households were about 50 percent more likely to vote for Obama than voters with similar characteristics who didn't have a union connection. They were also more likely to turn out on election day. In short, unions matter, and they matter, in substantial part, because they encourage their members to vote on the basis of pocketbook issues and to vote for Democrats—even for Democrats whose skin color might make them uncomfortable. Given that roughly a quarter of non-Southern voters hailed from unionized households in 2008 (the share was only half that in the South), this is a huge effect. The partisan gap between union and nonunion members is bigger, for instance, than the gap between those with and without a college degree.[28]

Studies of ethnic conflict in other countries have also stressed the pivotal role of elites. Scholars have identified a perverse form of political competition, ethnic outbidding, in which political leaders jockeying for support from an ethnically homogeneous group seek to outdo each other with ever more exclusionary appeals, fueling tribalism that can spiral into bloodshed. However, according to this body of research, ethnic hostility is a necessary but not sufficient condition for civil war: even in deeply divided societies, "mass-led violence cannot become a full-scale ethnic war without elite manipulation and mobilization of mass media," as one recent study puts it. Most dangerous is when outbidding occurs within a party that draws its support overwhelmingly from a nation's dominant ethnic group. In these cases, not only is there greater demand for ethnonationalism, there's also less likely to be pushback from minority voters (or elites courting those voters) within the party. Instead, the outbidders can "paint opposing moderate elites within one's own group as softies, cowards, and even traitors."[29]

The experiment at the commuter train station in Boston indirectly makes the same point. No one at the station made immigration an issue; the commuters were forming their own attitudes based on their own perceptions. Those attitudes, it turned out, softened as time wore on. Within ten days, the commuters were responding to the same questions about immigration with more welcoming views. By this point, it was impossible to be statistically confident their views were any different from those of commuters who hadn't encountered the two Hispanic men. "People have started to recognize and smile to us," one of the young Mexican Americans told the Harvard researcher. A passenger initiated a conversation with them by saying "the longer you see the same person every day, the more confident you feel to greet and say hi to them." Presumably, if the experiment had continued for months or years rather than weeks, attitudes would have softened further. They might even have turned positive.

Of course, two well-dressed men in a train station is a pretty mild threat. The response might have been different if many more commuters who looked like immigrants had shown up. Certainly, it would have been different if someone the passengers trusted had jumped on a soapbox to denounce Hispanic immigrants as a threat to white America.

AFTER DONALD TRUMP WON THE PRESIDENCY in 2016, the news site Vox proclaimed that the train station experiment was "Trump's electoral strategy in a nutshell." But the experiment says little about electoral strategy; its lessons concern mass psychology. Trump did exploit that psychology. But in the years prior to his ascent, alternative campaign strategies—ones that short-circuited in-group fear, rather than exacerbating it—were very much available to the Republican Party.[30]

The last major immigration bill that became law passed in 1986, when Ronald Reagan was president. It strengthened border and employer enforcement, but also allowed immigrants who had entered the country illegally to become citizens, a move now decried as "amnesty" among GOP politicians. During the 1984 campaign, Reagan told a pollster, "Hispanics are Republicans; they just don't know it yet."

As late as 2004, Reagan's quip seemed more optimistic than ironic. That year, George W. Bush won reelection with nearly 45 percent of the Hispanic vote, capturing Latino-heavy Arizona, Colorado, New Mexico, Nevada, Florida, and, of course, Texas. Moreover, Bush's appeal to Hispanic voters had strong backing within the GOP establishment, with the Republican National Committee spending more that year on outreach to Latinos than did the Democratic National Committee. As GOP consultant Lance Tarrance explained at the RNC's annual meeting in 2000, "For the last three decades, we've had a Southern strategy. The next goal is to move to a Hispanic strategy for the next three decades."[31]

Many Republican elites believed that the alternative was far worse. Senator John McCain, whose bipartisan immigration reform bill was the focal point of debate in the late 2000s and again in the mid-2010s, insisted the party's future hung in the balance. McCain ally Lindsey Graham, speaking in 2012, warned, "We're not generating enough angry white guys to stay in business for the long term." Within four years, however, Trump would keep the party in business by tightening the party's embrace of anti-immigrant outrage. Meanwhile, Hispanic voters (who, as late as 2013, had signaled surprising openness to Republican candidates in surveys) would give Hillary Clinton the same margins that they'd given an incumbent Democratic president in 2012, despite a much closer contest.[32]

What happened? The conventional answer is that Hispanic voters were a lost cause after anti-immigrant Republicans scuttled at least two serious attempts to pass immigration reform. Those repeated failures, in turn, emboldened anti-immigrant forces and candidates within the GOP. Without much prospect of attracting Hispanics, leading Republicans who sought to replicate the Bush 2004 strategy—among them his brother Jeb in 2016—were easily outflanked.

What this account leaves out, however, is how the party's embrace of plutocracy limited its options. The GOP's cratering among Latinos wasn't simply a result of the failure of immigration reform, or even of the anti-immigrant voices within the party. It was also a reflection of the party's continuing rightward movement on economic issues.

Latinos are far from single-issue voters. In the years that the

Republican Party debated immigration reform, surveys suggested that the issue was high on Hispanic voters' agenda. But other issues generally ranked higher. Beyond immigration, Latino voters generally didn't look so different from white Americans without a college degree: they held many conservative values, but their major concerns were economic security and upward mobility.[33]

The problem for Republicans was that Latino voters were not going to stick with a party that delivered on neither economic issues nor immigration reform. As Bush entered his second term, his top-heavy tax cuts had wrecked the budget, and his party was agitating for big spending cuts to close the gap. Reelected in 2004 with a record share of the Hispanic vote, Bush tried to spend his hard-earned "political capital" on privatizing Social Security, hardly a formula for building broader support on economic issues. His drive for immigration reform was launched only as the 2008 election neared—a late and ultimately fruitless attempt to reassure Hispanic voters that only succeeded in driving a deeper wedge within his own party.

Republicans lost Hispanics in part because they couldn't quit plutocrats. Corporate lobbies were supportive of a low-cost immigration bill that would help keep Republicans in power, but they weren't supportive of the party moving to the center on economic issues. What's more, their support for immigration reform was tepid, while their pursuit of their economic priorities was relentless. Low-wage employers that relied heavily on immigrants had rallied behind the 1986 reform bill, encouraging Republicans like Reagan to back it. But by the 2000s, many of these employers had moved overseas, mechanized their production, or gone out of business. The US Chamber of Commerce and other business groups issued press releases that expressed general support for immigration reform, but the amount they spent on the cause was a rounding error next to the money they spent lobbying for tax cuts, deregulation, and corporate subsidies.[34]

Nor did other organs of plutocratic influence contribute much to the effort. Just one prominent conservative think tank, the Cato Institute, was genuinely pro-immigration. Yet, by the 2000s, its libertarian rationale was destined to fall flat among GOP voters and the politicians who sought their favor. Another, the American Enterprise Institute, basically avoided engaging the issue at all.

The Heritage Foundation, by contrast, was engaged—on the hardliners' side. Though still committed to plutocratic stances on economic issues, its leadership and some of its donors saw the opportunity to gain influence by siding with the rising anti-immigrant voices within the party. Heritage became the intellectual hub of the opposition to comprehensive immigration reform, though "intellectual" is a bit of a stretch. Its virulently anti-immigrant spokesmen crafted the racialized framings that are now central to GOP rhetoric on immigration, describing the flow of migrants and refugees across the Southern border as an "invasion" that fed both foreign and domestic terrorism and voter fraud.

Heritage's move toward the fringe was the story of Republican-allied groups more generally. By the 2010s, right-wing organizations, conservative media, and enterprising nativists like Steve King and Michelle Bachmann were well into their successful campaign of ethnic outbidding. Bachmann, who ran for president in 2012 with a promise to deport the 10 to 12 million undocumented immigrants living in the United States, decried even modest efforts to provide temporary legal status to immigrants who'd come as children, prophesying that "the social cost will be profound on the U.S. taxpayer—millions of unskilled, illiterate, foreign nationals coming into the United States who can't speak the English language."[35]

In addition to the prominence that came with her presidential ambitions, Bachmann was one of the almost seventy House members who had come into office with the support of the Tea Party. The Tea Party was known as a grassroots movement, but it also had plenty of backing from conservative plutocrats who wanted to undermine the Obama agenda. Although the movement's central message was that government had grown too big, Tea Partiers in Washington also took extreme positions on social issues, including immigration: 70 percent of the House Tea Party Caucus also belonged to the euphemistically named Immigration Reform Caucus, the center of anti-immigration leadership in Congress.[36]

They knew their constituents: a national survey of voters conducted around the same time found that almost two-thirds of those who identified with the Tea Party wanted to get rid of birthright citizenship. More than 80 percent said they were "anxious" or "fearful" of immigrants who came to the country without legal authorization. These views weren't just to the right of those of most voters; they were to the right of those of conservatives who didn't embrace the Tea Party, less than half of whom believed in ending birthright citizenship.[37]

In 2013, these forces of backlash ran headlong into the mounting worries of those who feared the party was shrinking. In the wake of Mitt Romney's decisive defeat, the RNC issued a post-election analysis that reporters immediately labeled the "autopsy report." In it, top party insiders issued an urgent call: "America is changing demographically, and . . . the changes tilt the playing field even more in the Democratic direction. . . . [W]e must embrace and champion comprehensive immigration reform. If we do not, our Party's appeal will continue to shrink to its core constituencies only."[38]

The autopsy report appeared to send a clear message about what the Republican Party should do. But another message was sent when Eric Cantor, second in command in the House, unexpectedly lost his primary to an anti-immigration challenger. Right-wing media attacks were central to that loss, as they were to the defeat of immigration reform in both 2007 and 2013. (During the first fight, Republican senator Jeff Sessions expressed gratitude that his party's president had failed to push a bill through "before Rush Limbaugh could tell the American people what was in it.") As conservative media celebrities and the Tea Party celebrated Cantor's loss, the conservative political analyst Sean Trende of RealClearPolitics wrote an influential series of articles that argued that Republicans could win without strong Latino support so long as they energized the "missing white voters." The rest, as they say, is history.[39]

The rejection of the autopsy analysis (and of those, like Cantor, who favored it) revealed how siding with the plutocrats and opening Pandora's box had progressively narrowed Republicans' options. There was an alternative: more moderate positions on immigration *and* economics—the policy mix that George W. Bush had promised but failed to deliver. Yet this combination wasn't consistent with the party's plutocratic stances or its growing reliance on white backlash. Another mash-up, however, was: plutocratic populism. It would find its maestro in a candidate who had responded to the Republican National Committee's autopsy report with a tweet: "Does the @RNC have a death wish?"[40]

AFTER DONALD TRUMP'S IMPROBABLE VICTORY, pundits who had assumed his campaign was doomed set about trying to explain why it had succeeded. Journalists made pilgrimages to declining Midwest towns. Studies of the "white working class" became something close to their own literary genre. The plot of every story in that genre was that Trump won because he did something fundamentally different from Republicans before him.

Yet the most notable feature of the 2016 results wasn't how strange they were, but how familiar. Despite the many shocking aspects of Trump's campaign, most Republican voters did what they had done in 2012: they voted against the Democrat and for the Republican. Trump's performance affirmed the many studies showing that negative polarization had come to define his party—even Trump was preferable to Clinton for the vast majority of GOP voters. As late as the fall of 2016, roughly a quarter of GOP voters said they saw Trump as unqualified for the presidency. Still, on November 8, virtually all Republicans voted for him.[41]

Nor was Trump's strong performance among white voters who lacked a college degree without precedent. Over the course of a generation, as we have seen, Republican elites forged a distinctive strategy that combined increasingly conservative policies with increasingly resentment-laden campaigns. Mobilizing white voters with divisive identity claims, Republicans reached down the income ladder for support, rather than across racial, religious, and ethnic lines. Unwilling to moderate economically yet needing to motivate voters to stay in power, they embraced the three R's of resentment, racialization, and rigging. They went in pursuit of Atwater's populists so they could maintain their alliance with America's plutocrats.

Still, Trump did demonstrate what many in the party's leadership denied: a good share of those populists had little in common with the plutocrats on economic issues. "I'm not going to cut Social Security like every other Republican. And I'm not going to cut Medicare or Medicaid," Trump promised early in his campaign. On health care, he said, "I am going to take care of everybody. I don't care if it costs me votes or not. Everybody's going to be taken care of much better than they're taken care of now . . . the government's gonna pay for it." It is easy to dismiss these statements now. Yet polls conducted during the campaign show that voters heard and believed them: they had much more trouble placing Trump on the left–right spectrum than they did Clinton, and Trump was viewed as more left-leaning than any winning Republican candidate since Gallup started asking about candidate ideology in the 1970s.[42]

And while Trump's divisive appeals built on his party's long Southern Strategy, Trump exploited identity politics and affective polarization as no modern presidential victor had. For decades, Republican elites had refined their euphemisms, arguing that government was merely a vehicle for "welfare" and inflaming the resentment of white voters toward nonwhite "entitlements." Trump threw the euphemisms out. His anti-immigration and anti-Muslim rhetoric conjured up a vast army of dark-skinned criminals. He spoke of an "invasion" that not only threatened the safety and jobs of upstanding white citizens, but also their electoral majority. After the election, he claimed that he would have won the popular vote but for the illegal ballots of millions of undocumented immigrants, a charge that, like his others about voter fraud, was unfounded but effective at animating his supporters.[43]

Race wasn't the only identity card Trump played. He also split men and women as no modern candidate had before. On election day, the so-called gender gap was a record 24 points (Trump won men by 12 points and lost women by 12 points), with the increase over 2012 driven by unusually high support for the Republican candidate among white men. Here again, though, Trump intensified an ongoing trend: the gender gap in 2012 was 20 points (Obama won women by 12 points and lost men by 8 points), and in fact no Republican presidential candidate has won a majority of women's votes since George H. W. Bush in 1988. Trump's undeniable misogyny led many to predict he would crater among female voters. But negative polarization won out. Although nonwhite women gave Trump near-zero support, white women backed Trump, and Southern white women chose Trump over Clinton by a 25-point margin.[44]

Since the election, a mostly unproductive debate has taken place between those who insist Trump's victory was all about "racism" and those who, like us, think it had a lot to do with economics, too. The debate is mostly unproductive because it's framed as a binary choice. If the question is whether many Trump voters were motivated by racial resentment, the answer is yes. If the question is whether the rise of plutocracy contributed to the party strategies and voter mindsets that allowed Trump to tap that resentment, the answer is an equally emphatic yes.

Extreme inequality drove the Republican Party toward strategies of division and demonization to rally their white voting base. Extreme inequality was also a powerful contributor to the alienation of that base. The voters who swung to Republicans between 2012 and 2016 generally came from areas where the increasing riches of the plutocracy had coincided with long-term economic decline. Trump did well in areas where unemployment was higher, job growth slower, earnings lower, and overall health poorer. (One of the strongest county-level predictors of Trump's vote was the rate of premature death among white Americans.) Backlash against immigrants and racial minorities certainly does not require America's extreme inequality. But right-wing populism is most potent where, and among those who feel, opportunities for economic security and advancement have been lost.[45]

Was everyone who voted for Trump suffering economically? No. But Trump capitalized on the suffering there was. An economics research paper released two months before Trump won eerily foretold his victory: looking at areas of the country most affected by competition from China, the researchers found something that might have seemed odd in another political system. Where the bottom fell out of the local economy, moderate politicians disappeared from office. In a few such places, they were replaced with strongly left-leaning representatives—but only in those rare cases when an area was highly diverse, highly Democratic, or both. Everywhere else, radicalized Republicans gained power. The people in these places weren't obviously more racist or anti-immigrant than those that didn't get clobbered by Chinese competition—the study was designed in a way that ruled out such alternative explanations. But they were clearly much more prone to resentment once they had received that blow.[46]

There was a final irony in Trump's triumph: he was a plutocrat who ran against the plutocrats—so rich, he insisted, that he didn't want their money, so in tune with the working class that he wouldn't bow to their defenders. Trump would "drain the swamp." He would end the pay-to-play world of Washington. That world, above all, was what enraged Trump's working-class supporters. It was also the world in which the GOP's deep-pocketed allies had prospered.

When Trump won the nomination, many plutocrats were worried, not so much because they thought he was truly liberal (nor, revealingly, because they thought he was a race-baiter) but because they thought he was a loser. The party's plutocrats, including the Koch brothers, stuck with the GOP, pouring money into contested Senate races in states that Trump had to win. But most didn't offer rhetorical or financial support to Trump himself. There were big-money Trump donors: billionaire investors Carl Icahn and John Paulson, for example, and New York Jets owner Woody Johnson. But with a few conspicuous exceptions—Sheldon Adelson, Peter Thiel, the Mercers—they offered more money than praise.[47]

Then Trump won, and Republicans held onto both houses of Congress. The forces of the establishment had made the best of a bad situation, and they'd have to make the best of a Trump presidency. Little did they know just how awesome the best would be.

Chapter 5

A VERY CIVIL WAR

IN MOST ACCOUNTS OF THE 2016 ELECTION and its aftermath, Donald Trump tears down the old GOP and remakes it in his image. A standard trope is that the GOP establishment—whether by "establishment" one means prominent elected officials or the loose association of formidable organized interests that bankroll the GOP and mobilize its supporters—went to battle with Trump, and lost. Trump won the Republican base, forced equivocating politicians to declare their allegiance, and swept all before him. In the words of Paul Ryan, "The Trump wing beat the Reagan wing."[1]

The journeys of the vanquished varied. Some, including the commentators David Frum, William Kristol, and George Will, became "Never-Trumpers," going into exile and quickly losing any influence they once had on the right. Some joined Trump when it became clear he would win the party's nomination. Then there were the "November 9thers" who studiously refused to endorse Trump but switched to the winning side after his upset victory in the general election. Still others—Senators Bob Corker and Jeff Flake, for instance—attempted to maintain some distance and preserve their options. Corker and Flake soon left politics, followed by Paul Ryan himself, and it was the closure of this last path that signaled, to many observers, the end of the party's civil war. In the new GOP, public officials either bent their knee to Trump, retired from the scene, or were demolished.

Yet if the past few years have witnessed a Republican civil war, it has been a *very* civil war, in which the side allegedly losing has made gains it could have scarcely contemplated just a few years before. Among the biggest winners were right-wing plutocrats who had been at the heart of the establishment. When Trump took power, he handed much of that power to people loyal to these plutocrats, or to the plutocrats themselves. They brought their long-standing policy ambitions into the federal government and carried them out with a vengeance.

This plutocratic agenda was, and is, extraordinarily unpopular, and its unpopularity is a reminder of the fundamental clash between the priorities of the party's power elite and the interests of its voters. In two-party democracies, parties aren't supposed to pursue high-profile policies with only minority backing, much less policies that impose disproportionate suffering on people who give the party disproportionate support. Yet the self-styled tribune of workers in the White House has done just that, his embrace of economic elites even tighter than that of the last Republican president, George W. Bush.

The plutocrats have gotten huge tax cuts. They have reaped the benefits of an unprecedented attack on regulations that police big corporations and protect consumers, workers, and the environment. And they have seen the nation's powerful courts tilt even further in favor of elite economic interests. Looking back on the first year of the Trump presidency, establishment Republican and plutocrat ally Mitch McConnell pronounced it to be "the best year for conservatives in the thirty years that I've been here [in the Senate] . . . the best year on all fronts."[2]

DONALD TRUMP BEGAN HIS IMPROBABLE RUN for the presidency with no allies in the GOP establishment. His campaign was dismissed, reasonably, as a publicity stunt. He garnered almost no support during the "invisible primary" that operates alongside, and largely in advance of, the slate of caucuses and primaries where party voters weigh in. The invisible primary has had a pretty impressive track record. As in the McCain-Bush struggle of 2000, powerful figures within the party—big donors, prominent officials, leaders of aligned groups—decide which candidate to back, and the money and endorsements start flowing in even before the first primary vote. Once this process gains momentum, it generally pushes just one or two candidates to the head of the pack. More often than not, one of them receives the party's nomination.[3]

The invisible primary revolves around two questions: Can the candidate win the presidency? And will the candidate deliver what powerful interests want if victorious? No prominent presidential candidate has ever failed these two tests as miserably as Donald Trump. The journalist Tim Alberta, who had access to top Republican figures, reports that the "plotting" against Trump started on the day he announced his candidacy in mid-2015: "Senior members of Congress, governors, major donors, influential lobbyists, and many top conservative activists—all of them wanted to take Trump out."[4]

While Trump failed both tests, other major Republican candidates did not. Jeb Bush, Ted Cruz, Marco Rubio, Chris Christie—all had spent many years in Republican networks, were extremely familiar to the power brokers, and had contested multiple elections. They were known quantities; Trump was reckless and unpredictable. He was a former registered Democrat whose positions changed from week to week, sometimes from sentence to sentence. On issues dear to the power brokers—whether favorable to the plutocracy (free trade, "entitlement reform") or essential for key allied groups (abortion, guns)—Trump had taken stances during the campaign or in the recent past that were at odds with Republican orthodoxy.

Yet, as the campaign proceeded, Republican-affiliated organizations became increasingly confident they could thrive under a Trump presidency, if it somehow came to pass. Anti-elite salvos notwithstanding, many of Trump's campaign proposals were tilted toward the wealthy and corporate America. And the Trump campaign was working hard to provide reassurance. Before the convention, Trump broke with precedent in extraordinary and revealing fashion. After consulting with Leonard Leo (head of the Federalist Society) and campaign counsel Don McGahn (who had worked for the Koch-affiliated Freedom Partners), Trump publicly committed himself to appointing Supreme Court justices from a prepared list of conservative judges. Also telling was Trump's selection of Mike Pence as his running mate. Pence, a long-time Koch brothers favorite, was the walking embodiment of the plutocratic-evangelical alliance at the heart of the modern GOP.[5]

If Trump took tangible steps to forge ties to the party elite, an even greater source of reassurance to the GOP establishment had nothing to do with Trump. If Congress remained in Republican hands—and that looked likely even with Trump at the top of the ticket—he would have strong institutional incentives to go along with the party's program. In matters related to national security, presidents have formidable powers. In most areas of domestic policy, however, they are strongly dependent on Congress to break new ground. Party elites were confident that a Republican Congress would be reliable. In 2012, the head of Americans for Tax Reform, Grover Norquist, laid out the essential characteristic that movement conservatives should look for in a Republican presidential candidate:

> We are not auditioning for fearless leader. . . . We just need a president to sign this stuff. . . . The leadership now for the modern conservative movement for the next 20 years will be coming out of the House and the Senate. . . . Pick a Republican with enough working digits to handle a pen to become president of the United States.[6]

At the time, Norquist was trying to convince fellow conservatives not to worry about Mitt Romney's insufficient purity. Trump was not Romney, but the logic still held. He could change his mind, but not his role in the American constitutional system.

In the end, the establishment's big problem with Trump was not his supposed unreliability. It was the other part of the invisible primary test: electability. Knowledgeable observers thought Trump was unelectable and would bring the party crashing down on top of him. South Carolina senator Lindsey Graham's pronouncement was not atypical: "If we nominate Trump, we will get destroyed[,] and we will deserve it." Up until election day, party bigwigs were

terrified that their improbable candidate, with historically unprecedented negative poll ratings, was leading the party to disaster.[7]

Nor did they keep this view to themselves. Insiders expressed
remarkable contempt for the man who now garners unprecedented
approval from the party faithful. Rick Perry called his candidacy "a
cancer on conservatism." Ted Cruz said that he was "a pathological
liar." Marco Rubio called him a "con-man." Mick Mulvaney said he
was "a terrible human being." Paul Ryan deemed Trump's remarks
about a Latino judge "sort of like the textbook definition of a racist comment." After the *Access Hollywood* tapes became public,
he vowed not to campaign for the party's nominee. Yet, in all these
cases, the expressions of contempt lasted only as long as the certainty
Trump would lose. When he won, all of these insiders became Trump
allies, either going to work for him or offering dependable support
from Capitol Hill—even when Trump did things like blame "both
sides" for white supremacist violence in Charlottesville. The shift
was an acknowledgment of Trump's power. Even more, it reflected
an appreciation of what could be done with that power, and confidence that it would be used to advance the establishment's interests.[8]

WHAT THE REPUBLICAN ESTABLISHMENT wanted to do was not
in doubt. Over the prior two decades, since Gingrich led the GOP's
takeover of Congress in 1994, the party had pushed a consistent,
albeit ever more aggressive, policy agenda designed to advance plutocratic interests. Republican leaders sought to sharply cut taxes
on the wealthy and corporations, roll back expensive social welfare
programs, and remove irksome environmental and consumer regulations. And they sought to install judges who would extend and protect those achievements. In the broadest sense, they sought to tear
down the foundations of the relatively balanced economy (installing
some limits on the power of corporations and the wealthy) that had
taken shape in the United States and all other affluent democracies
after World War II.

With their electoral sweep, party leaders saw their chance.
"When I woke up the morning after Election Night 2016," Mitch

McConnell recalled, "I thought to myself, 'These opportuni-
ties don't come along very often. Let's see how we can maximize
[them].'" A week after the election, Ryan boasted to reporters,
"Welcome to the dawn of a new unified Republican government.
. . . This will be a government focused on turning President-elect
Trump's victory into real progress for the American people."[9]

Ryan's choice of the phrase "Trump's victory" rather than
"Trump's agenda" was telling. Trump had presented himself as
a very different kind of Republican than Ryan. But Ryan was not
promising to implement the president-elect's agenda. When he promised "real progress," he meant real progress on the policy agenda of
the plutocrats.

Ryan's efforts did not get off to an auspicious start. Republicans
had long railed against the Affordable Care Act, the most momen-
tous domestic policy achievement of Trump's Democratic predecessor. Obamacare was loathed in Republican circles; vowing to
repeal it had been a staple of conservative politics since the day it
had been enacted. Between 2011 and 2016, Republicans in Congress
had repeatedly voted to do so, each vote a symbolic effort, given the
certainty of an Obama veto. Now that veto threat was finally gone.

For much of the party base, the ACA was a symbol of unwanted
government intrusion and, for many, of unjustified largesse to racial
minorities. Obamacare had been racialized from the start, even if
its roots were in Mitt Romney's Massachusetts. For the powerful
economic interests within the Republican coalition, however, the
stakes were more concrete. Observers, including those on the left,
often failed to appreciate that the Affordable Care Act was the most
downwardly redistributive federal initiative in half a century. The
ACA extended health insurance to roughly 20 million low- and
moderate-income Americans. It lowered out-of-pocket expenses for
millions more, and it extended popular protections for those who
had or might develop "pre-existing conditions" to all Americans.
These benefits were financed in part through increased taxes on the
health care industry, but mostly through taxes on those in the very
top reaches of the income distribution.[10]

While the party's deep-pocketed backers helped pay the tab, tens of millions of those who voted for Trump reaped the benefits, even if many of them didn't know it. And many millions more would have benefitted, too, if the nineteen states still refusing the Medicaid expansion in 2017—in all cases, due to GOP opposition—had taken the generous federal deal on offer. Despite this, Republicans were determined to eviscerate the law.

They had larger ambitions, too. The House GOP plan (confusingly named the American Health Care Act, or AHCA) would have not only dramatically scaled back the ACA. It went beyond this to make big changes to the joint state-federal Medicaid program. Medicaid is now the largest public health care program in the United States, a source of health insurance for roughly 65 million Americans with low incomes. The AHCA would have essentially transformed Medicaid from an individual entitlement—something that gave all those eligible the right to a specified set of benefits—into a specific amount of funding. That amount could then be squeezed over time, requiring individual states to decide which recipients would lose their benefits. As Paul Ryan colorfully if undiplomatically put it, this was something he and other self-described "fiscal conservatives" in the party had "been dreaming of . . . since [we] were drinking at a keg."[11]

The proposed Medicaid reductions were projected to save the federal government more than $800 billion over ten years, with even bigger cuts thereafter. This huge retrenchment certainly wasn't designed to provide "insurance for everybody," as Trump had promised in January 2017. In fact, every time Republicans put forth concrete proposals, the nonpartisan Congressional Budget Office came back with the news that their bills would simultaneously raise premiums and out-of-pocket costs, lower the quality of insurance plans, increase the chances of insurance market death spirals, put new pressure on state budgets, and massively increase the ranks of the uninsured. These outcomes were not a result of policy ineptitude, but the inevitable consequence of the Republicans' overriding priority: the more health care spending could be slashed, the larger tax cuts could be.[12]

The House and Senate leadership's bills were as far to the right as any could be and still have a chance of passage. A spate of polls showed that less than one in five Americans supported them. Their unpopularity was no surprise. What was surprising was how close Republicans came to succeeding. In the end, Senate Republicans came just one vote shy of moving forward legislation that would have left roughly 16 million Americans newly uninsured.[13]

It was a remarkable display of hard-right hubris—brazenly trading in health care for tens of millions of Americans for yet more tax cuts for the very richest. Had Republicans succeeded, it would have constituted a social policy reversal unparalleled in advanced democratic societies. Tellingly, the GOP response to their bills' horrific polling was not to moderate their aims but to do everything they could to hide the party's biggest policy initiative from scrutiny. Despite their best efforts, their health care crusade provoked unprecedented public disapproval for a new administration's flagship economic legislation. It also provided the clearest possible evidence that plutocratic rather than populist forces were still running the party.

Through all this, Trump's support for the Republican effort never wavered. During the campaign, he had vowed to protect not just Social Security and Medicare but also Medicaid, an increasingly vital source of protection for many of the party's white working-class voters. Residents of declining rural and rustbelt regions were not only disproportionately insured under the ACA's Medicaid expansion; they were also more likely to benefit from the law's support for substance abuse treatment. All the GOP bills would have curtailed most of these benefits. The new and much less generous funding formulas in the GOP bills also permitted higher premiums for older Americans, a voting demographic that had leaned to Trump. The economic hit from these provisions would be especially large in rural areas, and among those over the age of fifty living on moderate incomes.[14]

It would have been hard to more precisely target the voters who had rallied behind Trump. In a startling interview with the president, Fox's Tucker Carlson noted that the House bill cut taxes for those making over $250,000 and that "middle class and working class" counties that voted for Trump would do "far less well" than more affluent counties that voted for Clinton. "Oh, I know," was the president's response. "It seems inconsistent with the last election," Carlson observed. "A lot of things aren't consistent," replied Trump.[15]

In July 2017, a mortally ill John McCain stepped to the floor of the Senate to cast the decisive vote against the GOP's final proposal. After six months of intense conflict, Republicans narrowly failed to pass a bill that would deliver on their seven-year promise to "repeal and replace" the 2010 health law. But the dramatic defeat of the GOP assault on millions of its own voters shouldn't obscure what they had tried to do, or how little effect the setback had on the party's priorities.

REPUBLICAN LEADERS REMAINED EAGER to exploit what might be a fleeting moment of unified control over the federal government. After the failure of ACA repeal, they went right back to the hard work of shifting money up the income ladder. For both congressional Republicans and the Trump administration, big tax cuts for corporations and the wealthy were the next major priority. There were wrinkles along the way, including Paul Ryan's hope to raise some offsetting revenue with a border adjustment tax—an idea that was crushed by a Koch-led rebellion within the GOP. Throughout, however, the upper-class tilt was overwhelming. The president falsely insisted to the public that the bill would hurt him financially. His treasury secretary and other leading Republicans maintained that the new law was aimed at the middle class. Yet every major change to the bill compounded its upward bias. At the very end, when exhausted congressional leaders scrambled to hold Republicans together, clean up their work, and push the legislation across the finish line, they did so by increasing that tilt even more.[16]

In the short run, most Americans outside the top 1 percent received smallish reductions in their tax bills. But that was as good as their news would get. Just as in the 2001 Bush tax cuts, these small savings were designed to phase out over time. Only the big benefits for the wealthy and corporations were made permanent. Under the law, by 2027 an astonishing 83 percent of the tax cuts were projected to go to the top 1 percent of income earners. That same year, 70 percent of those in the middle-income brackets would be paying *higher* taxes than if the law had never been enacted.[17]

Republicans were quick to point out that they hoped to extend the expiring benefits for middle-income Americans. Doing so, however, was projected to cost another $900 billion, and this would supposedly happen at a time when the federal budget was almost certain to be facing huge deficits. Republicans well understood that the tab for these massive cuts for the rich would eventually come due, requiring either cuts in spending or higher taxes, and there's no reason to think they intended corporations and the wealthy to fill the gap. Put simply, most of the bottom 90 percent of Americans were highly likely to be made worse off by the tax policies cheered on by their president.[18]

Just as with health care, Republican leaders kept details of the tax proposals hidden for as long as possible, reflecting concerns that such regressive policies could not withstand extensive public scrutiny. They were right to worry. Across a range of surveys, the House and Senate tax bills received about 30 percent approval. As with the GOP health plans, the hard part isn't explaining this stunning lack of support. Americans didn't consider tax cuts a high priority, and they were unenthusiastic about reducing taxes on the rich and large corporations.[19]

The hard part is explaining why politicians in a democracy just kept barreling on. By now, "Republicans eager to cut taxes on the rich" is a dog-bites-man headline. But it should be news when an entire party remains tenaciously committed to a hugely costly initiative that's so unpopular. As political scientists, we were trained to see initiatives like these as unicorns. Politicians just aren't supposed to act so openly, on such big public issues, in such blatant opposition to the clearly expressed views of voters. Yet, when given unexpected unified control of the government, Republicans conjured up two unicorns in less than a year.

Figure 6 shows the level of public support—averaging across all available polls—for major pieces of legislation over the past quarter century. It reveals that the Republican Party's two initiatives in 2017

Figure 6

PUBLIC SUPPORT FOR MAJOR PIECES OF LEGISLATION OVER THE PAST QUARTER CENTURY

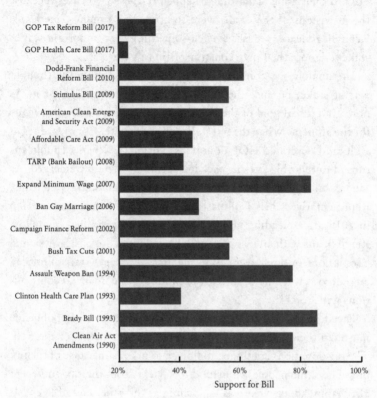

Source: Christopher Warshaw, George Washington University. Polls include ABC News/*Washington Post*, AP/NORC, Associated Press, CBS News/*New York Times*, CNN, Fox News, Gallup, Kaiser, *Los Angeles Times*, Monmouth, NBC News, NPR/PBS/Marist, Pew Foundation, Quinnipiac, *USA Today*/Suffolk, and YouGov.

Support for major pieces of legislation since 1990, averaging across all available polls. The Republicans' 2017 health care plan (which failed by a single vote) and tax cuts (which passed) were the two least popular pieces of major legislation over this nearly thirty-year period.

were stark outliers. The only major initiative less popular than the tax cuts that Republicans shoved through in 2017 was the health care bill that they tried to shove through just a few months before. Increasing polarization may have lowered the ceiling of public support for any bill, as voters whose party is out of power become more hostile to anything Washington does. But it should also have raised the floor of public support, as voters loyal to the party in power rally to their tribe. That didn't happen in these two cases, because the provisions of these bills were so grim for so many Americans. Republican leaders must have felt something very important was at stake to ignore their own constituents in this way.

Fortunately we don't have to guess what Republicans thought was at stake, because they were surprisingly candid about it. As noted, a critical goal of the health care bill was to deliver tax cuts for the affluent. When the bill stalled in the Senate, Cory Gardner of Colorado described GOP donors as "furious." When Republicans turned to their big tax-cut package, a similar dynamic emerged. As the tax bill struggled to gain sufficient support among Republicans, Representative Chris Collins from New York (who would resign in 2019 after pleading guilty to insider trading) rallied his fellow Republicans with an inspiring call: "My donors are basically saying 'Get it done or don't ever call me again.' " Lindsey Graham offered an ominous warning of the cost of failure: "The financial contributions will stop."[20]

Faced with this imminent danger, congressional Republicans mustered their courage and passed enormous tax cuts for the rich. The big donations continued to flow, and not just because of the tax bill. The same people who stood to benefit from the tax cuts were also happy about what was happening at the other end of Pennsylvania Avenue.

IN MOST AREAS OF DOMESTIC POLICY, Trump had to share power with the congressional GOP. As Norquist predicted, he used his working digits to sign the bills that came his way, though not as many landed on his desk as GOP stalwarts had hoped. But what about the areas where the president could take the lead or operate on his own? Trump's actions on trade and immigration have grabbed the most attention, and they are not ones that the establishment has greeted with enthusiasm. Elsewhere, however, long-held GOP priorities were safe. More than safe: Trump's only distinctiveness turned out to be his willingness to embrace the most radical versions of these priorities. When McConnell said "the best year on all fronts," he most definitely included the activities of the White House. The new president's team would prove to be extraordinarily responsive to the leading concerns of the Republican donor class.

That responsiveness was already evident in Trump's initial top-level appointments. Where Obama had constructed a "team of rivals," Trump assembled a "team of billionaires," including Treasury Secretary Steven Mnuchin (net worth actually only a few hundred million), Small Business Administration head Linda McMahon, and Education Secretary Betsy DeVos. The Department of Commerce received two billionaires, Wilbur Ross and Todd Ricketts (although Ricketts later withdrew). Gary Cohn, head of Trump's National Economic Council, left his prior job as president of Goldman Sachs. Goldman had also employed Mnuchin, not to mention Steve Bannon. Trump tapped billionaire financier Stephen Schwarzman to head his short-lived "Strategic and Policy Forum."[21]

In addition to the ultra-rich, Trump's nominees leaned toward the ultra-conservative. Especially notable were the appointees who brought congressional experience. Republicans in Congress have shifted sharply right over the last generation, yet Trump's picks still stood out. Virtually every member of the Trump administration who had served in the House or Senate—from Vice President Mike Pence, to Office of Management and Budget Director (and later acting Chief of Staff) Mick Mulvaney, to CIA head (and later Secretary of State) Mike Pompeo, to Health and Human Services Secretary Tom Price, to Attorney General Jeff Sessions—came from the rightward flank of the congressional GOP.[22]

These were just the highest-profile appointments. Much of the federal government's power rests in the "administrative state," where decisions with a massive influence on Americans' health and the economy are made daily. This power is an unavoidable consequence of the complexity of modern societies. Because Congress lacks the expertise, resources, and time required to manage these affairs, it is forced to delegate considerable authority to the executive branch.

Ironically, the creation of the modern administrative state

reflected reformers' hope that the presidency would provide greater protection for relatively independent and publicly minded action. Congress, so the thinking went, was acutely vulnerable to the pleading of powerful but narrow interests: what political scientists call "capture." Presidents, elected by and dependent on national majorities, were expected to be less inclined to let lobbyists run the government and more capable of protecting the public.

The Trump administration has turned this expectation on its head. On a pair of issues where Trump had modestly consistent views and an instinct to preserve his brand—trade and immigration—Trump has pursued a course clearly at odds with the preferences of the GOP establishment. On all other matters, however, Trump has invited capture, essentially handing over the administrative apparatus to the plutocratic and business interests that political reformers had hoped to dislodge from power.

Before Trump's victory, New Jersey Governor Chris Christie had been in charge of what seemed like a purely hypothetical exercise in transition planning. Once the hypothetical became real, Christie was unceremoniously ousted, his preparatory binders filled with prospective hires thrown in the trash. Authority over the staffing of Trump's administration transferred to Mike Pence. During the campaign Pence had become, in the words of Doug Deason, "the contact to the big donors." Deason's billionaire father Darwin was a mega-donor to the Trump campaign; by the son's count, there were "at least eight or nine" billionaires (including David Koch, Wilbur Ross, and Carl Icahn) celebrating in a VIP room upstairs at the midtown New York Hilton as Trump announced his election victory.[23]

Pence's selection as Trump's running mate thrilled evangelical leaders, but he was, as Trump adviser Kellyanne Conway put it, "a full-spectrum conservative." Pence had long cultivated close connections with the party's big funders. He was particularly close to the Koch brothers. Before Pence ran into political troubles as Indiana's governor, there had been speculation that he was their preferred candidate for president. Steve Bannon, perhaps the most outspoken right-wing populist in the administration, expressed fear that a hypothetical President Pence would "be a President that the Kochs would own." Bannon accepted Pence's selection as running mate as a painful but necessary concession to power: "The Kochs are a hundred percent with you, so long as it means cutting taxes for the Kochs. Anything that will help the middle-class people? Forget it."[24]

Many Pence affiliates rotated through the Koch political empire. Marc Short is emblematic. Pence had risen rapidly in the House GOP by attacking Speaker of the House John Boehner from the right. When he was selected as chair of the Republican Conference (the third-highest leadership position in the House GOP), he chose Short as the conference's chief of staff. Short followed his work for Pence with a five-year stint as head of Freedom Partners Chamber of Commerce, a central conduit for the vast flow of Koch money. His wife worked for the Charles Koch Foundation. Like most prominent Republicans, Short was a Trump skeptic in 2016, and he tried unsuccessfully to enlist the Koch brothers in an effort to derail Trump's campaign. When Pence joined Trump, however, so did Short. After serving as Pence's lieutenant in managing the post-election transition, he became Trump's director of legislative affairs, coordinating relations with congressional Republicans. A White House colleague described Short as "a pod person" who "really delivered Pence to the Kochs." In 2019, he came full circle when Pence named him his chief of staff.[25]

With Pence in charge of staffing the Trump administration, it's unsurprising that the Kochs' fingerprints turned up everywhere. CIA chief Mike Pompeo (nicknamed "the congressman from Koch"), Secretary of Education DeVos, Secretary of Energy Rick Perry, White House Counsel Don McGahn, and EPA chief Scott Pruitt (who resigned in 2018 after a long series of ethics violations) are just a few of the prominent figures with ties to the Koch empire. Lower level positions were filled with Koch affiliates, too, along with people vetted by the extremely conservative Heritage Foundation. In keeping with its earlier exploitation of anti-immigration sentiment to build its influence, Heritage had been one of the first major Republican organizations to lend support to Trump.[26]

Despite Trump's popular campaign pledge to "drain the swamp," his appointees were frequently plucked directly from the ranks of those who had built careers catering to economic elites. In agency after agency that provides important checks on powerful business interests and the wealthy, the story has been similar: a health policy consultant with strong industry ties to head the Centers for Medicare & Medicaid Services, an anti-labor lawyer to lead the Department of Labor, a drug industry insider to run the FDA. Trump swiftly moved to relax ethics rules for his appointees. He didn't just narrow rules about conflicts of interest that had been in place under Obama; he also granted a flood of waivers (five times as many as Obama had over an equivalent period) that allowed many of his appointees to participate on matters that they had lobbied on only a few months before.[27]

THE ENVIRONMENTAL PROTECTION AGENCY is a representative example, and a crucial one, both given the significance of its core mission and the considerable discretion it possesses under the country's extensive environmental statutes. The EPA has long been a leading target of the right, especially the fossil fuel industry, which is an influential part of the modern Republican coalition. The industry is heavily represented among top donors and in key Republican-affiliated organizations, including the US Chamber of Commerce and the Koch brothers' network. It has become increasingly active politically, as the challenges associated with global warming have made its products and practices subject to intensive regulatory scrutiny.[28]

Trump and Pence filled the EPA with appointees drawn from the network of business-funded groups hostile to its mission. They tapped Myron Ebell, a vocal opponent of action on climate change, to lead the transition. Ebell had directed the energy and environment program at the libertarian Competitive Enterprise Institute, a group funded in part by the Koch brothers and a number of fossil fuel companies. He would call for cutting half the EPA's budget and two-thirds of its staff to limit "regulatory overreach." Flanking Ebell as director of the energy transition was Thomas Pyle, former lobbyist for Koch Industries (and more recently head of the American

Energy Alliance, supported by money from the Kochs and other fossil fuel industry giants).[29]

The new chief of the EPA would be former Oklahoma attorney general Scott Pruitt, already known for his extremely close ties to the traditional energy sector, his antipathy to the EPA, and his skepticism about climate change. Deep ties to regulated industries united the members of Pruitt's team. The assistant administrator for air and radiation, for instance, had served as a lobbyist for oil, gas, and coal companies. A key official in the Office of Research and Development came over from Koch Industries. Pruitt worked assiduously to replace scientists (dinged by new "conflict of interest" rules if they had received EPA grants) on key advisory committees with industry allies (many of them recommended by big donors). Even some Republicans were shocked: George W. Bush's EPA head, Christine Todd Whitman, observed that "I've never known any administrator to go into office with such an apparent disregard for the agency mission definition or science." Pruitt's scandal-a-week record would eventually force his ouster. His replacement? Former coal lobbyist Andrew Wheeler.[30]

Pruitt and Wheeler led a sweeping effort to roll back environmental regulations, even as the threat of climate change loomed, and despite overwhelming evidence of the enormous benefits of federal environmental policies for public health. President Trump pulled out of the Paris climate accords. Pruitt began the process, finished by Wheeler, of reversing the Obama administration's ambitious Clean Power Plan and substituting an alternative that was arguably worse than taking no action at all. He rolled back his predecessor's fuel economy standards, adopting an alternative so toothless that it has actually met opposition from the nation's *automobile industry*. And he gutted enforcement: the number of inspections of industrial facilities carried out was half the total of 2010; monetary penalties on violators dropped 94 percent. Wheeler continued all these efforts, weakened rules on mercury and methane emissions, and intensified the push to strip California's long-established autonomy on air pollution regulation, which has been a catalyst for environmental progress.[31]

The EPA story is not unusual. Throughout the administrative state, the Trump team placed foxes in charge of the hen houses. At Energy, it was long-time oil industry ally Rick Perry. At Interior, Trump chose Montana congressman Ryan Zinke. David Bernhardt, former lead lawyer to the Independent Petroleum Association of America, was tapped to be his top aide. The IPAA's head then bragged to a room of laughing energy executives that "we have unprecedented access to people that are in these positions who are trying to help us, which is great." When Zinke's impressive efforts to match Scott Pruitt scandal-for-scandal finally forced his resignation, Bernhardt—a "walking conflict of interest" in the eyes of a coalition of 150 environmental groups—became secretary of the interior.[32]

In agency after agency, regulations that economic elites disliked were rolled back, enforcement efforts curtailed, and fines for violations reduced. Enforcement actions declined sharply at the Consumer Financial Protection Bureau, the Securities and Exchange Commission, and the Department of Justice. White-collar crime cases dropped by a third from the level of 2013. Monetary penalties imposed on the 100 largest public companies dropped *90 percent* from the annual average under President Obama, from $17.4 billion to just $1.8 billion. In 2010, the IRS audited 96 percent of the nation's largest firms; in Trump's first year, it audited less than half—and less than half the number of millionaires it had audited in 2010.[33]

As consequential as Trump's administrative actions have been, their long-term impact will depend on the durability of Republican rule. Just as Trump's EPA worked to reverse the regulatory actions of his predecessors, a future president could do the same to the work of Pruitt and Wheeler. Diminished administrative capacity and hollowed-out staffs will be harder to rebuild, but that too could happen in time. And it remains to be seen how much of the Trump administration's regulatory efforts will survive the court challenges they face. But this last uncertainty points to what may be the most significant and durable victory for plutocrats: the remaking of the federal judiciary.

IN NOVEMBER 2018, TWO THOUSAND PEOPLE gathered in Union Station's Main Hall for a $200-a-ticket celebration of the Federalist Society. On the stage for a "conversation" sat Senate Majority Leader Mitch McConnell and White House Counsel Don McGahn, symbols of the alliance that was remaking the nation's courts. In the audience were the most visible fruits of that alliance: five sitting Republican justices, two newly appointed, all with ties to the Federalist Society. McConnell and McGahn were not just taking a victory lap; they were promising more. "My goal," said McConnell, "is to do everything we can for as long as we can to transform the federal judiciary, because everything else we do is transitory."[34]

McConnell could rightly claim much of the credit. The Republican-controlled Senate had blocked Obama's judicial appointments during his last two years in office, and McConnell had done what no Senate leader had done before: refused to hold a vote, or even hearings, for almost a year when Antonin Scalia died and President Obama nominated the respected appeals-court judge Merrick Garland to fill his spot on the Supreme Court. The obstruction paid off, leaving the Trump administration perfectly positioned to move swiftly to refashion the courts. By August 2019, the Senate had confirmed forty-three new appeals court judges. This was far more than any recent president at the same point in his presidency, and more than twice as many as Obama had appointed (indeed, that number represented almost 80 percent of the total Obama appointed in his entire two terms).[35]

Those appointed were very conservative. Despite complaints that many of Trump's nominees were outside the judicial mainstream, the Senate confirmed almost all of his picks. And then there were the grand prizes: the appointments of fierce conservatives Neil Gorsuch and Brett Kavanaugh to the Supreme Court. The world's most powerful court, which would have leaned liberal if McConnell had not blocked Garland, is now firmly in the hands of the right, and is likely to remain so for a long time.[36]

Here again, Trump accepted the establishment's agenda. He had already signaled as much as the Republican nominee by publicly previewing a list of potential Supreme Court nominees generated by Leonard Leo and Don McGahn (with input from the Heritage Foundation). Once Trump was in office, he placed McGahn on the inside. As White House counsel, McGahn worked with Leo, who sat at the top of a very well-funded yet opaque network of organizations committed to remaking the judiciary. For the confirmations of Gorsuch and Kavanaugh, Leo temporarily left his post at the Federalist Society to advise the White House, just as he had for the nominations of John Roberts and Samuel Alito during the George W. Bush administration.[37]

Press coverage of battles over the courts typically portrays them as part of the broader culture war, highlighting social issues connected to gender, race, and religion. And certainly the prominence of these issues on the court's agenda helps explain why judicial appointments have been at the heart of the pact between Republican leaders and religious conservatives. Leonard Leo, for instance, is a deeply conservative Catholic. Tom Carter, who was director of media relations when Leo was the chairman of the US Commission on International Religious Freedom, has said that Leo's views on social issues are the driving force behind his career: "He figured out twenty years ago that conservatives had lost the culture war. Abortion, gay rights, contraception—conservatives didn't have a chance if public opinion prevailed. So they needed to stack the courts."[38]

The standard account of the Supreme Court and its impact dramatically downplays the plutocratic elements of the GOP's judicial agenda. Religious conservatives stress the battle for the courts in their efforts to mobilize supporters. Economic elites, by contrast, have no incentive to play up their legal ambitions, which probably have even less popular support than their quest for endless tax cuts. Yet the dominant economic interests within the party, including both the Koch brothers' network and the US Chamber of Commerce, have long seen the courts as a major strategic opportunity. For decades, and with growing urgency, they have spent a substantial share of their organizational resources to reconfigure the judiciary.[39]

An essential characteristic of the social conservative agenda is its compatibility with the plutocratic one. Situations where the courts must choose between the two groups are rare. To be viable for nomination, a prospective conservative judge must—and, crucially, can—satisfy both. When they are not weighing in on the culture wars, the courts offer ample opportunity for plutocrats to achieve victories they could not win more directly at the polls: scaling back regulations; curtailing the opportunities for class-action lawsuits, which help level the playing field for disputes between powerful corporations and workers or consumers; and blocking or offering corporate-friendly interpretations of federal laws. Just as important, conservative courts can shift the rules of political life in favor of their allies: easing the flow of dark money, protecting gerrymandering, allowing efforts to disenfranchise voters. Judicial restrictions on unions, which have proliferated in recent years, are particularly attractive, because they strengthen corporations in the private economy and weaken a key political ally of the Democratic Party (recall how much union membership has mattered in recent elections).[40]

To what degree do these plutocratic concerns shape judicial selections? Even though much plays out behind closed doors, the evidence suggests that plutocrats wield considerable power. Nobody would mistake McConnell for a committed social conservative. By contrast, his relationship to the GOP's donor class is long-standing and his commitment to its priorities unwavering. His former chief of staff Steven Law, for instance, went on to be general counsel at the US Chamber of Commerce before heading huge Super PACs affiliated with Karl Rove (American Crossroads) and McConnell himself (the Senate Leadership Fund). Prior to going to work for Trump, Don McGahn's most notable public work was the leading role he took, as a George W. Bush appointee, in obstructing the Federal Election Commission's efforts to regulate big donors. He also worked as an attorney for the Kochs' Freedom Partners.[41]

Another piece of evidence is the huge war chest the GOP's allies assembled to pursue their ambitious plans for the judiciary. Leonard Leo's empire took in a remarkable $250 million in donations between 2014 and 2017. Much of this bounty was run through the Judicial Crisis Network, which has led advocacy campaigns on Supreme Court nominations, donated to Republican Party groups active in judicial politics or to state-level judicial elections, and fun-neled money to other organizations (such as the NRA) that in turn involved themselves in judicial nomination fights. Leo's network also directed $1 million to the Trump inauguration, and combined a $20-million gift from an anonymous donor with a $10-million gift from Charles Koch to endow George Mason University's renamed Antonin Scalia Law School.[42]

Thanks in part to the rulings of a conservative Supreme Court, the funding for these ambitious undertakings is almost all dark. Though there are severe limits to what we can know, sums of this magnitude are far more characteristic of the party's economic donors than its religiously motivated allies. Most striking is a single anon-ymous contribution in 2016 of over $28.5 million to the Wellspring Committee, a group lacking any visible office. The organization's founding has been tied to the Kochs, however. Professed libertari-ans, the Kochs are clearly not motivated by the social conservative agenda. The Wellspring Committee in turn donated over $23 mil-lion to the Judicial Crisis Network (and an additional $17 million the following year).[43]

Nothing suggests the draining of Washington's swamp like a single anonymous contribution of $28 million to a group with no physical office. For "the forgotten men and women of our country" Trump invoked in his 2016 victory address, he had something a lot more visible, but no more beneficial, in mind.

To THESE FORGOTTEN AMERICANS, Trump promised great things. "We are going to fix our inner cities and rebuild our high-ways, bridges, tunnels, airports, schools, hospitals," he declared. "We're going to rebuild our infrastructure, which will become, by the way, second to none. And we will put millions of our people to work as we rebuild it."[44]

Trump did work to signal his populist identity, and nowhere more so than on the twin issues of immigration and trade, where his stances constituted big departures from the established agenda of GOP eco-nomic elites. Both issues lent themselves to a simple Bannon-esque message, in which Trump battled on behalf of working-class Americans from the heartland against foreign enemies (aided by greedy and corrupt domestic elites). And both were areas where Trump had significant authority to act unilaterally—authority delegated to presidents in the expectation that they would be more insulated from protectionist and nativist pressures.[45]

Immigration was at the heart of Trump's campaign from the moment he announced his candidacy. Although occasionally presented as a threat to American jobs, the dominant themes were threats to security—criminality, terrorism, disease—the costs to taxpayers, and the prospect that this "invasion," coupled with fraud, was a plot by Democrats to steal elections. In short, highlighting immigration was less about making an economic appeal to the base than about substituting a focus on ethnic threat for a concern with economic issues.

Trade was the clearest instance of Trump actually pursuing, rather than just promising, a distinctive stance on economics. There was at least some evidence that Trump's base found his posture appealing. By 2019, however, it was clear that trade wars were not so "easy to win," as he had tweeted in 2018. Rather, the short-term costs were substantial, and the medium-term risk that trade wars would trigger a painful economic downturn was growing. The burden fell largely on US consumers and producers. Economists suggested that just the China tariffs would cost American consumers $1,000 per year per household, wiping out the fleeting savings many would get from the 2017 tax cuts.[46]

What was striking about Trump's trade wars wasn't just the negative impact on the American economy; it was the pain they inflicted on Trump voters. Foreign retaliation to Trump's tariffs had the greatest impact in rural areas and small towns—precisely where Trump's support was strongest. Nor was this backfire effect distinctive to the administration's trade policies. Almost across the board, the flip side of the administration's fealty to the plutocrats was the damage its policies caused in the places that had given him the greatest support.[47]

A striking feature of the 2016 election was that the counties

Clinton carried—mostly well-placed cities and their surrounding suburbs—accounted for two-thirds of the nation's economic output. Trump, by contrast, did best in the places that were experiencing relative decline. Incomes in these areas lagged behind. Many of these locations also stood out as flashpoints for the "deaths of despair"— suicides and deaths from drugs and alcohol—that were skyrocketing among middle-aged whites. Declining longevity, which has not occurred among other demographic groups or in other rich nations, constituted the most striking indicator of spreading social dysfunction in much of the nation's heartland. Republican leaders in these same places typically complained that tax dollars were being sucked from their states and wasted in Washington. In fact, Trump-friendly states and locales relied on fiscal transfers from more affluent parts of the country to sustain local infrastructure, keep hospitals open, and provide social assistance to those on low incomes and the retired.[48]

A party needing these voters and presenting itself as a force aligned with the people against elites might be expected to use public authority to address the alarming social and economic challenges facing these "left-behind" communities. Not a chance. Trump's highly popular pledge of a massive investment in infrastructure, which could have been used to generate employment and development in struggling regions, was incompatible with the GOP fixation on high-end tax cuts. Plans for a major infrastructure initiative never got off the drawing board.

Here, as in so many areas of economic policy, Trump simply continued or intensified a pattern of Republican neglect for the party's voters. The devastating impact the GOP's plans to repeal the ACA would have had on millions of Trump voters was nothing out of the ordinary. Republicans in many red states had already rejected the ACA's Medicaid expansion, which would have provided huge benefits to local hospitals and millions of voters (one recent study estimated that the refusal to expand Medicaid in these states has caused almost 16,000 unnecessary deaths). Over the course of Trump's presidency, access to health care in rural areas continued to decline, with the biggest problems in states that had refused to accept the ACA's Medicaid expansion.[49]

Perhaps the most telling example was the GOP's striking passivity with respect to the horrific opioid epidemic, whose devastating impact has been deepest in many of the communities that rallied to Trump's promise of working-class renewal. Republicans, with unified control over Washington, faced not just a moral imperative but a seemingly easy opportunity to demonstrate concern for their constituents. Instead, they mostly turned a blind eye. In a rare moment of bipartisanship, Congress did pass legislation designed to tackle the crisis in 2018. Republicans were self-congratulatory. Yet, the main thing to know about the bill to address the biggest public health crisis since the AIDS epidemic was that it was "revenue-neutral." "How much money was Congress willing to spend on the worst opioid epidemic in U.S. history?" asked Keith Humphreys, a Stanford psychiatry professor and former adviser at the White House Office of National Drug Control Policy. "None." As part of its budget deal that year Congress did allocate $6 billion over two years, but that was still a small fraction of what most experts considered necessary to confront the crisis.[50]

Despite President Trump's vow that "we will never stop until our job is done," Republicans have resisted meaningful action to help these hard-hit communities. Instead, they fell back on a consistent excuse: the nation couldn't afford big plans. In the fall of 2017, as Republicans rushed their tax cuts to the floor, they had dismissed any concern about the deficits that might ensue. Just before passage, despite the skepticism of independent experts and the clear weight of historical evidence, Mitch McConnell was reassuring: "We are totally confident this is a revenue-neutral bill and probably a revenue producer." Administration officials offered extravagant claims about the boost to growth that would follow. It took no time for the pessimism of less partisan observers to be more than vindicated, and for federal deficits to reach levels unprecedented in a peacetime economy with low unemployment.[51]

McConnell didn't miss a beat, turning something he had promised wouldn't happen into an argument for massive cuts to programs essential to the economic security of the GOP's aging electoral base. Rising federal deficits, he said, made it essential to "reform" (that is, cut) Medicaid, Medicare, and Social Security—"the real drivers of the debt." Ryan's House GOP concurred, passing a budget in 2018 that would have cut major social programs that offer assistance to poor and moderate-income households by about one-third over a decade. The bill would also have raised the age for Medicare eligibility. Trump's proposed budgets similarly offered savage cuts in spending on the less affluent, as well as massive reductions in the discretionary spending that funds everything from national parks to medical investment. Meanwhile, no GOP politician suggested the high deficits they had promised to avoid might warrant revisiting their enormous tax cuts for corporations and the wealthy.[52]

In his recent book *Kochland*, the business journalist Christopher Leonard observes that "the politics that Koch stoked in 2010 became the policies that Trump enacted in 2017." Charles Koch evidently agreed. In 2018, he told one of his regular meetings with donors that "we've made more progress in the last five years than I had in the previous fifty." He didn't mean tariffs or aggressive actions against asylum seekers.[53]

Yet, while Koch was exuberant, Republican congressmen and women fretted. Unlike Trump, they had to face the voters that year. When they did, they ran up against the realities of the Conservative Dilemma.

The unpopularity of the GOP's economic agenda had been evident all along. It wasn't just the unprecedented negative polling around the flagship health care and tax bills. It was the damage those initiatives did to the president's image. In August, a Quinnipiac poll indicated that, by 58 percent to 38 percent, voters agreed the president was not doing enough for the middle class. Despite the warning signs, the GOP's campaign to retain the House in 2018 began with the notion that Republicans could run on the tax cuts. Soon campaign consultants concluded that the party could not rely on economic appeals to mobilize its voters. David McIntosh, president of the Club for Growth, confessed that polls showed that the group's favored economic issues fell flat with the party's base. Heritage

Action head Tim Chapman said the "fiscal issues are a complete wasteland . . . and the donors know it." He added that the party's Wall Street backers were urging a pivot to red-meat social issues.[54]

Meanwhile, Democrats found health care in particular to be a potent campaign issue. As the midterm elections approached, when Republicans did talk about economic matters, their claims became untethered from their actual agenda. They insisted they were committed to preserving protections against pre-existing conditions that they had tried to kill in 2017 and continued to target in a federal lawsuit. They promised that they were just about to lower prescription drug prices and invest in infrastructure, goals they had not pursued in their first two years and would show no interest in pursuing after the midterm election.

Mostly, though, they fear-mongered over immigration—or, as they claimed, invasion. As the British newspaper the *Guardian* reported, "a review of nearly five dozen Republican-backed TV ads revealed a messaging strategy rooted in painting a dark portrait of immigrants, with a fixation on violence and crime." President Trump repeatedly talked of a "caravan" traveling northward in Mexico, a development Fox News hyped in the weeks leading up to the election and then promptly forgot about. Newt Gingrich called it an "invasion," while noting that "voters are motivated by fear and they're motivated by anger." The US Chamber of Commerce's political strategist Scott Reed acknowledged that it was "a standard tactic to use fear as a motivating choice. . . ."[55]

It didn't work. Despite the mobilization of fear—and despite geographic advantages, aggressive gerrymandering, and the name recognition and superior funding that typically give incumbents an edge—the Republican House majority was washed away. Nancy Pelosi was now positioned to become Speaker again, something she may have envisioned the day House Republicans had passed the American Health Care Act. Just before the vote she had issued this warning from the House floor: "You have every provision of this bill tattooed on your forehead. You will glow in the dark with this one, you will glow in the dark." And they did.[56]

During its two-year run, a unified Republican government had labored to redistribute income and economic and political power toward those already at the top. Time and again, the GOP's agenda diverged sharply from the preferences of ordinary Americans, and even from those of the majority of Republicans. But the goal was not to serve the public; it was to serve the plutocrats. If Trump's arrival presented new challenges, diversions, and unseemly compromises, it also smoothed the way for rapid progress in cutting taxes, rolling back regulatory restraints, and remaking the courts—all outcomes giant corporations and the wealthy had long coveted.

EVEN BEFORE REPUBLICANS LOST THE HOUSE, Paul Ryan was heading for the exit. He had some regrets. He could see that the immediate policy window was closing, and he had failed to advance "entitlement reform," a fixation that, like all his budget initiatives, belied his oft-repeated commitment to helping the disadvantaged. Like John Boehner before him, he was tired of skirmishing with the Trumpian forces in the House and having to avert his eyes from or explain away Trump's behavior. Yet Ryan could count some big victories for his agenda; in the words of a long-time friend, he "made a calculation that to get through the policies he cares about meant that he had to muzzle himself." The French Huguenot who would become France's Henry IV supposedly rationalized his conversion to Catholicism by quipping that "Paris is well worth a Mass." For Ryan, tax cuts were apparently well worth a Charlottesville.[57]

After his retirement, Ryan defended his cohabitation with Trump, claiming that he had "felt a major onset of responsibility to help the institutions survive . . . to build up the country's antibodies . . . to have the guardrails up, to drive the car down the middle of the road, and don't let the car go off into the ditch." The weight of these responsibilities did not stop him from accepting a position (with an annual compensation of $335,000) on the board of Fox Corporation, parent company of Fox News, the epicenter of resentment politics. There were certain to be other lucrative opportunities. Ryan had long insisted that his heart remained in his hometown of Janesville, Wisconsin—a community still reeling from the closure of its fabled GM factory in 2010. Throughout his time in Congress, Ryan had signaled his allegiance to his hometown by sleeping in his office. "I just work here. I don't live here" was his familiar refrain. Shortly after his retirement, he rented a house in suburban Maryland and moved his family from Janesville.[58]

Some, including Ryan himself, interpreted his exit as the end of a civil war, with Trumpian forces having defeated the "establishment." Yet in Congress, the executive branch, and the courts, it would be hard to find a two-year period in which plutocrats had made such decisive gains. And even as Ryan cashed out and Republicans lost their House majority, the interests of economic elites were robustly protected in the Senate. In the White House and the courts, these interests were better represented and better tended than they had been in nearly a century.

Still, the tumultuous events of the previous two years reinforced a consistent message of recent American politics: ordinary citizens were decidedly unenthusiastic about the party's plutocratic agenda. One possible response was to focus voters' passions on other matters. In the 2018 midterms, that option had failed. Another option— that Republicans would pull away from the plutocrats and "pivot" to address the economic worries of ordinary Americans—had by this point become simply unthinkable. Republicans, however, had a third option, and it was one they were already pursuing: make voters' voices less relevant.

Chapter 6

TYRANNY OF THE (WEALTHY AND EXTREME) MINORITY

ALTHOUGH REPUBLICANS DECISIVELY LOST the House of Representatives in 2018, they did not turn to moderation. There was no post-election "autopsy," no statement of presidential contrition of the sort provided by Obama in 2010 ("a shellacking"), Bush in 2006 ("a thumpin'"), and Clinton in 1994 ("a clear message"). The day after the election, Trump tweeted, "Yesterday was such a very Big Win, and all under the pressure of a Nasty and Hostile Media!" Less than two months later, he would precipitate the longest government shutdown in American history.[1]

Yet if the president's response to losing the House wasn't contrite, it was consistent with his party's transformation in response to the Conservative Dilemma. For more than a generation, the GOP had expanded its support for plutocracy while stoking its base into ever-greater outrage, relying on right-wing organizations to do much of the outrage-stoking. For the plutocrats and the surrogate groups alike, building popular majorities was less important than building power for extreme ends. They recognized the widening gap between their priorities and those of the broader electorate. But they saw this growing divergence not as a problem with their priorities, but as a problem with their strategies. To these intense and focused factions, electoral and policy setbacks did not mean that Republicans had to attract wider support. They meant Republicans had to figure out how to win without it.

The fundamental problem is now familiar. The Republican Party is ever more committed to the narrow and unpopular priorities of corporations and the superrich. It is ever more dependent on radical surrogate groups to mobilize voters its economic policies do not help. And among those voters, it is ever more reliant on a demographic group in relative decline: older whites without a college degree living outside urban areas, particularly older white men.

None of these trends is sustainable. Or at least none is sustainable in the context of free and fair elections and majority rule. Unfortunately, these pillars of political accountability are now crumbling, as Republicans have exploited the weaknesses in America's eroding constitutional order to short-circuit its safeguards against sustained rule by extreme minorities.

SINCE THE 2016 ELECTION, concerned commentators have focused on the threat of creeping authoritarianism posed by Trump's presidency. This focus is understandable, even though it has tended to obscure how his party's long-term transformation laid the groundwork for Trump's rise and rule. As shown by Daniel Ziblatt and Steven Levitsky in their 2018 book, *How Democracies Die*, elected strongmen who gradually close down political competition lie behind much of the democratic erosion of our era. Autocratic executives concentrating power in their hands—whether Brazil's Jair Bolsonaro, Hungary's Viktor Orbán, or Donald Trump—now constitute our prevailing image of democratic backsliding.[2]

Yet there is another form of backsliding, and it is a form that our political system distinctively encourages: counter-majoritarianism, or sustained minority rule. As their goals have become more extreme, Republicans and their organized allies have increasingly exploited long-standing but worsening vulnerabilities in our political system to lock in narrow priorities, even in the face of majority opposition. The specter we face is not just a strongman bending a party and our political institutions to his will; it is also a minority faction entrenching itself in power, beyond the ambitions and careers of any individual leader. Whether Trump can break through the barriers against autocracy, he and his party—with plutocratic and right-wing backing—are breaking majoritarian democracy.

Just as America's distinctive form of right-wing populism reflects the combination of extreme inequality and our unusual political institutions, so too does the distinctive threat of counter-majoritarianism. In most accounts of our present crisis, America's skyrocketing inequality receives at most cursory notice. (It is barely mentioned in Ziblatt and Levitsky's book, despite its role in Ziblatt's work on the early twentieth century.) Yet extreme inequality creates powerful incentives for democratic backsliding, because it encourages economic elites to see democracy as a threat to their growing power and diverging interests. Elites themselves do not have to actively fight democracy for it to be imperiled. Rather, their insistence that conservative parties aggressively protect their privileges, if heeded, leads those parties to rely on incendiary appeals, outrage-generating groups, and anti-democratic tactics to maintain their hold on power.[3]

This is the less noticed danger we face today: a party that is committed to an unpopular policy agenda has figured out how to achieve many of its goals without popular support, or even without majority control of all elected branches of government. The danger is distinctive, because unlike would-be autocrats, the party and its allies do not seek power for its own sake. They seek it for very particular aims, rooted in plutocracy and enabled by right-wing populism. In pursuit of these goals, Republicans have proved willing to bow to Trump's authoritarian impulses, in part because Trump now commands the radicalized base they cultivated. This itself represents a considerable threat to our democracy. But Republican political elites and their allies have also worked for years to make their policies and power resistant to normal sources of democratic accountability, whether or not they hold the White House. Creeping counter-majoritarianism and creeping authoritarianism emerge from the same source—plutocratic populism—but defeating one will not necessarily defeat the other.

Creeping counter-majoritarianism is less noticed not only because it lacks the drama of an aspiring autocrat, but also because it exploits long-standing features of the American political system. Three, in particular, have proved particularly vulnerable. First, our system of territorially grounded elections places the more urban Democratic party at a systematic disadvantage, and our decentralized system of electoral administration has facilitated GOP efforts to augment that advantage. Second, the increasing tilt of the Senate toward low-population states has also increasingly favored Republicans, as has the growing role of the filibuster within that body. Third, our system's reliance on three branches serving as "checks and balances" on each other has proved highly vulnerable to a radicalized Republican Party—a party willing and able to stack the federal courts in its favor, yet mostly unwilling to protect congressional powers or police the executive branch when the presidency is in their hands.

The dangers these three distinctive features of our system pose are not symmetrical: like partisan polarization itself, the big story is on the Republican side. Democrats have at times benefited from one or more of these features, but the Republican Party has, in recent years, benefited from all of them. In 2016, they allowed Trump—a candidate with historically unprecedented negative ratings—to win the nomination of one of the nation's two parties and then to win the presidency despite receiving a minority of the national vote. Once Trump entered office, these features allowed him to pursue unpopular priorities and undermine democracy with little congressional or judicial pushback. If Hillary Clinton had narrowly won instead, not only would she have done so with a popular vote majority; more important, she would have also faced an opposition party in Congress (as well as a closely divided Supreme Court) more than capable of placing checks on her power, especially in the Senate.

Because these distinctive elements of our political system are long-standing, it is tempting to think that what's happening today is what the Constitution's framers intended. Yet the institutions now being exploited by powerful minorities to lock in power were not designed for that purpose. Our system was designed to make it difficult for *majorities* to rule without broad agreement. It was certainly not constructed to make it easy for a cohesive, powerful, and extreme minority to control things on its own. Yet that is precisely what plutocratic populism now seeks to achieve.

Civics students have long learned that the framers of the Constitution feared "tyranny of the majority"—rash and impulsive policymaking by temporary majorities, particularly when those majorities threatened individual rights. Yet the framers also feared what might be called "tyranny of the minority"—sustained rule by a cohesive minority—and they recognized that this threat was greatest when minorities had outsized economic and political power. The opportunities that the American constitutional order now creates for minority rule were not part of the framers' original design. Instead, they were largely unforeseen, reflecting unanticipated interactions or constitutional bugs that have become more consequential over time.

The biggest oversight of the framers concerned parties. Deeply suspicious of parties, they designed the Constitution around the idea that political allegiances would be multiple, overlapping, and cross-cutting—a diversity of alliances that would, in turn, facilitate compromise. Of course, the effort to avoid parties altogether was destined to fail. Yet for most of American history, the two parties that dominated American politics were riven with regional and ideological fissures. It is only in the past three decades that we have seen intensifying partisan polarization up and down America's entire federal system.[4]

The framers also largely took for granted that resources and representation would be relatively equally distributed (among white men). The Constitution of 1787 was a distinctively "middle-class constitution" that presumed inequalities of wealth were not so large that one class would be tempted to deploy the counter-majoritarian features of the American system against another. The framers also assumed that territorial inequalities in representative clout would remain relatively small. Toward the end of his life, the "father of the Constitution," James Madison, came to recognize just how mistaken these assumptions had been, as he contemplated the nation's growing disparities in population and prosperity. Yet Madison, at least, could say he was not responsible for the growing inequalities in representation that he now feared, having argued that Senate apportionment should be based on population, as in the House.[5]

To all the framers, the essential feature of the Constitution was its combination of enhanced federal power and a delicate system of checks and balances. Congress, the subject of Article I of the Constitution, was at the center of this system. Not only was it designed to govern a far-flung nation while representing a wide range of interests; it was also equipped to exercise its extensive powers independently of the executive. The framers' greatest fear was of "demagogues"—presidents who exploited popular passions to crash through the system's protections. As a result, they divided the central government even as they empowered it, not just to prevent the emergence of tyrants, but also to keep any single powerful faction from dominating lawmaking.[6]

The rise of extreme polarization and extreme inequality has undermined this balance. Indeed, if one wanted to design a stress test for America's aging constitutional order, it would be hard to think of a more effective one than today's radicalized GOP. Seeking to stay in power while serving narrow factions, Republicans have capitalized on the representational biases that favor them in the Senate, House, and Electoral College. They have used these advantages to stack the federal courts with extremists, thwart responsive lawmaking in Congress, and turn election rules and redistricting into finely honed partisan weapons. The Trump presidency has greatly increased the stress, but the weaknesses of the system were apparent well before he arrived. More frightening still, some of the most powerful elements of American society do not see these vulnerabilities as problems to be fixed but as opportunities to be exploited.

THE ESTABLISHMENT OF DEMOCRACIES in Europe required taking power from economic elites and those who spoke for them in government. Conservative parties and their patrons had to accept the legitimacy, or at least inevitability, of newly enfranchised voters and a strengthened opposition. That process took time. It's bracing today to read the arguments against mass democracy made at its birth. Criticizing the expansion of the franchise in Britain, for example, the Irish conservative William Edward Hartpole Lecky insisted, "In every field of human enterprise, in all the competitions of life, by the inexorable law of Nature, superiority lies with the few, and not with the many, and success can only be attained by placing the guiding and controlling power mainly in their hands."[7]

Today, contempt for democracy necessarily takes more subtle forms. Yet, as the Conservative Dilemma has resurfaced in the United States, so too has the conservative case against popular rule. Arguments against majoritarian democracy play poorly, and so they've mostly remained veiled or indirect. But, as the gap has grown between what economic elites want and what popular rule is likely to produce, so too has the volume of these complaints.

Consider an increasingly common refrain on the right: "We're a republic, not a democracy." The slogan apparently traces back to the head of the radically anti-government John Birch Society, who employed it in 1961 to decry the "centralization of governmental power in a simple majority . . . which the enemies of our republic are seeking to impose on us today." Its message is simple: those who think a "simple majority" should generally get what it wants (democracy) are subverting the framers' vision (republic). But the framers used the terms "democracy" and "republic" in a completely different way. When they said "democracy," they meant direct democracy, as in ancient Athens. They used "republic" to describe democratically elected representative government—that is, the form of government that every democratic state has today. The distinction had nothing to do with whether elections should be decided by majority vote or whether those elected representatives should operate on the basis of majority rule.[8]

But the historical misreading isn't the real problem with the democracy/republic slogan. The real problem is that those who invoke it are not, as a rule, making the reasonable argument that the rights of vulnerable minorities should be protected or that some decisions should require supermajorities. They are arguing that democracy itself is a problem, because it threatens the property and power of powerful minorities, and that any departures from democracy that serve to protect against that threat should be preserved. This complaint with majority rule is far from the framers' concern that unfiltered majority rule might allow rash policymaking. It is closer to ultra-libertarian Ayn Rand's description of democracy as "a social system in which one's work, one's property, one's mind, and one's life are at the mercy of any gang that may muster the vote of a majority at any moment for any purpose."[9]

Randian distrust of democracy is a particular temptation for those on the favored side of a widening economic divide. According to ex-libertarian columnist Will Wilkinson—who spent years at the Koch-funded Cato Institute—the conservative movement of which he was part grew more and more "skeptical of the legitimacy of redistribution-enabling democratic institutions" as inequality became a more pressing issue. Wilkinson's association of democracy with "redistribution-enabling . . . institutions" is itself telling. Democracy is not a zero-sum game, and redistribution is not the only thing, or even the biggest thing, that democracies do. But it's apparently one of the biggest sources of fear on the right—at least among the "libertarian-leaning donors, intellectuals, and politicians" whom Wilkinson argues have gained increasing power within the GOP.[10]

In the era of shared prosperity after World War II, such thinking was much rarer, or at least much less mainstream. Importantly, one source of its marginalization was economic elites themselves, particularly the leading spokesmen of the business community. When Birchers began talking about the dangers of rule by a "simple majority," establishment gatekeepers kept them far from the corridors of power. The Koch brothers grew up in a household suffused with their Bircher father's loathing of Dwight Eisenhower. Yet business leadership at the time thoroughly ignored and sidelined Fred Koch. Like his sons, he was a successful businessman who bankrolled right-wingers. Unlike his sons, he had no influence within the Republican Party. Eisenhower, in a private letter to his arch-conservative brother, scoffed at reactionary businessmen like Koch. "The Federal government cannot avoid or escape responsibilities which the mass of the people firmly believe should be undertaken by it," he insisted. Then he reminded his right-wing sibling that most business leaders agreed: "There is a tiny splinter group, of course, that believes you can do these things. . . . Their number is negligible and they are stupid."[11]

Their number is not negligible today. More important, those most skeptical of democracy appear much closer to political power than they were in Eisenhower's era. This may seem obvious given the central role of groups like Americans for Prosperity and ALEC in advocating restrictive voting laws and aggressive Republican gerrymandering. Yet what's often missed is that these efforts are not just about partisan gain. They shade from anti-Democratic strategies into anti-*democratic* strategies in part because democracy itself is a threat to plutocratic resources and power. To the ex-libertarian Wilkinson, conservative plutocrats and right-wing Republicans came to denigrate electoral democracy and majority rule because electoral democracy and majority rule potentially enabled nonaffluent Americans to challenge the growing rewards at the top. This fear, Wilkinson observes, "made it seem morally okay, maybe even urgently necessary, to do whatever it takes—bunking down with racists, aggressively redistricting, inventing paper-thin pretexts for voting rules that disproportionately hurt Democrats, whatever—to prevent majorities from voting themselves a bigger slice of the pie."[12]

Those who think such things don't publicly say them. Except when they do: the first two years of the Obama administration featured a remarkable litany of libertarian laments from corporate and financial leaders. In one well-publicized example, Blackstone cofounder (and later Trump appointee) Stephen Schwarzman described a Democratic proposal as "like when Hitler invaded Poland." That proposal, which failed, sought to close the so-called carried interest loophole, which allows private equity billionaires like Schwarzman to pay just over 20 percent federal tax on the untold millions they earn managing other people's money. Another Wall Street billionaire, Leon Cooperman, explained that President Obama would "never get the business community behind him" as long as he was responsive to "the forty or fifty percent of the country on the dole that support him." His fellow financier Tom Perkins suggested a fix: "You pay a million in taxes, you get a million votes."[13]

Around the same time, Peter Thiel—the plutocrat made rich by

PayPal—offered a more refined case against rule by the masses. Writing for the Cato Institute, he explained, "Since 1920, the vast increase in welfare beneficiaries and the extension of the franchise to women—two constituencies that are notoriously tough for libertarians—have rendered the notion of 'capitalist democracy' into an oxymoron." As a result, Thiel concluded, "I no longer believe that freedom and democracy are compatible." No surprise, perhaps, that Thiel was the first prominent tech entrepreneur to back Trump.[14]

But perhaps the most revealing dismissal of democracy came from Trump's aborted nominee to the Federal Reserve, Stephen Moore. An omnipresent conservative analyst who served for years as the lead economic spokesman for the Heritage Foundation, Moore explained in 2007 that the income tax was "the most evil act that has passed in a hundred years." Such evil may be why Moore later felt moved to confide, "I'm not even a big believer in democracy. I always say that democracy can be two wolves and a sheep deciding what to have for dinner."

Sensing that he might be losing his audience, Moore added, "Look, I'm in favor of people having the right to vote and things like that." Even as he was speaking, though, much of his party was going after that right.[15]

THE POWER OF THE BALLOT is as fundamental as any right guaranteed by a democracy. Yet we are witnessing the most sustained and coordinated assault on voting rights since Reconstruction, over a century ago, and it's being led by one party. The inflection point was 2010, when Republicans—urged on and funded by conservative forces and often touting model legislation to restrict voting developed by ALEC—used their newly expanded control over statehouses to pass a wave of voter restrictions. In the following years, roughly half of state legislatures put in place restrictive laws. Some of these laws required forms of identification that many poor and minority voters lacked; some made it harder to register to vote or stay registered; some cut back early or absentee voting. In virtually every case, these restrictions were put in place by Republicans.[16]

Scholars debate how effective these laws are, but there is little question about why they get adopted. Their timing and content have no relationship to voter fraud, which is vanishingly rare. They do, however, have a strong relationship to partisanship and race: Republicans pass them when they have unified control, and especially when the nonwhite share of the electorate is large. Nor is there doubt about the direction of their aggregate effect. Across nations and states, voter turnout is higher where registering and voting are easier. The differences are large: more than ten percentage points between states with the most facilitative and most restrictive laws, even after controlling for other characteristics.[17]

Gerrymandering—the drawing of district lines to favor one party—can be even more effective than voter restrictions. Carried out aggressively, it can transform a 50–50 landscape into a landslide for one party. Gerrymandering has been part of American politics from the start. Yet a number of factors—enhanced technology, the growing concentration of Democratic voters in cities, the dominance of Republicans in Southern and sparsely populated states, the emergence of GOP-allied organizations capable of coordinating multistate efforts—have made gerrymandering increasingly feasible and rewarding for Republicans. At both the state and federal levels, district maps have augmented the already-significant advantages that Republicans enjoy because their voters are more geographically diffuse. Even as Republicans have struggled to win the presidential vote, they have gained a decisive edge in House elections—an edge that, in the mid-2010s, amounted to a six- to eight-point higher Republican vote share in the typical House district than the share received by Republican presidential candidates nationwide. Roughly half that advantage appears to be a result of gerrymandering.[18]

Recent GOP moves in North Carolina show what's possible in a closely balanced state. Republicans first took the statehouse in 2010. They quickly enlisted the leading Republican architect of extreme partisan gerrymanders, Thomas Hofeller. A mostly anonymous figure until his death in 2018, Hofeller liked to describe gerrymandering as "the only legalized form of vote-stealing left in the United States." He once told an audience of state legislators, "Redistricting is like an election in reverse. It's a great event. Usually the voters get to pick the politicians. In redistricting, the politicians get to pick the voters." In 2018, North Carolina Republicans won their "election in reverse," keeping hold of the statehouse even while losing the statewide popular vote. In North Carolina's races for the US House, Republicans won half the statewide votes and 77 percent of the seats. A global elections watchdog ranked North Carolina's "electoral integrity" alongside that of Cuba, Indonesia, and Sierra Leone.[19]

It turns out that Hofeller wasn't just advising North Carolina Republicans. He was also working for the Republican National Committee, receiving over $2.4 million from the party in just over a decade. And, it turns out, he was simultaneously advising Commerce Secretary Wilbur Ross. In March 2018, Ross—the second-richest member of Trump's gold-plated cabinet—announced his intention to add a new question to the decennial census: "Is this person a citizen of the United States?" Ross's stated reason for adding the question (never before asked of the full population) was to allow better enforcement of the Voting Rights Act of 1965. Career Census officials, however, opposed the question, arguing that in immigrant-dense communities fear of repression and even deportation would lead to an undercount, which the bureau's own experts estimated could exceed 8 million US residents.[20]

Ross's true reason did have a lot to do with voting rights, only his intent was to undermine rather than enforce them. Shortly before his death, Hofeller had urged Ross to add a citizenship question to the Census so that states could have better data for redrawing electoral maps. Hofeller's request stemmed from a 2015 private report he'd prepared on redistricting in Texas. At issue was whether Texas could draw state districts based on the number of voting-age citizens, rather than all residents, or even all citizens. In his secret study, Hofeller said no, yet not because it was illegal but because it was "functionally unworkable"—the data just didn't exist. Add a citizenship question to the Census, however, and Republicans could pursue what Hofeller himself described as "a radical departure from the federal 'one person, one vote' rule." The results, he estimated, "would be advantageous to Republicans and Non-Hispanic Whites."[21]

Who paid for that 2015 report? The hedge fund manager Paul Singer, who saw it as a potential precursor to hiring conservative lawyers to jump into the redistricting wars. This, too, only came to light after Hofeller's death, because Singer had funneled the money through the Washington Free Beacon, a conservative media outlet. The conservative website's money laundering was meant to keep Singer's effort out of view. The rest of right-wing media—blaring racially charged accusations of voter fraud that Republican politicians used to justify electoral restrictions—undermined democracy out in the open.[22]

IN 2019, THE SUPREME COURT weighed in on Ross's stated rationale, and a majority of the court—Chief Justice John Roberts along with the court's four more liberal justices—declared it a lie ("contrived" was the exact wording). Most observers took comfort in the rebuff. The Supreme Court had played its essential role as a protector of vulnerable minorities, ensuring the 2020 Census would go forward without the citizenship question.

This role is a counter-majoritarian protection that Americans cherish. Unelected judges with lifetime appointments should not be in the business of everyday lawmaking. But when elected majorities try to take away individual rights or bully vulnerable minorities, courts are meant to step in and provide a check. Yet, as conservatives have shifted the courts in their favor, this vital counter-majoritarian role has been gradually turned upside down—especially in the court ultimately responsible for determining the law of the land. Today, rather than protecting powerless minorities disadvantaged by the rules, the Supreme Court is more likely to be standing up for powerful minorities who want to rig those rules to institutionalize permanent minority control.

Chief Justice Roberts has memorably likened his conservative judicial philosophy to umpiring, promising at his confirmation hearings, "I will remember it's my job to call balls and strikes, not to pitch and bat." But for the Roberts Court, all the strikes seem to be thrown by plutocratic interests and the GOP's right-wing surrogates, and all the balls seem to be coming from groups with a credible claim to represent broad cross-sections of citizens. The court has weakened the power of labor unions with rulings that deprive them of the ability to require dues of workers who reap the rewards of collective bargaining. It has weakened the power of consumers and workers with rulings that permit companies and employers to insist they submit any future legal dispute—whether it concerns cell phone contracts or wage theft—to business-friendly individual arbitration. And it has weakened the power of ordinary citizens with rulings that allow public officials to rig elections and groups with enormous resources to sway campaigns and policymaking, whatever popular majorities desire.[23]

Of course, by "public officials" and "groups with enormous resources," we mean Republicans and conservative plutocrats. The Republican appointees on the Supreme Court are among the most consistently conservative and pro-business justices to sit on the court in the past seventy-five years (in contrast, the court's liberals don't stand out as distinctly to the left in historical perspective). With the sometimes-moderate Anthony Kennedy no longer on the bench, they now have increased scope to entrench Republicans in power and challenge an active federal government. In the balance are policies that enjoy widespread support—just not among conservative plutocrats and intense GOP-allied groups.[24]

In 2019, for example, Roberts was able to write a decisive 5–4 decision on gerrymandering, essentially declaring that so long as the court remains in conservative hands, it will not step in regardless of how biased redistricting is. Roberts did not mince words about gerrymandering's affront to fairness: "Excessive partisanship in districting leads to results that reasonably seem unjust. But the fact that such gerrymandering is 'incompatible with democratic principles' does not mean that the solution lies with the federal judiciary." And where did the solution lie? Roberts suggested that friends of democracy look to the very state governments that were already eviscerating those principles.[25]

More significant still, Roberts elided the fact that he and his fellow conservatives had recently stepped in to *promote* partisan gerrymandering. With its 5–4 *Shelby County v. Holder* decision in 2013, the conservative majority effectively gutted the federal requirement that states with a history of voter disenfranchisement "pre-clear" their maps with the Justice Department (all of these states except Alaska were in the South). Roberts wrote the majority opinion in that case, too, chiding Congress for failing to fully recognize that "due to the Voting Rights Act, our Nation has made great strides." The very next day, Republicans in North Carolina showed which direction they were walking. They announced plans to pass an "omnibus" election bill and requested government data on the use of various election provisions by race. Based on that data, they made a series of restrictive changes, every one of which hurt black voters. A federal appeals court concluded that the law would "target African-Americans with almost surgical precision."[26]

Roberts and his conservative colleagues chose to stay out of that particular fight. But their role in facilitating vote rigging has been fundamental, and perhaps nowhere more so than in the realm of campaign finance. By now, *Citizens United* has become a shorthand for the flood of money into American politics, more and more of it coming from the wealthiest donors. But, in truth, the real problem is deeper than one or a few blinkered rulings. Technological and organizational advances in influence-wielding have combined with skyrocketing inequality to make big money vastly more influential. The Supreme Court—the only institution capable of acting independently on a highly partisan issue—has not just acquiesced in the face of these undemocratic developments. It has actively fostered them, and it has done so without any acknowledgment of the institutionalized corruption these arrangements facilitate, much less the imbalances of power they reinforce.

These imbalances are far greater than most realize. For example, by allowing unlimited deployment of corporate "resources" to influence elections, *Citizens United* freed employers to use their own workers as political pawns. Before the ruling, corporate PACs could contact employees only in writing and only twice a year. Now, they can make unlimited appeals in any form, including face-to-face meetings, and they can require that employees use work time to support candidates and parties. In most states, they can even discipline or fire workers if they don't obey. Some 16 percent of workers, according to a recent study, claim they have witnessed such retaliation.[27]

The centerpiece of these efforts is the Prosperity Project of the Business-Industry Political Action Committee (BIPAC). More than seven thousand corporations and industry associations participated in the project in 2014, using BIPAC's specialized software for targeting workers to send an astounding 238 million messages to their employees. A 2015 survey of all business managers (not just those working with BIPAC) found nearly half admitting to having mobilized their workers in some way—a practice they believe is as effective as lobbying in influencing government. In the run-up to the 2016 election, a parallel survey of workers showed that 30 to 40 percent of workers said they had received political communications from their employers. The overwhelming majority of these messages supported conservative positions and GOP candidates. As that recent study concludes, corporations are becoming "political machines," freed by the Supreme Court to recruit their workers as a kind of mercenary grassroots army.[28]

The consequences of the court's intervention are also evident in the states. Because *Citizens United* wiped out campaign finance laws on the books in nearly half of states, it acted as something of a natural experiment—changing policy overnight against the wishes of those legislatures. The effects? An enormous increase in outside political spending at the state level, particularly in affected states; a sharp shift toward Republicans in that spending; a major uptick in Republicans' electoral success (without any corresponding change in voters' opinions); and a large movement of elected Republicans further to the right—again, particularly in states where regulations were overturned. All these trends helped Republicans consolidate state power, pass voter restrictions, redraw district maps, and resist federal laws. They may also help explain the notable finding of a new survey of state legislators: Republican legislators think their constituents are much more conservative than they actually are. The business lobbies and intense GOP-allied groups they are hearing from *are* extremely conservative, but they're not representative of ordinary voters.[29]

That the priorities of the court's conservative justices strengthen entrenched minorities completes a circle, for those same influential minorities played a crucial role in placing those justices on the court in the first place. We have already seen the Federalist Society's mutually beneficial bargain between conservative plutocrats and social conservatives, whose unpopular agendas don't really come into conflict in the courts. But the debt of the court's majority to counter-majoritarian politics is far bigger. Of the five-man conservative majority, four were appointed by a president who had received a minority of the popular vote. The two most recent were also confirmed by senators representing states with a minority of the US population—in the case of Neil Gorsuch, a minority of just 42 percent. So too was Clarence Thomas. In other words, every one of these five conservative justices embody America's creeping counter-majoritarianism. Yet their lack of majority support has hardly tempered their jurisprudence. To the contrary, they are now poised to defend plutocratic and right-wing priorities even as the nation's attitudes and demographics inexorably shift against these priorities. Broad but disorganized majorities and vulnerable minorities will be on their own, while reactionary plutocrats and right-wing populists will have friends on the court for a long time coming.

As THOSE COUNTER-MAJORITARIAN confirmation votes suggest, the Supreme Court isn't the only institution increasingly tilted in favor of plutocratic populism. The Senate is, too. America's upper house has always been biased toward low-population states. Yet this bias has grown much larger and more consequential. As the population differences across states have increased, the Senate has become the most malapportioned legislature in any rich democracy. (Wyoming gets sixty-seven times more representation per person than California; even affluent democracies with upper houses feature much smaller ratios—in Austria, the ratio is 1.5 to 1; in Australia, it's 13 to 1.) The same demographic and geographic trends that have made gerrymandering easier (particularly the growing association between the urban-rural divide and the Democratic-Republican divide) have made this rising rural bias a rising Republican bias, too. And because blacks and nonwhite immigrants are scarce in low-population states, the Senate vastly overrepresents not just red America, but *white* America. Hispanics, for example, are effectively given half as much representation in the Senate as the typical white American, and the disparity is large for African Americans as well.[30]

In short, Senate malapportionment has become a GOP bulwark that has much the same effect as gerrymandering and voter restrictions (with the added bonus that this bulwark is hardwired into the Constitution): it helps a party confronting the Conservative Dilemma to hold onto power even as its agenda becomes less popular and its core voters less numerous. Since the 2000s, Republicans have routinely elected Senate majorities that represent a minority of the votes cast in Senate elections. By 2016, Trump finished 2.1 points behind Hillary Clinton. Yet Republicans finished 3.6 points ahead in the median Senate race. What's more, Trump found himself working with a Senate in which almost half the body hailed from states he'd won by at least five points—again, despite finishing second in the popular vote. If Clinton had eked out a win by narrowly carrying the pivotal states she lost, less than a third of senators would have come from states she'd won by at least five points.[31]

In the actual 2016 contest, Trump won because a big part of the Senate bias carries over to the Electoral College—another counter-majoritarian bug that now favors conservative plutocrats and right-wing groups. Because of the Electoral College's malapportioned formula (each state gets votes equal to the number of senators and representatives combined), a vote cast in Wyoming, with its single congressional district, is worth 3.6 times a vote cast in California. Before 2000, only three times had the Electoral College handed the presidency to a candidate who had not received the plurality of popular votes, and all three times predated the twentieth century. Since then, it has happened twice in just five elections. Looking forward, projections suggest it's more and more likely to be the route by which Republicans win. In an age of very close elections, the findings of a recent study are disquieting: 40 percent of tight contests are forecasted to result in the popular vote winner losing in the Electoral College. The vast majority of these scenarios involve a GOP victory. No surprise, perhaps, that in 2019 the conservative *Washington Examiner* ran a story entitled, "Republicans resigned to Trump losing 2020 popular vote but confident about Electoral College."[32]

But if a rural bias helps Republicans in the Electoral College, the impact on the powerful Senate is more acute. There, Republicans often have a majority of seats based on a minority of votes. And even without a majority of seats they can often block majority preferences because of the greatly expanded role of the filibuster. For most of American history, the filibuster—a Senate procedure, not a constitutional provision—bore no resemblance to the all-encompassing "rule of sixty" we see today. The current gridlock-friendly version of the filibuster emerged out of 1970s rule changes and increasing polarization. In the 1990s, Senate Republicans took advantage of those rules to launch an unprecedented wave of minority-party obstruction against President Clinton's agenda and nominees. With polarization rising and incentives to compromise declining, the next Republican Senate minority facing a Democratic president, led by Mitch McConnell, launched over five hundred filibusters in six years. In effect, if a significant bill wasn't protected from a filibuster, McConnell filibustered it.[33]

Both parties have used the filibuster, but as with so many other hardball tactics, Republicans have proved the main innovators. The zigzag escalation of the filibuster follows a clear pattern: Republican Senate minorities ramp things up, Democratic minorities more or less maintain the new levels. And due to the malapportionment of the Senate, even when Democrats are in the minority, governance under Republicans is much more likely to reflect the votes of senators representing a minority of the population. That was especially true in 2017 and 2018. Over the twenty months between Trump's election and the Kavanaugh vote, the average bill or nominee receiving at least 50 votes in the Senate drew the support of senators representing just 44 percent of the population. These majority votes included the confirmation of five circuit court judges and several other of President Trump's nominations, the 2017 tax cuts, and nine laws rolling back Obama-era regulations. The agenda of conservative plutocrats didn't just pass without the support of voters; it passed without the support of elected officials representing popular majorities.[34]

Senate Majority Leader McConnell has no problem with this equation. Though often portrayed as a Republican operative only interested in winning, he has a very particular definition of "winning." Over his career in national politics, McConnell has fought campaign finance rules with vigor, taken any step necessary to get ultraconservative justices on the federal courts, and worked to pass policies favorable to corporations and the superrich. Whenever he hasn't, he has worked tirelessly to ensure that challenges to right-wing priorities die in the Senate. It's not for nothing that McConnell is called "the Grim Reaper," an epithet he embraces. The Senate that he has helped create is a graveyard for policies opposed by conservative plutocrats, right-wing groups, and rural red states—whether these be efforts to address climate change, to help workers organize, to regulate firearms, or some other measure with majority support among the electorate but not within the Republican coalition.

In a gridlocked environment, power shifts from Congress toward the other branches, which are more likely to have the first and last say on fundamental issues. So long as the courts are in Republican hands, that suits McConnell just fine, too. When it strikes down a statute, the conservative majority on the Supreme Court always insists that Congress is perfectly free to amend it. Given what the Senate has become during the Grim Reaper's reign, this is a bit like saying that a commuter caught in bumper-to-bumper traffic is always free to gun the engine.

Yet the danger is gravest precisely where the founders voiced the greatest fears, the presidency. Unchecked presidential aggrandizement is a fundamental threat to democracy. It's especially so when the aggrandizing president has plutocratic and right-wing allies who aren't just standing by, but egging him on.

IN EARLY 2019, the nonpartisan watchdog group Freedom House reported, "Trump has assailed essential institutions and traditions, including the separation of powers, a free press, an independent judiciary, the impartial delivery of justice, safeguards against corruption, and most disturbingly, the legitimacy of elections." The group that usually spends its time worrying about democracy in developing nations concluded, "We cannot take for granted that institutional bulwarks against abuse of power will retain their strength, or that our democracy will endure perpetually. Rarely has the need to defend its rules and norms been more urgent."[35]

Rarely, however, has the willingness of Congress to defend those rules and norms looked so anemic. The framers saw Congress (the subject of the Constitution's first and by far longest article) as the heart of American government, and they expected it to be a jealous defender of its prerogatives. During the 2016 campaign, Mick Mulvaney—then a GOP congressman representing South Carolina—celebrated the coming battle to preserve congressional power:

> We've been fighting against an imperial presidency for five and a half years. Every time we go to the floor and push back against an overreaching president, we get accused of being partisan at best and racist at worst. When we do it against a Republican president, maybe people will see that it was a principled objection in the first place. So we actually welcome that opportunity. It might actually be fun, being a strict-constitutionalist congressman doing battle with a non-strict-constitutionalist Republican president.[36]

After Trump's election, many Republicans did a Mick Mulvaney—going to battle for rather than "with a non-strict-constitutionalist Republican president." Almost all of them did a half-Mulvaney. The more blatant a Trump assault on democratic norms, the quieter the response from Republicans. During Trump's first two years in office, the White House was filled with tweets; the Congress, crickets.

For sheer rhetorical whiplash, nothing compared to the hasty retreat from independence made by Senator Lindsey Graham. The Republican from South Carolina and McCain confidant who excoriated Trump during the 2016 campaign had, by 2018, become one of the president's most loyal defenders. Whatever his motives, the descent of the GOP under Trump could be told in the series of quotes that *Harper's* assembled, tracing Graham's changing assessment of "the world's biggest jackass." They run from "race-baiting, xenophobic bigot" to "potential recipient of the Nobel Peace Prize."[37]

Not many Republicans could match Graham's example. But nearly all of them fell in line. Their embrace of a rogue president was the logical outcome of their embrace of an alliance of extreme minority factions. In response to the Conservative Dilemma, Republicans had made the priorities of the conservative plutocrats their own, and most of Trump's domestic agenda pursued those priorities. They had also opened Pandora's box, and now had to wrestle with its contents. With Fox News operating as a PR department for the administration, a single tweet from the president could mobilize a well-funded primary challenge or trigger a right-wing media onslaught. Contemplating all this, Republicans either cowered or joined the attack.[38]

In effect, Trump had called his party's bluff. Were they willing to take their alliance with intense minority positions to its logical anti-democratic endpoint? The answer, alas, was yes. When Trump required defense, Republicans rallied to the side of a president trampling democratic norms—even when that meant trampling Congress's own prerogatives. The conservative adviser and commentator Bill Kristol, a never-Trumper critical of his party's submissiveness, opined, "They have made their bed and are trying to sleep in it and hope they don't have nightmares."[39]

Whether they had nightmares, the results were fearful. Even the most blatant executive overreach was tolerated. Frustrated with his lack of authoritarian power, Trump did what no president before him had done: he issued an emergency declaration to redirect federal spending toward his cherished border wall, using a 1970s statute designed to allow quick presidential action in response to a true crisis. No clearer abrogation of Congress's power of the purse could be imagined. The closest prior example was President Nixon's efforts to "impound" funds Congress had authorized. Back then, leading Republicans condemned an "imperial presidency," and the Senate voted eighty to zero to forbid the practice, with every Republican present voting aye. Trump's much more aggressive seizure of congressional prerogatives prompted just twelve Senate Republicans to push back—an empty gesture since they all knew it was far too few to overcome a presidential veto.[40]

Republican solidarity in the face of the Ukraine scandal poses far greater dangers—and, as we write, looks even stronger. Whatever happens, we run the risk of focusing too much on Trump and too little on the broader forces associated with his party's long-term transformation. Republican elites and their allies were weakening democracy well before Trump. So long as that alliance remains what it is, the increasing entrenchment of a resourceful, well-organized, and favorably positioned minority will continue to pose a profound threat.

AS THE 2016 ELECTION APPROACHED, an essay published in the conservative but usually staid *Claremont Review of Books* went viral. Dubbing the approaching contest "The Flight 93 Election," it argued that the United States was hurtling toward catastrophe. The specter of a Clinton victory was so terrifying it was time to rush the cockpit—which is to say cast a vote for Donald Trump. According to the anonymous author (later revealed to be a former finance executive who had worked in the George W. Bush administration and would go on to work for Trump), the result, if this heroic effort failed, would be a "permanent victory" for "the Left, the Democrats, and the bipartisan junta that will forever obviate the need to pretend to respect democratic and constitutional niceties."[41]

By 2016, such thinking was ascendant in all the dominant power centers of the GOP. Each group had their particular concerns, but all of them saw catastrophe looming. Evangelical leaders argued they were being persecuted and faced extinction. NRA leaders warned that only a short step separated the most modest efforts to regulate

firearms from the Gulag. Plutocrats sitting on unprecedented fortunes and wielding unprecedented influence feared that popular
majorities would expropriate their riches. Right-wing media fanned
these flames. In the summer of 2019, one of Trump's Fox News favor-
ites, Jeanine Pirro, insisted that Democrats' "plot to remake America is to bring in the illegals, change the way the voting occurs in
this country, give them licenses, they get to vote maybe once, maybe
twice, maybe three times. . . . Think about it, it is a plot to remake
America. To replace American citizens with illegals who will vote
for the Democrats."[42]

Today, all of these groups see a growing risk that they will be out-
voted. GOP surrogate groups such as the NRA have every incentive
to amplify that risk. It keeps the troops energized and the contributions flowing. Yet if the dismal futures they forecast are fantasies, the potential loss of power is real. For plutocrats, this fear is as
old as democracy: the lack of public enthusiasm for their agenda is
what gives rise to the Conservative Dilemma. But now the surrogate
groups see the same looming threat. The older, whiter, and more
rural electorate that the modern GOP relies on is in demographic
decline. Among younger, more educated, and more urban Americans, the Republican agenda is toxic.

What makes democracy even more threatening is that the views
associated with these conservative factions—on tax cuts for the rich,
on gay marriage, on gun control, on climate change—are increasingly unpopular. This has left them even more invested in protecting
a political alliance that is committed to advancing those policies.
The allure of prizes they cannot otherwise win encourages them
to look the other way when their allies engage in anti-democratic
practices—or even to embrace the notion that democracy threatens
something they consider more important.

"The Flight 93 Election" correctly noted that extreme partisans
had lost interest in "democratic and constitutional niceties." Only
those extremists were in the Republican Party. Less than forty-eight
hours after the election, North Carolina's Republican legislature held a lame-duck session to strip the incoming Democratic
governor of many of his key powers. Two years later, the North

Carolina playbook would reappear in Wisconsin and Michigan, states where voters had also repudiated Republican governors after a hard-right turn.[43]

In Wisconsin, corporations had showered money on Republicans during the campaign. The drugstore giant Walgreens, fighting to preserve an unpopular but lucrative tax loophole, had directly funded the state House Speaker, Representative Robin Vos. Defending the power grab, Vos said, "If you took Madison and Milwaukee out of the state election formula, we would have a clear majority. We would have all five constitutional officers, and we would probably have many more seats in the Legislature." Republicans in other states made similar anti-urban claims—invoking the heretofore unknown democratic principle of "one person, one vote, unless that person lives in a city."[44]

Within a year, many of the Wisconsin legislature's lame-duck restrictions on an elected governor of the other party would be tied up in court. But the message had not been lost. In closely divided states as well as in Washington, a party allied with extreme inequality and extreme positions would use counter-majoritarian tactics to protect its narrow agenda—even when that meant undermining democracy.

CONCLUSION

IN AN AGE OF DEEPENING POLITICAL DYSFUNCTION in which economic elites have outsized power, we should not be surprised that some look to the plutocrats themselves for leadership. Those who do can find signs of promise: in August 2019, the Business Roundtable, the four-decade-old lobby representing CEOs, issued a high-profile "Statement on the Purpose of the Corporation." It was signed by executives from almost two hundred of the nation's largest companies, including Amazon, Apple, General Motors, Pepsi, and Walmart. Noting the pressures facing American workers, the signatories expressed their commitment to environmental sustainability, social diversity, worker dignity, and local communities. Using the old-fashioned language of "stakeholders," the statement implicitly rejected the inequality-celebrating doctrine of "shareholder value," which insisted that the sole concern of CEOs was maximizing the price of their companies' stock.[1]

The following month, nearly 150 business leaders—including the CEOs of Airbnb, the Gap, Levi's, and Lyft—sent a letter to Senate leaders urging action to address America's "gun violence crisis." A headline in *Chief Executive* heralded a "New American Revolution" in which, the writer explained, CEOs had issued "a historic call to action." When Walmart announced it would no longer sell ammunition for military-style weapons, a breathless article in *The Hill* called its CEO a "corporate hero."[2]

Even the Koch Network, which had done so much to push the

nation's economic governance rightward, seemed to be rethinking things. Key figures within the network sent highly public signals—dubbed "the shift"—that they intended to keep Trump and the GOP at arm's length, were eager for bipartisanship, and wanted to focus on issues like criminal justice reform and reducing foreign military adventures. With the passing of David Koch, some observers also touted an impending generational shift (to Charles's son Chase) and speculated that the result might be a kinder, gentler libertarianism.[3]

Given the clout of the American business community, any sign that executives are reorienting their political practices to address the nation's growing political and social dysfunction is welcome. A few years ago, we wrote a book, *American Amnesia*, in which we argued that the GOP's increasingly aggressive government-bashing was bad for capitalism in the long run. It might be good for top CEOs, or short-term profits, or industries that imposed big social costs (like climate change). But it was entrenching incumbent elites rather than promoting opportunity and dynamism, while curtailing social investments in education, population health, research and development, and other public goods central to shared prosperity in the twenty-first century.[4]

The evidence for that conclusion is far stronger now. The Trump administration and its cronies don't just create and deepen social divisions. They encourage corporate plunder rather than social investment. They seek to subsidize the digging of coal while doing all that they can to sabotage the rise of clean energy. They rely on the votes of declining regions (without addressing their economic needs) and attack the nation's most dynamic regions. Plutocratic populism is plainly not delivering much to ordinary voters, but it's also an increasing threat to the policy predictability and long-term focus that a healthy capitalist economy needs.

A business community that truly pushed the GOP to moderate its policies and support a more balanced form of capitalism would be extremely helpful. Yet it would be naïve to expect it. A few business leaders decry the vulgarities and authoritarian impulses of Donald Trump. Many more take the popular side on issues that repel their customers and alarm their own workforces. (It is hardly heroic to give rhetorical backing to universal background checks that more than 90 percent of voters support.) Corporate leaders can tout their commitment to diversity and their embrace of sustainability all they want. Their political expenditures mostly tell a different story. Until they invest seriously in changing the course of American politics and the Republican Party, their talk is cheap.[5]

The Business Roundtable, with its signature brand of corporate statesmanship, is a spent force. Statements of purpose notwithstanding, it saves its major organizing efforts for matters that directly affect executive compensation (spoiler: the Roundtable has vigorously opposed policies that might limit CEO pay). Clout has long since shifted to other large business organizations, especially the US Chamber of Commerce and the Koch Network. These powerful groups aren't big on petitions, they mostly avoid the limelight, and their leaders never give memorable speeches. What they have done is devote billions of dollars to driving the GOP's long rightward march.

Large companies have diverse interests. Most present a public face of nonpartisanship. Yet for corporations, as for the wealthy, their private political behavior is generally much more conservative than what they display in public. Many companies split their modest contributions to political action committees, which represent their most visible political spending, fairly equally between the parties. The larger and less-visible flows of money—often funneled through organizations like the US Chamber of Commerce, ALEC, and state party committees—tilt much more heavily toward the GOP. None of these groups, or their funders, seems overly troubled by climate change, gun violence, or the unavailability of health insurance. Any concerns they might have about partisan gridlock, Trump's racism, or even assaults on core democratic institutions are not serious enough to meaningfully alter their behavior.[6]

Recall the three threats posed when inequality increases to extreme levels: power shifts to economic elites; their interests diverge from those of their fellow citizens; and they become more apprehensive about democracy. This is why the Conservative Dilemma intensifies and becomes more dangerous as inequality grows. As the preferences and power of elites diverge from those of ordinary citizens, the steps that plutocrats and their champions must take to sustain their influence grow uglier.

A few months before the 2016 election, a leading plutocrat faced this frankly at a private event in Park City, Utah, hosted by Mitt Romney and attended by Paul Ryan. Ed Conard, Romney's former partner at Bain Capital, later posted his remarks online. Conard, author of *The Upside of Inequality*, argued that "leaders of business and advocates of free enterprise" were facing a critical moment, requiring "tough, even odious compromises." He maintained that to "regain control of the Republican Party," economic elites needed a "new coalition" to replace the one they had built "with the religious right after *Roe v. Wade* . . . which we used to lower the marginal tax rate from 70 percent to 28 percent." Conard noted that "the demographics of that coalition have eroded." The new coalition would be with "displaced workers" and would require "advocates of free enterprise" to concede to restrictions on immigration and trade.[7]

Conard framed this "new coalition" as an alternative to what he called "Trumpism." In truth, it sounds a lot like Trumpism. The "odious compromises" may have been more odious than Conard acknowledged. But the benefits had been enormous as well, though not for those displaced workers. With Trump in the White House in 2017, the Republican Party, ignoring the clear preferences of the nation's citizenry, was laser-focused on cutting the corporate tax rate from 35 percent to 21 percent. America's largest corporations and wealthiest citizens received massive windfalls from the GOP's increasingly aggressive stances on taxes and deregulation. Also hugely beneficial for economic elites was the flow of pro-business appointments into the courts. Conard's plutocrats got their policies and then some.

These changes are bad for American capitalism in the long run. They are bad for democracy right now. But they don't seem so bad for the holders of great wealth. We should not stop making the case to the economically powerful that long-term prosperity must be shared prosperity, but it would be foolish to rely on the enlightened self-interest of economic elites, or expect that they will correct course out of some sense of noblesse oblige. As in the past—during the New Deal and the reforms of the 1960s, or when Eisenhower rebuffed business conservatives because he knew voters were with him—moderation from economic elites is most likely to emerge in response to growing pressure from below.

WHERE, EXACTLY, WILL THAT PRESSURE come from? The most hopeful observers look to the inexorable force of demography, forecasting an "emerging Democratic majority" of the kind that transformed California from a Republican stronghold into a Democratic one. In 1983, when Lee Atwater wrote his memo to the presidential campaign of Ronald Reagan, California's former governor, the GOP dominated politics in the Golden State, as it had since World War II. Today, voter registrations in California show Republicans as the third party, not only far behind Democrats but also behind "decline to state" (that is, independents). And the majority of independents lean toward the Democrats. Republicans remain competitive in only a handful of still-red Congressional districts, Democrats hold all statewide offices, and they have a two-thirds majority in both houses of the state legislature.

What happened? In 1994, Republican governor Pete Wilson was facing a difficult reelection campaign. To beat back the challenge, Wilson settled on a strategy of whipping up the base. He rallied Republicans around Proposition 187, which would set up a state office to verify citizenship and prohibit the undocumented from gaining access to public education and nonemergency health care. Ads from that year have a Trump-era style—grainy black and white images of people flooding across border crossings.

Wilson's plan was a tactical success. The base came out (in what was, nationally, a Republican year), and he cruised to reelection. For his party, however, Wilson's stance was a strategic catastrophe. How much Proposition 187 itself mattered remains unclear: it passed, but was quickly blocked in the federal courts and eventually ruled unconstitutional. In any event, it was emblematic of the broader trajectory of the California GOP. The party sided with demographic groups that were in decline, and it attempted to leverage the fear associated with that decline into political mobilization. That posture alienated demographically ascendant groups—Asian Americans, Latinos, and college-educated whites—with profoundly negative and lasting effects on the party's reputation. Yet with the national Republican Party following an increasingly fevered version of the Wilson script, California Republicans found it hard to reverse course. In 2016, Donald Trump would win the lowest percentage of the vote in the state of any Republican in eight decades—the year FDR buried Alf Landon in a landslide.[8]

And still the California GOP hadn't hit bottom. Kevin McCarthy, who was about to take over for Paul Ryan as leader of the House Republicans, held his California colleagues in line behind the president despite Trump's evident hostility to the state and his deep unpopularity there. In the 2018 elections, Republicans would be swept out of Orange County, the epicenter of Reagan Republicanism. Having previously ceded three of the county's seven seats, the GOP now lost their remaining four. In the nation's largest state, the GOP was annihilated outside the rural enclaves that most resembled areas of GOP strength elsewhere. All told, Republicans would retain just six of California's fifty-three seats in the House. It was their lowest share of California representatives since 1883, when the state had just six total seats in Congress.

With the same broad demographic trends evident nationally, many Democrats see California's trajectory as a harbinger. The GOP leans ever more heavily on votes from older whites, especially those distant from major urban centers, and especially those without a college education. These demographic groups are in steady decline. Meanwhile, the party continues to lose ground among racial minorities, the college educated, people in or near major cities, and people under the age of fifty. The journalist Ron Brownstein, who has been skillfully charting the Republican Party's trajectory for decades, describes an ongoing, demographically grounded conflict between a white, nonurban "coalition of restoration" and an urban, diverse "coalition of transformation."[9]

The veteran Democratic pollster Stanley Greenberg has argued forcefully that California represents the Republican future. In *RIP GOP*, Greenberg suggests that Trumpism is a last-ditch resistance to overwhelming demographic trends that are about to swamp the party. To see the plausibility of Greenberg's case, one need look no further than Texas. The same year Pete Wilson was holding off a rising Democratic star (Kathleen Brown) in California, George W. Bush was taking down an established one, easily defeating incumbent governor Ann Richards. Texas rapidly became the power center of the post-1994 GOP, with Texas conservatives Dick Armey, Tom DeLay, and Bill Archer helping lead the Gingrich revolution.[10]

Today, Texas is fast approaching battleground status. In 2018, Beto O'Rourke came just a few percentage points short of winning Ted Cruz's Senate seat, while Democrats captured two Republican House seats and came close to winning several more. Will Hurd, the GOP's lone black member in the House, barely survived. He offered his own succinct autopsy report: ". . . the only way you stop that trend is by appealing to a broader base of people. If the Republican Party in Texas ceases to look like voters in Texas, there will not be a Republican Party in Texas." A year later, the forty-one-year-old Hurd announced he would not run for reelection.[11]

IN KEY RESPECTS, the *RIP GOP* analysis is an optimistic reprise of the two conventional accounts of Trumpism we discussed in the introduction to this book—interpretations that place the decline of the white working class at the heart of our politics. One narrative focuses on the divide within the party between its business-oriented establishment and insurgent voting base; the other on how that insurgency fits into the nation's long and treacherous struggle for racial equality. But both see in the emergence of Trump the anguished cry of voters grappling with their declining status in a rapidly changing society.

We do not question the importance of this demographic transition, or the reality that it helps create a ready audience for the politics of white backlash. In modern societies, political conflicts focused on racial divisions are common. Scholars of comparative politics have long noted that creating and sustaining democratic political systems in a multiracial society is very difficult. The challenges only intensify when the demographic balance is becoming less favorable to the currently dominant group.

It is a troubling fact that American party dynamics have been most stable, at least on the surface, when racial minorities have been politically excluded. The two main attempts to more fully incorporate African Americans—after the Civil War and following the civil rights movement—generated furious white backlash, fierce conflict, and ongoing resistance that roiled American politics. And these conflicts took place in a country where whites constituted the overwhelming majority and economic inequality was historically low. How fraught will such conflicts be as diversity and inequality both increase?[12]

The experience of other nations suggests that they will be very fraught. As we saw in Chapter 4, it is easy for previously dominant groups to interpret demographic changes as a threat, especially if influential figures encourage them to embrace this view. Other societies have experienced the ugly effects of ethnic outbidding, when the politically ambitious or simply opportunistic stoke feelings of threat and force people to choose sides. Even when societies hold together, the results are not pretty.

The core of the *RIP GOP* case is that if something can't go on, it won't. Yet saying that it won't go on is not the same as saying Brownstein's "coalition of transformation" is destined to prevail. The nation's demographic trajectory suggests that as a *majoritarian* strategy, white ethnonationalist populism is doomed. This is essentially a question of math. Yet what will follow as that strategy collapses is a question of politics. Coalitions can be remade. Or the political system can be remade in ways that prevent the inexorable demographic logic from translating into effective political power. If something has to give, it will. Whether that something is ethnonationalist populism or the American experiment with majoritarian rule is the crucial matter.

If conditions were otherwise favorable, America's demographic transition would be daunting. Sadly, conditions are not favorable, which is why framing our political challenge as all about demography is inadequate. We face an additional formidable obstacle: plutocracy. Moreover, plutocracy is powerful in part because it has exploited yet another formidable obstacle: the vulnerabilities in our political institutions. A conservative party that has embraced the priorities of a tiny slice of our society is trying to use and magnify these vulnerabilities, as well as deep social divisions, to fend off popular majorities. To get past these obstacles, we need to fully comprehend why our democracy is at risk, and why the "coalition of transformation" remains so embattled despite the powerful demographic trends on its side.

THE PLACE TO START is with American political institutions. The framers could hardly have predicted our current circumstances. Yet some of their choices now serve to prop up those most committed to resisting democracy. We saw in the last chapter that three features of our political system have proved most congenial to anti-democratic strategies: our system's emphasis on representing particular geographic areas, the tilt of the Senate toward low-population states, and the separation of powers—the fragmentation of political authority among Congress, the president, the courts, and state governments.

The first two of these features have created a pronounced rural bias that increasingly favors Republicans. That bias has always been a feature of our system, but it is now far more consequential. It isn't just that it has gotten much worse as the nation has urbanized and modernized; it is also that it matters much more, because the urban/rural divide now demarcates so much of our political conflict. Denizens of nonurban America are older, whiter, less educated, more likely to be evangelicals, more likely to own guns, more likely to produce a high carbon footprint—and more likely to be Republicans. And this is becoming more and more true with each passing election. In sharply advantaging rural areas, the Constitution now sharply advantages the GOP.

Moreover, the rural bias in representation now interacts in troubling ways with the Constitution's separation of powers. In two fundamental ways, our fragmented institutions greatly advantage the Republican hybrid of plutocracy and right-wing populism.

First, our institutions are making it ever harder to wield public authority for any constructive purpose. A united party uninterested in compromise almost always has opportunities to block reforms, especially now that the expanded use of the filibuster makes a group of just forty-one senators an insurmountable obstacle. This can cut both ways, but it is the party that wants to harness the capacities of democratic government that is damaged the most. And the diminishing capacity to govern only plays into the anti-government rhetoric that has fueled rising discontent with our institutions. It is a vicious circle: make it impossible for government to do anything, and then rage at government for not doing anything. Imagine for a moment how the GOP would have responded to a President Hillary Clinton, regardless of how cautiously she proceeded. Steve Bannon, echoing Newt Gingrich's approach to the moderate Republican George H. W. Bush, was blunt during the 2016 campaign: "Our back-up strategy is to fuck her up so badly that she can't govern."[13]

Even worse is the second problem: our institutions, combined with rural bias, now prop up creeping counter-majoritarianism. The Senate now tilts so heavily toward the GOP that losing the overall popular vote in Senate elections but holding the Senate majority—often by a substantial margin—has become the norm. Because of this tilt, along with some good luck and a willingness to run roughshod over long-established norms, Republican appointees control the Supreme Court, even though the GOP has won the popular vote for president just once in the last thirty years.

In the American system, these are formidable and durable positions of power. They are unlikely to disappear even if Republicans do poorly in future national elections. Republicans' control of the Senate gives them the capacity to block a Democratic president's appointments, as they did with Merrick Garland. Even if they lose their majority, they can use the filibuster to kill ordinary legislation. Senators representing as little as 17 percent of the nation's population can bring Congress to its knees, preventing even extremely popular or desperately needed bills from becoming law.

As problematic as this is for democratic practice, the current Supreme Court majority might be even more of a threat. It has allowed conservatives to strike down important and highly popular policies. Chief Justice Roberts had last-minute qualms about killing the Affordable Care Act in its entirety, a bill that virtually every lawmaker on both sides treated as unquestionably constitutional throughout the long public fight over the ACA. Yet if Roberts had proceeded as most expected him to, the law would have fallen. And the court did make it possible for many Republican-controlled states to kill one of the most popular pieces of the ACA, the expansion of Medicaid.

Even more significant than their blocking role, however, is the conservative majority's willingness to render decisions about political rules that bolster the Republican right-wing alliance. Although it is considered bad manners to bring it up, we should not forget that in *Bush v. Gore* Republican appointees (relying on reasoning they explicitly said would apply to no other cases) handed the presidency to the man who lost the national popular vote. In just the past few years, the conservative majority has allowed the virtually unlimited flow of dark money into elections, gravely weakened the organizing capacity of unions, sharply restricted class-action lawsuits (weakening another big Democratic ally, as well as the key means by which ordinary consumers and investors bring legal action against corporations), effectively gutted the Voting Rights Act (encouraging GOP voter suppression), and refused to put any limits on party-based redistricting (encouraging GOP partisan gerrymandering). There is now reason to worry that Republican justices will prove to be strong allies of executive power, so long as that executive hails from the correct party.

The Supreme Court has always been a bastion of counter-majoritarianism. Never before, though, has it been so tightly aligned with a party that is *also* committed to counter-majoritarianism. Holding the last word on the rules, the Supreme Court is perfectly placed to help the GOP get a bigger boost out of whatever share of votes it does get. If that proves insufficient, it is well placed to defang political majorities.

GIVEN THESE INSTITUTIONAL ROADBLOCKS, efforts at reform must be focused on the fundamental problem. The place where inequalities of economic power, intensifying social conflict, and mounting political dysfunction all come together is the contemporary Republican Party. This is why we have focused on that party's alarming trajectory. It is the GOP that has faced a modern form of the Conservative Dilemma. It is the GOP that has responded by fomenting tribalism, distorting elections, and subverting democratic institutions, procedures, and norms. It is the GOP that is badly failing a test that American democracy needs it to pass.

We know many consider it partisan to point a finger at one party. So be it. One reason we have brought historical examples to bear is to clarify the deep structural roots of our contemporary challenge. Viewed from a distance, so much of what is unfolding could have been anticipated. It is unsurprising that a dramatic increase in inequality, especially in a country that has other deep social cleavages, would lead to worsening political conflict and tribalism. And it is also unsurprising that in a two-party system facing these particular challenges, the deepest fissures in our politics and gravest threats to democratic stability would arise from the conservative party.

Attributing our dysfunction to both sides is based on the fallacy that the two parties are mirror images. On the contrary, they face distinctive pressures in an era of extreme inequality. Democrats look like a conventional center-left party—actually more center than left by international standards. Republicans have increasingly moved to the right not just of conservative parties in other nations, but even some far-right parties, too. But even if the Democratic Party moves left, it will aspire to address social problems through governance and thus remain more or less open to compromise. At the same time, Democrats will be constrained rather than emboldened by the disproportionate power of the wealthy and large corporations.

Republicans, by contrast, have been emboldened rather than constrained, becoming a radically disruptive force our political system is ill equipped to contain. The deep racial cleavages in our society leave us open to some of the most dangerous temptations associated with the Conservative Dilemma, while American institutions reward a political strategy of stoking grievance. The result is a double crisis: a party committed to unpopular policies that further concentrate wealth and power at the top, but also one that can potentially treat broad public disapproval not as a powerful demand necessitating a course correction but as a mere speed bump as it barrels ahead.

Despite this harsh verdict, we stress that the goal should not be to make our politics more Democratic; it should be to make our politics more democratic. As in other nations a century ago, the core challenge is finding a path that brings the conservative party into the democratic fold and encourages it to stay there. So long as the party most affiliated with very powerful elites does not believe it can survive the rigors of fair electoral competition, democracy will be under threat. The only lasting way out of our challenge is to make the Republican Party once again a contributor to a healthy polity, capable of helping the nation address pressing public problems.

AT A MOMENT WHEN THE GOP has offered such unquestioning support for the Trump administration's assault on our institutions, many will see our concern with repairing the Republican Party as distasteful. Many will see it as unrealistic as well. Yet we need to remember that the journey of the Republican Party to plutocratic populism has been unsteady and contested. Prominent figures within the party have advocated a different answer to the Conservative Dilemma, one that would diminish the GOP's responsiveness to the wealthy and expand its appeal to those of more limited means, that would reach out to racial minorities rather than use them as instruments to incite fear. The challenge is to resurrect those calls for inclusiveness and strengthen the forces working for them.

At the same time, the marginalization of GOP moderates, and the long absence of any serious organizational effort among them, show how completely the forces of plutocratic populism now dominate the party's inner circles. If modern American government needs a capacity for bipartisanship to function—and it does—something must shift the incentives of a considerable subset of ambitious Republican politicians. This will be an uphill struggle given the presence of a large and intense Republican base, reinforced by well-resourced organizations and an extremist media.

The road up that hill begins with a decisive electoral defeat for Trumpism. Not only would this slow the dangerous march toward counter-majoritarianism and unchecked executive power. A clear and sharp electoral repudiation of plutocratic populism would send the loudest possible signal to important forces within the GOP that they need a new approach. An essential quality of democracy has always been the capacity of voters to tell politicians that what they're doing must stop. Even as democracy's check on the Republican Party has dangerously weakened, fierce electoral retribution remains the best hope to motivate a fundamental rethinking of the party's priorities.

A decisive defeat may also open opportunities for meaningful political reforms. There is no end to the list of proposals for reform, but many are based on faulty diagnoses. Too often they ignore rather than address the corrosive effects of stark inequalities of wealth and power. Too often they emerge from a superficially neutral and non-partisan stance, treating the problem as one of "polarization" in which "both sides" are to blame. Getting legislators to have lunch together, changing the rules of party primaries, electing a handful of moderates, empowering a third, centrist party—none of these would improve our situation, and some could make it worse.

Instead, the existence of extreme inequality and asymmetric polarization should direct us to two broad priorities: we need aggressive efforts to reform an economy whose benefits go so disproportionately to the plutocrats, and we need a more robust and inclusive democracy. Even if Democrats rebound politically, fundamental economic reform will be extremely difficult given the entrenched influence of economic elites in both parties and the plutocrats' particular power bases in the Senate and on the Supreme Court. The irony is that the astonishing concentration of contemporary economic rewards creates the opening for valuable first steps. The wealthiest 400 families now pay a lower rate of overall taxes than at any time since World War II, despite the meteoric increase in incomes at the top. Reformers could use redistribution from the very top to provide visible and concrete benefits to the overwhelming majority of Americans. Raising taxes on the superrich substantially and spending the proceeds on programs that provide tangible and widespread benefits would send a powerful affirmation of how government can help working families. These efforts also could be carried out through the budget reconciliation process, which cannot be filibustered, and they should withstand scrutiny from even a hostile Supreme Court.

Much more fundamental changes in what has become a dangerously unbalanced economy will be necessary, too. Over the medium run, the goal must be to strengthen the middle class and build organizations that can put checks on economic elites. There are creative efforts under way, especially at the local level, to develop new models of civic organizing and new forms of worker representation, but this is a slow, hard process. Even modest progress, however, may have salutary effects. Meaningful economic reforms can lay the foundation for further reforms, strengthening supporters and weakening opponents. Progress in addressing the acute economic challenges facing ordinary Americans—progress that voters can see—would place increasing pressure on the GOP to compete by doing the same. Indeed, the country's best hope is that the vicious circles that have appeared on the right will give way to more virtuous ones.

Political reform could reinforce this dynamic. Opening doors to more democratic participation and ensuring fairer elections would not only engage more citizens and ensure their votes counted; it would change the incentives for Republicans, pushing them to build a bigger tent. Similarly, reducing the sway of money—or at least taking steps to make it more visible—could also help replace a vicious circle with a more virtuous one.

Right now, the GOP looks monolithically Trumpian. The challenge is structural, not merely personal. Just as we cannot wait for plutocrats to fix the problems that their own vast wealth helps create, we cannot expect that once Trump exits the stage, his party will somehow revert to a saner, more moderate version of itself—at least not so long as it can exploit America's aging political institutions for counter-majoritarian ends. But a stinging electoral defeat, backed by reforms that empower voters and improve their lives, could lead to such a shift. Parties want to win elections, and if electoral competition can be opened up, the GOP will face mounting pressures to adapt. In particular, it will face mounting pressures to become a truly multiracial party. That would mean backing away from its current embrace of ethnonationalist appeals. But no less important, backing away from these incendiary tactics would put increased pressure on the party to offer plausible responses to the economic needs of ordinary citizens.

The hope is not that the GOP gets relegated to permanent minority status. Our institutions create very strong incentives to have just two major parties, and it is neither realistic nor desirable to expect only one of them to rule. The goal is to prod Republicans to turn toward the future rather than the past, to build a more economically moderate and racially inclusive coalition. The current Republican voting base—old, white, rural—is on the losing side of the major demographic trends in American society. Although the biases of American political institutions offer considerable protections to this base, they do not provide a basis for the long-term competitive success of the current GOP coalition in a relatively open political system.

One can see a glimpse of a viable and democratic Republican future, and its salutary effects on our politics, in some unlikely places. Four of the five most popular governors in the country share a common storyline: they are Republicans in predominantly blue states. Charlie Baker of Massachusetts, Larry Hogan of Maryland, Chris Sununu of New Hampshire, and Phil Scott of Vermont have succeeded by establishing themselves as reasonably moderate counterweights to Democratic legislatures. All have tried to stay within sight of the political center and keep their distance from the national party. These governors have advantages that Republicans in Washington currently don't. In these blue states, the contours of the electorate require Republican politicians to reach for the middle, and the local right-wing outrage-stokers aren't strong enough to stop them.[14]

Once a demographic tipping point is reached nationally, more and more Republican politicians will face similar pressure to adapt—and perhaps quickly. If this seems implausible, it is worth emphasizing that what currently looks like a monochromatic "red state" coalition masks considerable underlying heterogeneity. Ours is an immense and extremely diverse country. There are extraordinary differences in the circumstances of the Deep South, the Mountain West, the sparsely populated plains states, and the deindustrializing Midwest. It would be a challenge to hold together such a diversity of interests under any circumstances. It becomes especially so given the GOP's fealty to extreme groups like the NRA and its intense commitments to economic elites. These attachments leave Republicans hard-pressed to address the aspirations of ordinary citizens in any of these settings.

The party's challenge is most immediate, though, in the traditionally Republican "sunbelt" areas (Arizona, Texas, Florida, Georgia, and North Carolina). These states contain 109 Electoral College votes, along with large and growing Latino populations and expanding outposts of the high-tech knowledge economy. Here is where we can anticipate the tipping point beyond which the party will face ever-greater pressure to repudiate its current course.

AMERICAN PLUTOCRACY WANTS what majorities won't provide. Right-wing populism decries changes it can't stop. The Republican Party's rhetoric conjures up a mythical past because the party as currently constituted cannot survive in a democratic future. There is a path before us in which the intensity of the Conservative Dilemma gradually diminishes. If political and economic reforms weaken the disproportionate clout of elites, our political leaders will find it harder to ignore the demands of ordinary citizens. If those who resist such reforms cannot construct counter-majoritarian bulwarks, our society will rediscover how to identify and pursue shared interests, even among those with very different economic circumstances.

The challenge is to get there. The GOP has turned to a polarizing and counter-majoritarian strategy precisely because it knows it is in a race against time. The forces of reaction cannot win forever in a reasonably open and competitive political system, but this very fact endangers that open and competitive system. We face the nation's gravest political crisis since the Great Depression. Donald Trump contributes to this danger, but he neither caused it nor is it dependent on him. Entrenched minority rule remains a very possible future—a future that we can avoid only if we recognize and address the profound inequalities that have made it possible.

EPILOGUE

ON NOVEMBER 3, 2020, AMERICANS voted in unprecedented numbers despite a global pandemic. By a margin of over 7 million votes, they chose to deny Donald Trump a second term. It was only the third election defeat of an incumbent president since 1932.

The removal of a would-be authoritarian from office is no small accomplishment. Authoritarian-minded leaders elected to power in other countries, such as Jair Bolsonaro in Brazil, have cemented their control during the COVID-19 crisis. But as we have emphasized throughout this book, the risks to our democracy posed by plutocratic populism emerged well before Donald Trump and extend well beyond his dangerous role. Trump was the potentially fatal metastasis of a malignant cancer. American voters removed the tumor, but our democracy is still very sick.

Though the vote was clear, Trump came much closer to victory than pre-election polls, or his catastrophic response to the pandemic, suggested he would. A swing of less than fifty thousand votes across key states might have allowed him to again win in the Electoral College. Down-ballot, Republicans did better than expected—beneficiaries of Trump's remarkable turnout of the party's base, GOP gerrymandering, and the rural tilt of our electoral system. Democrats held the House and captured the Senate by the slimmest possible margin in two runoff elections. But Republicans took heart in their vigorous minority position, their continuing strength at the state level, and the prospect of GOP gains in the 2022 midterms.

216 LET THEM EAT TWEETS

In short, the election did not deliver the decisive repudiation of plutocratic populism that might have created strong pressure on elite Republicans to steer the party toward a more moderate and multiracial path. Instead, the result was a mixed verdict: although Trump was removed from office, the prospects for an immediate GOP change of course looked slight. Refusing to concede, Trump signaled he would remain a radicalizing force in Republican politics. Even as former Vice President Joe Biden prepared for office, Republicans hoping for a future in politics overwhelmingly sided with (or at least tolerated) lies about a stolen election, feeding a dangerous myth that would spawn a violent assault on the Capitol on January 6, 2021. There was no sign that the party would, or perhaps could, close Pandora's Box.

Equally significant, the failure of Democrats to gain a strong hold on Congress reduced the possibility of a wave of political reforms that would have allowed them to govern with their popular majorities and created greater pressures on Republicans to shift direction. In our increasingly sclerotic polity, windows of opportunity to address fundamental failings through normal institutional channels are rare, and typically emerge at the beginning of a new president's term. Democrats' current window is narrow, and it might emerge.

The problem, as we have insisted, is structural. Our aging political institutions have not proved capable of preventing a party radicalized by America's ever-worsening extreme inequality from burrowing into those sites of governance most resistant to popular control. The election delivered a transfer of power. It did not deliver the transformation of power necessary to vanquish plutocratic populism. Whether that transformation takes place will depend, more than ever, on creating the conditions and case for meaningful democratic reform.

THE NEED FOR SUCH REFORM is more evident today than ever. As its human costs mounted, COVID-19 brought all the darkest aspects of plutocratic populism into vivid display. The financial toll of the pandemic ruptured American society along the very lines that had radicalized the Republican Party, separating ordinary Americans and small businesses from the super-wealthy and the titans of consolidated corporate sectors. The greatest health and economic costs were borne by those working on the front lines and those living on the social periphery. Disproportionately nonwhite, their jobs were devastated, families upended, health threatened, lives ended. Death, dislocation, and despair spread through black and Latino communities across the nation, helping to spark a massive wave of protests (and counterprotests) focused on racial injustice.

Amid this trauma, the extent to which the three Rs of Republican base-building came out into the open was shocking, if sadly unsurprising. Trump's entire campaign centered on resentment, racialization, and rigging. He offered no vision, only division. In an unprecedented move, the party did not even adopt a new platform at its national convention. The president's now-ironic reelection pledge "Keep America Great" said it all.

Especially after the Black Lives Matter protests of midsummer—sparked by video of a policeman slowly suffocating an unarmed black man in Minneapolis—Republican leaders had an opportunity to acknowledge the realities of systemic racism. Instead, they stood with Trump as he condemned the overwhelmingly nonviolent protests and encouraged armed right-wing rallies against them, as well as against state measures to limit the spread of COVID-19.

Indeed, the strategies we referred to as racialization increasingly gave way to unveiled racism. Trump's number one charge against his Democratic rival—besides the calumny that he was a closet socialist—was that, by supporting affordable housing, Biden wanted to encourage low-income minorities to move into the suburbs. At the GOP convention, a wealthy white couple that had threatened a group of mostly black protesters with weapons ominously warned, "Make no mistake: No matter where you live, your family will not be safe in the radical Democrats' America."[1]

Alongside the resentment and racialization was rigging. From early on, the president and his allies knew he would only win through an Electoral College inversion, and that his chance of eking out such a win depended on making the election as disreputable and chaotic as possible.

The moment it became obvious the pandemic would require mail-in voting the president used his bully pulpit to delegitimate the process. He fought federal measures to ensure the election went smoothly (while rushing a big-dollar GOP fundraiser into the role of postmaster general), and encouraged Republicans to show up on election day not just to vote but to "watch very carefully." "The only way we're going to lose this election is if the election is rigged," Trump declared months before voting began. His son, Donald Trump Jr.—a rising right-wing star in his own right—called for an "Army for Trump" to prevent "the radical left" from robbing Trump Sr. of his certain victory.[2]

The strategy was as transparent as a bank robber sending the police his plans in advance. If mail-in votes were delayed, the votes of those Trump urged to go to the polls in person would loom large in the initial count. Creating an early impression of a Trump win could help Republicans make the case for contesting mail-in ballots that disproportionately favored Biden. Republican legislatures abetted this ploy, refusing proposals to speed the counting of what everyone knew would be an unprecedented flood of mail-in ballots.

THAT THIS ANTI-DEMOCRATIC STRATEGY FAILED should not blind us to its significance, and not just because it facilitated the political right's construction of a dangerous myth of a stolen election. If the margins had been slightly closer, the election might really have been stolen—by Republicans. A president used the power and prestige of his office to undermine the most fundamental of democratic rights. Those in his party with the influence to push back either cheered him on or looked the other way.

As the election neared, an independent research group released a chilling report showing that the United States was very much part of a worldwide trend toward "autocratization," in which elected leaders undermined democratic safeguards like checks on executive power and free elections. The central problem? The Republican Party, whose "lower commitment to political pluralism, demonization of political opponents, disrespect for fundamental minority rights and encouragement of political violence" made it "more similar to autocratic ruling parties such as Turkey's AKP and Hungary's Fidesz than to typical center-right governing parties in democracies such as the Conservatives in the United Kingdom or CDU in Germany."[3]

In the end, though, the party's standard-bearer lost. Nonwhite voters in GOP-controlled states overcame the many barriers placed in their way, often at considerable personal risk. And Joe Biden obtained a sizable enough margin in key states to make post-election challenges futile. In virtually every state, Biden did a little better than Clinton had in 2016—and that was enough.

The result was a rebuke but not a realignment. Trump received 47 percent of the vote. His demonization of minorities, scapegoating of China, and transformation of public health measures into culture-war weapons energized the core GOP electorate. Trump's intense backing rested on all the familiar divisions: rural vs. urban, college vs. non-college, white vs. black, men vs. women. Mocking Biden for wearing a mask while extolling his own virility after contracting COVID-19, Trump essentially portrayed concern for one's fellow citizens as weakness and indifference as manliness. (The role of toxic masculinity in Republican base-building is a topic that deserves far more attention than we have given it in this book.) An economic crisis and nearly a quarter million lives lost barely shook Trump's base. It was a chilling signal of how irradicable Republicans tribalism had become—a signal that became far more chilling on January 6.

And it suggested a frightening possibility: Had Trump done just a bit more to cultivate his popularity through tangible expressions of humanity, he might well have been reelected. Divisive strongmen in other nations, from Brazil to India to Turkey, coupled right-wing rhetoric with generous doses of government assistance. Trump took credit for an early wave of aid spearheaded by House Democrats, even delaying the sending of relief checks to ensure his name was on them. Yet his erratic response to the crisis left additional rounds of relief dependent on Mitch McConnell and his caucus—that is, on the establishment stalwarts who had spent much of 2017 trying to take health care away from their own constituents. The same statesmen of the Senate who had insisted on massive tax cuts for the superrich and corporations, deficits be damned, now postured as guardians of fiscal probity.·

Had more relief been forthcoming, it could have made the difference. After the election, analysts found that counties that experienced the greatest spikes in unemployment at the height of the crisis leaned toward Biden.[4] In an alternate world in which another round of Trump-signed stimulus checks had arrived in October, or in which 2016 infrastructure promises had actually been carried out, the close outcomes in critical rustbelt states might easily have tipped the other way. In other words, if plutocratic populism been less plutocratic and more populist, Donald Trump might well have had four more years to tear apart American democracy.

CERTAINLY, PLUTOCRACY'S CORROSIVE EFFECTS WERE everywhere to see. The initial round of relief was chock full of giveaways to corporations and the wealthy, including $135 billion in special tax breaks for hedge-fund billionaires and (wait for it) real estate magnates. Once that had passed, Republicans led by Mitch McConnell insisted only modest additional efforts had any chance in the Senate, though that didn't stop them from including in their demands a provision doubling the tax deduction for business meals. (It was unclear how executives were going to enjoy those three-martini lunches as the pandemic raged.) Meanwhile, McConnell mocked state and local fiscal relief that governors of both parties were pleading for as a "blue-state bailout." Nothing better summed up Senate Republicans' continuing commitment to plutocracy than the spectacle of Speaker of the House Nancy Pelosi trying in vain to convince them to take steps to rescue the economy that would surely have helped Trump be reelected.[5]

Equally telling was Republicans' number one precondition for any new aid: broad liability relief for corporations, shielding them from future lawsuits over any failures to protect workers or consumers from the pandemic. Such failures were already rife. A watchdog group identified a dozen "pandemic profiteers" whose wealth had ballooned even as their workers struggled to stay safe. They included John Tyson, the billionaire owner of Tyson Foods, where 11,000 workers had become infected with COVID-19; and Rob, Jim, and Alice Walton, whose combined personal wealth increased $48 billion between March and November, even as Walmart resisted providing workers with ongoing hazard pay. Siding with the US Chamber of Commerce, Trump refused to use the Defense Production Act to make protective medical gear. Yet he invoked the act to require that meat-packing plants stay open, even as tens of thousands of workers in the industry were sickened and hundreds died.[6]

But the poisonous tendrils of plutocracy went much deeper. Over the prior decade, corporations had poured hundreds of millions into shadowy nonprofit groups enabled by *Citizens United*. Though these "527 organizations" were meant to keep spending anonymous, investigative spadework showed that roughly two-thirds of the money went to groups on the right. Amid the tragedies of 2020, the reasons why corporations were hiding their contributions became obvious. It was these business-backed groups that pushed a lawsuit led by Texas's attorney general that threatened the entire Affordable Care Act in the midst of the pandemic. It was these business-backed groups that fought to overturn federal efforts to limit carbon emissions even as corporate heads finally expressed concern about the problem. It was these business-backed groups that helped engineer the extreme gerrymandering and voter suppression laws—all disproportionately affecting nonwhite voters—that helped Republicans maintain control of state legislatures even in states where Trump lost.[7]

The debilitating effects of the long plutocratic assault on government capacity were also apparent in the faltering federal response to the pandemic. Not since World War II had competent public authority based on scientific expertise looked so essential—or so elusive. Business groups lamented COVID denialism, but right-wing skepticism built on the infrastructure of junk science they had helped build in the long fight against government efforts to address threats ranging from smoking and lead poisoning to the existential challenge of climate change. Corporate "merchants of doubt" were not peddling this particular product line, but they shared a good deal of the blame for the strength of the market.

For conservative plutocrats, the item that loomed largest as the election approached was not COVID-19 but SCOTUS 6. By filling the seat left vacant by the sudden death of liberal icon Ruth Bader Ginsburg, the right had the opportunity to create a 6–3 conservative supermajority that could simultaneously guard against progressive economic policies and pursue the plutocratic-populist agenda of market and moral fundamentalism. Playing constitutional hardball as always, Mitch McConnell quickly ditched the freshly minted principle he had invoked to block Merrick Garland for almost an entire election year. Leonard Leo's Judicial Crisis Network—with its deep ties to both the Federalist Society and culturally conservative groups like the NRA—deployed the usual tens of millions in anonymous conservative cash. By the end of October, the conservative plutocrats had another reliable ally on the court.

Yet they were also discovering the limits of their influence within the party they had helped radicalize. The large tax cuts in their pockets and plutocrat-friendly federal courts could not obscure the endless uncertainty and continuing pileup of governance failures, along with Trump's ever less deniable racism. With Trump's defeat looking more and more likely, an increasing share of economic elites openly distanced themselves from the Trump administration. Biden himself received substantial financial support from the more progressive precincts of corporate America, as well as from moderate-minded denizens of Wall Street. Republican-allied business groups like the US Chamber of Commerce hedged more than usual. Though the Chamber mostly supported Republicans—only three of the top twenty-five beneficiaries of its PAC contributions were Democrats—its spokespeople called for a more conventional, if no less conservative, approach.[8]

After the election, even Charles Koch publicly lamented what he'd wrought. "Boy, did we screw up! What a mess," he confessed in a coauthored book entitled *Believe in People*. Apparently, his belief in people didn't extend to Georgia voters, as within weeks Americans for Prosperity had poured a half million dollars into ads and canvassing to support the Republican side in the high-stakes Senate runoffs.

It was hardly the first time Koch had tried to soften his public image by expressing support for bipartisanship while privately continuing a decades-long practice of boosting hard-right Republicans. Nonetheless, economic elites within the party had good reason to worry about the increasingly wild products of the GOP's outrage machinery.

BEFORE THE 2012 ELECTION, PRESIDENT Obama, battered by two years of obstruction and wild accusations from Tea Party Republicans, predicted the "fever" that had gripped the GOP would "break" if he won.[9] Eight years later, it is clear that "fever" was the wrong metaphor. The disease that now saturates the GOP is more like an addiction. Party leaders had boosted the energy of the party's supporters by injecting ever-larger doses of outrage. Now, they found themselves unable to break with an extreme form of identity politics ever more weakly tethered to reality.

Many within the party who worried about this trend believed that Trump's defeat would halt it. Judged from the election's immediate aftermath, the opposite was true. As Trump brazenly insisted he had won, all but a handful of Republicans in national office rallied behind him or stayed silent. Nearly two-thirds of Republicans in the House, including House Minority Leader Kevin McCarthy, signed onto a lawsuit to overturn the 2020 election by tossing out the results of four states, disenfranchising twenty millions Americans. The bid was so egregious that even the conservative Supreme Court supermajority swiftly and curtly refused to hear it. In a move without precedent, most national representatives of one of the country's two major parties allowed a defeated president speaking in their name to trash public confidence in America's representative institutions, stoke racialized grievances about a stolen election, and hinder a smooth transition of power amid an intensifying pandemic. Some stood up as well as stood by: Lindsey Graham—the Trump critic turned sycophant—tried to intervene in Georgia's vote-counting, a crime that if committed by an ordinary citizen would likely have put him in jail.[10]

They knew what the election results showed: the GOP base—a

minority of the electorate but a majority of the party—was thoroughly Trumpian. The president's racial divisiveness appeals to tribalism, and efforts to delegitimate the election and his opponent may not have saved him, but they unquestionably helped Republicans lower on the ballot. Republican candidates for the House and Senate benefited from Trump's ability to bring his voters out, without themselves suffering the drop-off among Trump-weary suburbanites that cost the president his reelection.

Trump's voting base wasn't chastened by the election; they were convinced a vast antifa conspiracy (that included, apparently, scores of GOP officeholders and election workers) had ripped victory from their hands. This was a pretty modest misbelief compared with others that conservative outrage-stokers had encouraged. The QAnon conspiracy theory, popular in right-wing circles, cast Trump as the last line of defense against Satan-worshipping pedophiles who controlled the Democratic Party. But whether it was QAnon or "stop the steal," elected Republicans recognized that efforts to challenge these fantasies could lead the party to implode.

As in the post-Gingrich past, right-wing outrage didn't just bubble up from below. It rested on organizational surrogates on which the party had become increasingly dependent—from the NRA and Christian right to the ever more extreme fringes of right-wing media. Whether their goal was power or profit, these forces found no cause to slacken their outrage-stoking in the turmoil of 2020. To the contrary, the greatest danger they confronted was accusations from even further right that their extremism was not pure enough. Fox, for example, immediately faced defections and attacks when its embattled "news" side called the election for Biden. The spectacle of Rupert Murdoch's conservative empire furiously accused of excessively moderation suggested there were still new precincts of extremism into which orchestrated outrage could go.

THE RIGHT-WING DRAMATICS ALSO SUGGESTED it was Trump who would be leading the way, as he signaled his intention to remain a dominant presence within the GOP—and even, perhaps, to challenge Biden in 2024. In the weeks after his loss, the defeated president turned his lies about election fraud into massive fundraising. (Ostensibly raised to challenge the results, most of the money would be available to fund Trump's activities going forward.) Like his allies in right-wing media, he understood how lucrative the business of outrage could be. Unlike them, Trump controlled the levers of executive power, which he deployed to purge and pardon, politicize and propagandize, as no defeated president had before. Trump's continuing assault on democratic norms and institutions heightened the risks for any ambitious Republican who might favor a turn to moderation, or even just a recognition of reality. The base was loyal to Trump, and Trump would continue to demand loyalty from politicians who hoped to earn its support. Anyone wanting a future in the party would still have to bend the knee. Electoral rebuke and insurrectionist violence notwithstanding, the prospects for a GOP course correction looked dim.

The intensification of GOP radicalism is especially ominous given the mixed outcome of the election itself. By the end of January 2021 Democrats will control all three of the nation's elected lawmaking bodies: the presidency, the Senate, and the House. Yet Democrats confront an ugly truth: the majoritarian institutions that favor them are increasingly hostage to the counter-majoritarian institutions that don't. Even though Democrats picked up both Senate seats in Georgia—and hence have a majority by virtue of the tie-breaking vote of Vice President Kamala Harris—their agenda hangs by a slender thread. They will need to hold together their entire caucus, and even then their opponents can turn to the Senate filibuster on every issue but the budget. Failing that, Republicans have Mitch McConnell's greatest piece of plutocratic-populist engineering: a 6–3 Supreme Court sitting atop a federal legal system stacked with Trump appointees.

Republicans understand what the fight is about: power. Shortly before the election, Jerry Taylor—the former head of the Cato Institute and staff director of the American Legislative Exchange

Council—offered candid reflections about the movement he had left behind. "Regardless of what the campaign that brought them into office was about," Taylor observed, "conservatives invariably attend to policy initiatives designed to cripple Democratic power. Right-to-work statutes, public-employee contracts, campaign finance regulation, the promotion of conservative judges: all are top priorities for a right that understands the long-term political advantages that accrue from hobbling muscular Democratic constituencies and the future scope of liberal lawmaking."[11]

Far more than Democrats, Republicans benefit from the features of our system that make it easy for powerful minorities to block what popular majorities demand. Especially now that Republicans have locked in large tax cuts for corporations and the wealthy, they will be more than happy to focus on obstructing the use of government to address social problems—from climate change, to deep racial inequalities, to a frightfully expensive and inadequate health system. A party that wants to pursue structural changes in the economy and polity needs active government. A party that wants to preserve and deepen already embedded structural biases mostly doesn't. Indeed, for Republicans, obstruction is a twofer: it allows them to defend their corporate and wealthy allies and intense conservative factions like the NRA; and it breeds popular resentment and distrust in government they can exploit in coming elections.

Democrats, by contrast, need to pass bold laws to pursue much of their agenda. But even with control of the House and Senate, passing bold laws is very hard given inevitable Democratic defections and the filibuster. James Madison called the House "the grand depository of the democratic principle of government."[12] But after Democrats took the House in 2018, they found that their resounding vote win provided little governing power. Nancy Pelosi's majority passed a broad range of reforms. They ended up in a rather less grand depository: gathering dust on Mitch McConnell's desk. Now they face Mitch McConnell's filibuster.

Even the House's vaunted power of impeachment fizzled. In December 2019, the House passed impeachment charges in response to Trump's brazen attempt to use the American military to encourage foreign interference in the election on his behalf. Given lockstep GOP loyalty and the two-thirds Senate vote required, a conviction was never in the cards. In the wake of the insurrection of January 6, the House impeached Trump again. The near-certainty the Senate will again fail to convict him suggests that impeachment is a chimerical power today.

Our Constitution has enabled these undemocratic outcomes, but they aren't the "checks and balances" the framers had in mind. They saw the popularly elected House as central rather than peripheral. They believed impeachment could and should be used to stop demagogues. They adopted only a limited number of super-majority requirements, and none as sweeping or as consequential as the "rule of sixty" now in force under Senate rules. They believed the separation of powers would force shifting majorities to build broad alliances, not that it would allow a durable national coalition, reliant on a popular minority, to obstruct governance and lodge power deeply in institutions insulated from popular pressures.

Yet this is precisely what is happening. Plutocratic populism has given rise to two threats—one highly visible, one more insidious. The threat of an authoritarian demagogue we know and see. The threat of what we called "counter-majoritarianism"—but now think is more accurately termed "minoritarianism"—is the less visible but no less dangerous development.

Democrats have won the popular vote for president in seven of the last eight elections—a run of victories without precedent. In the Senate, they have represented states containing a majority of the nation's population for all but two of the past twenty years.[13] The growing diversity of the electorate and their dominance among younger voters continues to favor them.

But while these demographically rooted advantages are real, so too is the narrowness of their geographic reach. As noted by *The Atlantic*'s Ronald Brownstein, Biden won all but a handful of the nation's hundred largest counties. Yet while Democrats gain ground in the "most economically vibrant metropolitan areas, their support in exurban, small-town, and rural regions has collapsed." There are roughly 3,000 counties in America—Biden won just over 500.[14]

So long as polarization continues to cleave urban areas from non-urban areas, density and diversity from rurality and resentment, Republicans will enjoy a large edge in the Senate and a smaller but still significant one in the Electoral College. Since 2000, Democrats have twice won the popular vote for president while losing the presidency, and Biden fairly narrowly avoided a similar fate. Unless Democrats' geographic bases of support shift substantially, the combination of the Electoral College and Republican efforts to tilt the electoral playing field will require that their presidential nominees win by big margins to be guaranteed victory.

The Democratic majority in the House is also fragile. Although the body's rural bias is nowhere near as severe as the Senate's, the concentration of left-leaning voters in urban districts means Democrats need to win the overall popular vote in House elections by several percentage points to consistently hold a majority. With decennial redistricting based on a shambolic Census set to begin, Republicans can use their control of state legislatures—itself often a result of extreme legislative gerrymandering—to win extra congressional seats by drawing biased maps. National Republicans can add to these efforts by continuing to pursue the Trump administration's aggressive attempts to bolster GOP representation by redrawing electoral lines to reflect the estimated number of legal residents, rather than total population. Derailed by the Supreme Court but not declared unconstitutional, this radical change would bring GOP vote rigging squarely onto the national stage.

Republican redoubts, by contrast, look more secure. Congressional elections are increasingly driven by partisanship, irrespective of the qualities of candidates.[15] This gives Republicans a clear upper hand in the Senate, even as the nation's population balance continues to shift from red to blue states. The conservative Court majority seems likely to last for many years, if not decades. For Republicans, control of the courts is central not just to their policy aims, but also to their ability to maintain and widen distortions in our political system that favors GOP minority rule—from laws that favor the political power of the wealthy and weaken labor unions to those allowing the continued suppression of minority voters and extreme partisan gerrymandering.

These aren't checks and balances; they are affronts to democracy. Representative government rests on the promise that all citizens can exercise their right to vote without fear or suppression. And it requires that those votes have meaning—that they are not debased by large and persistent gaps between majority preferences and electoral outcomes. The emergence of electoral and political institutions that systematically favor one party even as it consistently receives less popular support threatens to turn this fundamental right into an empty promise.

DEFEATING DONALD TRUMP WAS A big win not just for Democrats, but for democracy. His authoritarian aspirations, sanctioned by virtually all elected Republicans at almost every turn, posed an enormous danger to representative government. But we still face the grave threat of persistent rule by a plutocratic-populist minority exploiting the weaknesses of the American constitutional design. And this threat will be much more difficult to dislodge.

At least the problem is now understood. Reformers are discussing an ambitious set of changes designed to make American democracy more majoritarian and responsive. These include eliminating the filibuster, ensuring the right to vote, limiting the role of big money, reducing the capacity for state parties to do extreme gerrymandering, and reducing the sway and tilt of a stacked Supreme Court. Such reforms could start to rebuild the virtuous cycle of democratic governance that we wrote about in the conclusion, in which popularly elected majorities have the power to govern, do popular things, and regain office to do more of them.

We still believe that slow but steady demographic change offers hope. Biden received six of ten votes among those under thirty years of age.[16] While there were surprising areas of Latino support for Trump, Biden still won close to twice as many votes within this rapidly growing demographic group. And his strong support among white voters near major metro centers showed the limits of Trump's strategy of open racial demonization. Such trends will both strengthen the Democrats' coalition and put pressure, eventually, on the GOP to rethink the dangerous path it is pursuing.

The election results also offered a reminder that while Republicans have entrenched themselves in power, many of the policies that they back are deeply unpopular. Voters who cast their ballot for GOP candidates also voted for ballot measures to raise the minimum wage, expand Medicaid, and even raise taxes to fund education. Plutocratic populism rests on outrage because it does not push back against extreme inequality, and there is no sign that GOP leaders who recognize this bind are poised to emerge. So long as the "populists" with the party respond to the conservative dilemma by offering right-wing extremism rather than economic moderation, the party will have difficulty moving beyond its intense minority base.

Because the crisis facing American democracy is structural, rooted in the collision of extreme inequality with our aging political institutions, better strategies or messages will only get us so far. Those who believe in fundamental reform will need to do their own power-building: sparking and strengthening new grassroots movements, fighting the good fight for political reform with boldness and clarity, and using tangible help clearly identified with government to slowly build new bonds with potentially persuasible citizens. The seeds for broader change are there: galvanized labor unions, broad social movements, get-out-the-vote campaigns in states like Georgia and cities like Philadelphia, led by black and brown organizers who understand the stakes. To grow those seeds will require a challenging blend of passion and patience. Above all, it will require a clear-eyed recognition of the problem and the stakes.

ACKNOWLEDGMENTS

We want to begin with a deep thanks to all the intrepid scholars and journalists whose investigations are essential for a work of real-time social science like this. As the endnotes attest, we could not have written this book without their varied and valued efforts.

We are also grateful to the many brilliant colleagues who generously shared their time and insights. Dan Ziblatt has greatly shaped our thinking about the role of inequality in transforming the Republican Party, and Paul feels fortunate he was his office mate in Paris at "MaxPo" (the Max Planck Sciences Po Center on Coping with Instability in Market Societies). Dan and his coauthor Steven Levitsky also graciously vetted the book with a group of their students when Jacob was a fellow at the Radcliffe Institute for Advanced Study. Jacob thanks the other Radcliffe fellows for their friendship and feedback; the executive director of the program, Meredith Quinn, for her splendid leadership; the social science director Daniel Carpenter, for his influence on both of our thinking; and Humza Jilani and Meena Venkataramanan for their able research support. He also notes with sadness the passing of the prior director, Judy Vichniac, a beautiful person who headed Harvard's Social Studies program when he was an undergraduate.

Many other colleagues helped us with this book when it was still a work in progress, including Daniel Goldhagen, Dan Galvin, Ruth Collier, Jake Grumbach, Alex Hertel-Fernandez, Peter Hall, Rob Mickey, Eric Schickler, Steve Teles (who deserves credit for the "Bond villain" reference in the introduction), Chloe Thurston, and Kathy Thelen. At an idyllic workshop in Italy organized by the Social Science Research Council and German Research Foundation, we were fortunate to discuss our ideas with Marius Busemeyer, Nick Carnes, Lea Elsasser, Peter Enns, Jane Gingrich, Silja Häusermann, Staffan Kumlin, Frank Nullmeier, Jonas Pontusson, Philipp Rehm, Kay Schlozman, Laura Seelkopf, Jale Tosun, Jessica Trounstine, Margaret Weir, and Jonathan Wolff. At the 2019 meeting of the American Political Science Association, we gained additional insights from Robert Lieberman, Suzanne Mettler, Megan Ming Francis, Leah Wright Rigueur, Theda Skocpol, and Rick Valelly. Theda has had a special impact on our ideas, and we want to thank her for illuminating the path we follow.

Jacob also received great feedback from presentations at Northwestern University and Trinity College, and Paul from presentations at Columbia University, Cornell University, and the New America Foundation. Paul is especially thankful for many discussions of this work with the wonderful members of the Successful Societies Program of the Canadian Institute for Advanced Research, and owes a particular debt to Peter Gourevitch, Peter Hall, Michele Lamont, and Anne Wilson. Finally, we are grateful to Tom Mann for his close reading of the book, for our many (surprisingly enjoyable) conversations about the (highly disturbing) state of American politics, and for his remarkable joint books with Norm Ornstein and E. J. Dionne.

At Yale's Institution for Social and Policy Studies (ISPS), three stellar research assistants helped us (and saved us from many errors): Jack Greenberg, Benjamin Waldman, and Sam Zacher. Jacob also thanks ISPS's terrific staff, especially Pamela Lamonaca.

Our agent, Sydelle Kramer, showed herself once again to be a master of her craft. We could not have moved forward without her support, encouragement, and advice. Sydelle helped connect us with Norton and the amazing team at Liveright, headed by Bob Weil. Our editor, Dan Gerstle, was an author's dream: passionate, supportive, hard-working, and thoughtful. So too, our publicity team: Peter Miller and Cordelia Calvert. We are also grateful to Haley Bracken, Rebecca Homiski, William Avery Hudson, Gina Iaquinta,

Amy Medeiros, and Anna Oler. We feel honored our book bears the Liveright imprint.

Above all, we feel grateful for the love of our families. We know that many authors don't have the great good fortune of having siblings who will offer extremely astute feedback on their work, as Paul's brothers Mike and Kit do. We also know that authors writing a book on a short timeline aren't always fun to be with. For not just putting up with us but showing far more understanding than is the norm for teenagers, we want to thank our children: Ava and Owen (Jacob) and Sidra and Seth (Paul).

Our greatest debt, however, is to the two women who, notwithstanding the associated demands and stresses, have wholeheartedly supported our collaborations from the beginning, Oona and Tracey. We have dedicated books to them before, but we can never do so often enough, or show the true depth of our gratitude—much less the full measure of our love.

NOTES

INTRODUCTION

1. Gabriel Zucman, "Global Wealth Inequality," *Annual Review of Economics* 11 (August 2019): 109–138.
2. Jacob S. Hacker and Paul Pierson, "Confronting Asymmetric Polarization," in *Solutions to Political Polarization in America*, ed. Nathaniel Persily (New York: Cambridge University Press, 2015), 59–72; Thomas E. Mann and Norman J. Ornstein, *It's Even Worse Than It Looks: How the American Constitutional System Collided with the New Politics of Extremism* (New York: Basic Books, 2012); Christopher Ingraham, "This Astonishing Chart Shows How Moderate Republicans Are an Endangered Species," *Washington Post*, June 2, 2015, https://www.washingtonpost.com/news/wonk/wp/2015/06/02/this-astonishing-chart-shows-how-republicans-are-an-endangered-species/.
3. Didi Kuo and Nolan McCarty, "Democracy in America," *Global Policy* 6, no. S1 (June 2015): 53; Jacob S. Hacker and Paul Pierson, *American Amnesia: How the War on Government Led Us to Forget What Made America Prosper* (New York: Simon & Schuster, 2016); Michael Tomasky, "The GOP's Legislative Lemons," *New York Times*, December 14, 2017, https://www.nytimes.com/2017/12/14/opinion/the-gops-legislative-lemons.html; Emily Ekins, "The Five Types of Trump Voters: Who They Are and What They Believe," Democracy Fund Voter Study Group, June 2017, https://www.voterstudygroup.org/publication/the-five-types-trump-voters#toc-appendices. See also Martin Gilens and Benjamin I. Page, "Testing Theories of American Politics: Elites, Interest Groups, and Average Citizens," *Perspectives on Politics* 12, no. 3 (September 2014): 564–581.
4. Jacob S. Hacker and Paul Pierson, "Abandoning the Middle: The Bush Tax Cuts and the Limits of Democratic Control," *Perspectives on Politics* 3, no. 1 (March 2005): 33–53.

Notes to Pages 4–9

Notes to Pages 4–9

5. Ibid.; "Distributional Analysis of the Conference Agreement for the Tax Cuts and Jobs Act," Tax Policy Center, December 18, 2017, 5, 8.
6. Fareed Zakaria introduced the term "plutocratic populism" in his discussion of an article one of us wrote. Fareed Zakaria, "Maybe Trump Knows His Base Better Than We Do," *Washington Post*, December 9, 2017; Paul Pierson, "American Hybrid: Donald Trump and the Strange Merger of Populism and Plutocracy," *British Journal of Sociology* 168, no. S1 (November 2017): S105–119.
7. For representative examples of this genre, see Tim Alberta, *American Carnage: On the Front Lines of the Republican Civil War and the Rise of President Trump* (New York: HarperCollins, 2019); Jeremy Peter, "The Tea Party Didn't Get What It Wanted, but It Did Unleash the Politics of Anger," *New York Times*, August 28, 2019, https://www.nytimes.com/2019/08/28/us/politics/tea-party-trump.html; Shane Goldmacher, "How David Koch and His Brother Shaped American Politics," *New York Times*, August 23, 2019, https://www.nytimes.com/2019/08/23/us/politics/david-koch-republican-politics.html; Jeremy W. Peters, "Charles Koch Takes on Trump. Trump Takes on Charles Koch," *New York Times*, July 31, 2018, https://www.nytimes.com/2018/07/31/us/politics/trump-koch-brothers.html.
8. Paul Krugman, "Notes on Excessive Wealth Disorder," *New York Times*, June 22, 2019, https://www.nytimes.com/2019/06/22/opinion/notes-on-excessive-wealth-disorder.html; Matthew Yglesias, "Billionaire Trump Donor Explains He's in It for the Tax Cuts, Not the Racism," Vox, August 8, 2019, https://www.vox.com/2019/8/8/20782269/stephen-ross-soulcycle-equinox-trump-donor; Jonathan Chait, "'American Carnage' Exposes the Republican Slide Into Trumpism," *New York*, August 24, 2019, http://nymag.com/intelligencer/2019/08/american-carnage-review-tim-alberta-trump.html; Jane Mayer, *Dark Money: The Hidden History of the Billionaires behind the Rise of the Radical Right* (New York: Anchor Books, 2017).
9. Benjamin I. Page, Jason Seawright, and Matthew J. Lacombe, *Billionaires and Stealth Politics* (Chicago: University of Chicago Press, 2018); Benjamin I. Page, Larry M. Bartels, and Jason Seanwright, "Democracy and the Policy Preferences of Wealthy Americans," *Perspectives on Politics* 11, no. 1 (March 2013): 51–73.
10. Page, Bartels, and Seawright, "Democracy and the Policy Preferences of Wealthy Americans"; Alexander Hertel-Fernandez, *State Capture: How Conservative Activists, Big Businesses, and Wealthy Donors Reshaped the American States—and the Nation* (New York: Oxford University Press, 2019). See Chapter 2 for more evidence.
11. Hacker and Pierson, "Confronting Asymmetric Polarization"; Mann and Ornstein, *It's Even Worse Than It Looks*; Ingraham, "This Astonishing Chart Shows How Moderate Republicans Are an Endangered Species."
12. For representative examples, see Eduardo Porter, *American Poison: How Racial Hostility Destroyed Our Promise* (New York: Random

House, 2020); Marisa Abrajano and Zoltan L. Hajnal, *White Backlash: Immigration, Race, and American Politics* (Princeton, NJ: Princeton University Press, 2017); Ashley Jardina, *White Identity Politics* (New York: Cambridge University Press, 2019); John Sides, Michael Tesler, and Lynn Vavreck, *Identity Crisis: The 2016 Presidential Campaign and the Battle for the Meaning of America* (Princeton, NJ: Princeton University Press, 2019).

13. Alvin Rabushka and Kenneth Shepsle, *Politics in Plural Societies: A Theory of Democratic Instability* (Columbus, OH: Charles E. Merrill Publishing Company, 1972); Kanchan Chandra, "Ethnic Parties and Democratic Stability," *Perspectives on Politics* 3, no. 2 (June 2005): 235–252; Stuart J. Kaufman, "Spiraling to Ethnic War: Elites, Masses, and Moscow in Moldova's Civil War," *International Security* 21, no. 2 (Fall 1996): 108–138; Zack Beauchamp, "'Ethnic Outbidding': The Academic Theory That Helps Explain Trump's Anti-Muslim Rhetoric," Vox, December 10, 2015, https://www.vox.com/world/2015/12/10/9881876/trump-muslims-ethnic-outbidding; Shiping Tang, "The Onset of Ethnic War: A General Theory," *Sociological Theory* 33, no. 3 (October 2015): 256–279.

14. Theda Skocpol and Vanessa Williamson, *The Tea Party and the Remaking of Republican Conservatism* (New York: Oxford University Press, 2016); Christopher Parker, "The (Real) Reason Why the House Won't Pass Comprehensive Immigration Reform," Brookings, August 4, 2014, https://www.brookings.edu/blog/fixgov/2014/08/04/the-real-reason-why-the-house-wont-pass-comprehensive-immigration-reform/.

15. Thomas Piketty, Emmanuel Saez, and Gabriel Zucman, "Simplified Distributional National Accounts," World Inequality Database (working paper, January 2019).

16. Nico Grant and Ian King, "Big Tech's Big Tax Ruse: Industry Splurges on Buybacks," Bloomberg, April 15, 2019, https://www.bloomberg.com/news/articles/2019-04-14/big-tech-s-big-tax-ruse-industry-splurges-on-buybacks-not-jobs; Emily Stewart, "Apple Took the GOP Tax Cut and Turned It Into a \$100 Billion Stock Buyback," Vox, May 2, 2018, https://www.vox.com/policy-and-politics/2018/5/2/17310770/apple-stock-earnings-buyback-dividend-tax-tim-cook-iphone.

17. Daniel Ziblatt, *Conservative Parties and the Birth of Democracy* (New York: Cambridge University Press, 2017).

Chapter 1: **THE CONSERVATIVE DILEMMA**

1. John Adams, "Defence of the Constitutions of Government of the United States," in *The Founders' Constitution*, ed. Philip B. Kurland and Ralph Lerner, vol. 1 (Chicago: University of Chicago Press, 1986); Alexis de Tocqueville, *Democracy in America*, ed. and trans. Harvey C. Mansfield and Delba Winthrop (Chicago: University of Chicago Press, 1986), 201.

2. See, e.g., Daron Acemoglu and James A. Robinson, *Economic Origins of Dictatorship and Democracy* (New York: Cambridge University Press, 2005).

3. As quoted in Irving Dillard, *Mr. Justice Brandeis, Great American* (Saint Louis: Modern View Press, 1941), 42. There are doubts as to whether Brandeis is the source of the quote, but it seems he said it or something similar to Congressman Edward Keating. Peter Scott Campbell, "Democracy v. Concentrated Wealth: In Search of a Louis D. Brandeis Quote," *The Greenbag* 16, no. 3 (Spring 2013): 251–256.

4. Frederick Douglass, "Address at the Celebration of West India Emancipation, Rochester, N.Y.," August 1, 1848, Library of Congress, https://www.loc.gov/item/mfd.21023/.

5. See Arthur A. Goldsmith, "Economic Rights and Government in Developing Counties: Cross-National Evidence on Growth and Development," *Studies in Comparative International Development* 32, no. 2 (1997): 29–44; Adam Przeworski and Fernando Limongi, "Political Regimes and Economic Growth," in *Democracy and Development*, ed. Amiya Kumar Bagchi (New York: Palgrave Macmillan, 1995), 3–24; John E. Roemer, "On the Relationship between Economic Development and Political Democracy," in *Democracy and Development*, 28–55.

6. Steven Levitsky and Daniel Ziblatt, *How Democracies Die* (New York: Crown, 2018).

7. Daniel Ziblatt, *Conservative Parties and the Birth of Democracy* (New York: Cambridge University Press, 2017), 33.

8. William Harbutt Dawson, *Bismarck and State Socialism: An Exposition of the Social and Economic Legislation of Germany Since 1870* (London: Swan, Sonnenschein & Co., 1890).

9. Daniel Schlozman, *When Movements Anchor Parties: Electoral Alignments in American History* (Princeton, NJ: Princeton University Press, 2015).

10. Ziblatt, *Conservative Parties*, 28, citing Paul Smith, ed., *Lord Salisbury on Politics: A Selection from His Articles in the Quarterly Review, 1860–1883* (Cambridge, Eng.: Cambridge University Press, 1972), 155.

11. Ziblatt, *Conservative Parties*, 55.

12. Ziblatt, *Conservative Parties*, 105–110.

13. Andrew Gimson, "Why the Tories Keep Winning: Inside the World's Most Ruthless—and Successful—Political Party," *New Statesman*, May 15, 2017, https://www.newstatesman.com/politics/elections/2017/05/why-tories-keep-winning.

14. *The Times* (18 April 1883), 11, quoted in Moisei Ostrogorski, *Democracy and the Organization of Political Parties,* trans. Frederick Clarke, vol. 1 (New York: Macmillan, 1908), 257.

15. Suzanne Fagence Cooper, *Effie: The Passionate Lives of Effie Gray, John Ruskin and John Everett Millais* (New York: Macmillan, 2010), 200; Ziblatt, *Conservative Parties*, 122.

16. Ziblatt, *Conservative Parties*, 168.

17. Ziblatt, *Conservative Parties*, 141–149.

18. Michael S. Rosenwald, "Fact-Checking 'The Crown': Did the Duke of Windsor Plot with Hitler to Betray Britain?" *Washington Post*, December 30, 2017, https://www.washingtonpost.com/news/retropolis/wp/2017/12/30/fact-checking-the-crown-did-the-duke-of-windsor-plot-with-hitler-to-betray-britain/.

19. Ziblatt, *Conservative Parties*, 176, 215–224, 266.

20. Ziblatt, *Conservative Parties*, 176–179; Sarah Binder and Thomas E. Mann, "Slaying the Dinosaur: The Case for Reforming the Senate Filibuster," *Brookings Review* 13, no. 3 (Summer 1995): 42–46.

21. Isabela Mares, *From Open Secrets to Secret Voting: Democratic Electoral Reforms and Voter Autonomy* (New York: Cambridge University Press, 2015), 117.

22. Ernst von Heydebrand, Stenographische Berichte, Haus der Abgeordneten 77 Sitzung, 21 Legislative Period, May 20, 1912, quoted in Ziblatt, *Conservative Parties*, 242.

23. Ziblatt, *Conservative Parties*, 198.

24. Ziblatt, *Conservative Parties*, 273–274; the quoted historian is Thomas Mergel, "Das Scheitern des deustschen Tory-Konservatismus. Die Umformung der DNVP zu einer rechtsradikalen Partei 1928–1932," *Historische Zeitschrift* 276 (2003): 323–368.

25. Ziblatt, *Conservative Parties*, 286–296. The discussion to follow draws on Ziblatt, *Conservative Parties*, 291–333.

26. Hermann Beck, *The Fateful Alliance: German Conservatives and Nazis in 1933: The Machtergreifung in a New Light* (New York: Berghahn Books, 2008), 25.

27. Beck, *Fateful Alliance*, ch. 1.

28. Edward Gibson, *Class and Conservative Parties: Argentina in Comparative Perspective* (Baltimore: Johns Hopkins University Press, 1996), 17, 210; Guillermo O'Donnell and Philippe C. Schmitter, "Tentative Conclusions About Uncertain Democracies," in *Transitions from Authoritarian Rule: Prospects for Democracy*, ed. Guillermo O'Donnell, Philippe C. Schmitter, and Laurence Whitehead, vol. 4 (Baltimore: Johns Hopkins University Press, 1986), 62–63.

29. Jeffrey G. Williamson and Peter Lindert, *Unequal Gains: American Growth and Inequality Since 1700* (Princeton, NJ: Princeton University Press), 2016.

30. John Markoff, "Where and When Was Democracy Invented?" *Comparative Studies in Society and History* 41, no. 4 (1999): 660–690; Williamson and Lindert, *Unequal Gains*.

31. Suzanne Mettler, "Democracy Under Siege: Backsliding in the 1890s," paper presented at the American Political Science Association Meeting, Washington, DC, 2019.

32. Mettler, "Democracy Under Siege"; Richard Franklin Bensel, *The Political Economy of American Industrialization, 1877–1900* (New York: Cambridge University Press, 2000), 285; David Brian Robertson, *Capital, Labor, and the State: The Battle for American Labor Markets from the*

Civil War to the New Deal (New York: Rowman and Littlefield, 2000), ch. 3; Matthew O'Brien, "The Most Expensive Election Ever . . . 1896?" *Atlantic Monthly*, November 6, 2012, https://www.theatlantic.com/business/archive/2012/11/the-most-expensive-election-ever-1896/264649/.

33. Richard B. Baker, Carola Frydman, and Eric Hilt, "From Plutocracy to Progressivism? The Assassination of President McKinley as a Turning Point in American History" (unpublished manuscript, September 2014).

Chapter 2: REPUBLICANS EMBRACE PLUTOCRACY

1. Jerome M. Rosow, "The Problem of the Blue-Collar Worker," Department of Labor, April 16, 1970, 4–9.

2. See Jefferson Cowie, "Nixon's Class Struggle: Romancing the New Right Worker, 1969–1973," *Labor History* 43, no. 3 (2002): 257–283. Nixon saw the parallel; he told Daniel Patrick Moynihan, "You know very well it is the Tory men with liberal policies who have enlarged democracy." "Daniel Patrick Moynihan," *Economist*, March, 27, 2003, https://www.economist.com/obituary/2003/03/27/daniel-patrick-moynihan.

3. John C. Whitaker, "Nixon's Domestic Policy: Both Liberal and Bold in Retrospect," *Presidential Studies Quarterly* 26, no. 1 (Winter 1996): 131–153; Richard P. Nathan, "A Retrospective on Richard M. Nixon's Domestic Policies," *Presidential Studies Quarterly* 26, no. 1 (Winter 1996): 155–164; Hugh Davis Graham, "Richard Nixon and Civil Rights: Explaining an Enigma," *Presidential Studies Quarterly* 26, no. 1 (Winter 1996): 93–106; "Nixon Reportedly Says He Is Now a Keynesian," *New York Times*, January 7, 1971, https://www.nytimes.com/1971/01/07/archives/nixon-reportedly-says-he-is-now-a-keynesian.html.

4. Benjamin Waterhouse, *Lobbying America: The Politics of Business from Nixon to NAFTA* (Princeton, NJ: Princeton University Press, 2014), 108.

5. Waterhouse, *Lobbying America*, 122; Cowie, "Nixon's Class Struggle," 271, 273.

6. Kevin P. Phillips, *The Emerging Republican Majority* (New Rochelle, NY: Arlington House, 1969), 232.

7. Richard Nixon, "1968 Acceptance Speech," C-SPAN, August 8, 1968, https://www.c-span.org/video/?4022-2/richard-nixon-1968-acceptance-speech.

8. Rosow, "Problem of the Blue-Collar Worker," 3.

9. Jacob S. Hacker and Paul Pierson, *Winner-Take-All Politics: How Washington Made the Rich Richer—And Turned Its Back on the Middle Class* (New York: Simon & Schuster, 2010), 16, 45–46.

10. Hacker and Pierson, *Winner-Take-All Politics*, 19–28; Thomas Piketty, Emmanuel Saez, and Gabriel Zucman, "Simplified Distributional National Accounts," World Inequality Database (working paper, January 2019).

11. Jacob Bor, Gregory H. Cohen, and Sandro Galea, "Population Health in

an Era of Rising Income Inequality: USA, 1980–2015," *America: Equity and Equality in Health* 389, no. 10077 (April 2017): 1475–1490; Fabian T. Pfeffer, "Growing Wealth Gaps in Education," *Demography* 55, no. 3 (June 2018): 1033–1068; "The State of the Nation's Housing 2019," Joint Center for Housing Studies, https://www.jchs.harvard.edu/state-nations -housing-2019.

12. Jon Bakija, Adam Cole, and Bradley T. Heim, "Jobs and Income Growth of Top Earners and the Causes of Changing Income Inequality: Evidence from U.S. Tax Return Data" (working paper, April 2012), https://web .williams.edu/Economics/wp/BakijaColeHeimJobsIncomeGrowthTopE arners.pdf, 1–2.

13. Thomas Piketty, *Capital in the Twenty-First Century*, trans. Arthur Goldhammer (Cambridge, MA: Belknap Press, 2014).

14. According to the most recent data, the level of private-sector unionization in fifteen Western European countries (not weighted by population) is 33 percent (countries included are Austria, Belgium, Denmark, Finland, France, Germany, Greece, Iceland, Ireland, the Netherlands, Norway, Spain, Sweden, Switzerland, and the United Kingdom). See Jelle Visser, "Database on Institutional Characteristics of Trade Unions, Wage Setting, State Intervention and Social Pacts in 55 countries between 1960 and 2018," *Amsterdam Institute for Advanced Labour Studies* (November 2019). In the United States, unions represent just 6.4 percent of private workers. "Union Members Summary," Bureau of Labor Statistics, January 18, 2019, https://www.bls.gov/news.release/union2.nr0.htm. For historical data, see the Union Membership and Coverage Database, www.unionstats.com.

15. See Margaret C. Rung, "Richard Nixon, State, and Party: Democracy and Bureaucracy in the Postwar Era," *Presidential Studies Quarterly* 29, no. 2 (June 1999): 421–437.

16. Steven Pearlstein, "Income Gap Is Issue No. 1, Debaters Agree," *Washington Post*, December 7, 1995, quoted in Leslie McCall, *The Undeserving Rich: American Beliefs about Inequality, Opportunity, and Redistribution* (New York: Cambridge University Press), 70.

17. E. J. Dionne, "George H. W. Bush represented a different kind of Republicanism," *Washington Post*, December 1, 2018, https://www .washingtonpost.com/opinions/the-virtues-of-a-public-spirited-patri cian/2018/12/01/41bc3292-f57b-11e8-bc79-68604ed88993_story.html; Perry Bacon Jr., "The Republican Party Has Changed Dramatically Since George H. W. Bush Ran It," FiveThirtyEight, December 1, 2018, https://fivethirtyeight.com/features/the-republican-party-has-changed -dramatically-since-george-h-w-bush-ran-it/.

18. Pearlstein, "Income Gap Is Issue No. 1."

19. McKay Coppins, "The Man Who Broke Politics," *Atlantic Monthly*, October 17, 2018, https://www.theatlantic.com/magazine/ archive/2018/11/newt-gingrich-says-youre-welcome/570832/. For the seminal text on anti-system parties, see Giovanni Sartori, "Opposition

and Control Problems and Prospects," *Government and Opposition* 1, no. 2 (January 1966): 149–154.

20. Zach Smith, "For Newt: 'Nixon's the One!'" *Politico*, January 19, 2012, https://www.politico.com/story/2012/01/for-newt-nixons-the-one-071684; Dan Balz and Charles R. Babcock, "Gingrich, Allies Made Waves and Impression," *Washington Post*, December 20, 1994, https://www.washingtonpost.com/archive/politics/1994/12/20/gingrich-allies-made-waves-and-impression/b4f6216a-5377-4887-9c73-289421a069f5/.

21. Omnibus Budget Reconciliation Act, Pub. L. 101-508 (1990); Gingrich quoted in Dan Balz and Ronald Brownstein, *Storming the Gates: Protest Politics and the Republican Revival* (Boston: Little, Brown, 1996), 121.

22. The "stalwart" was John Kasich, a close Gingrich ally (who would come to be seen as a moderate as his party moved right but was well to the right of the center of his party at the time). Steve Kornacki, "The Decade the GOP Hopes You've Forgotten," Salon, April 19, 2011, https://www.salon.com/2011/04/19/republicans_deficit_taxes/. See also Omnibus Budget Reconciliation Act, Pub. L. 103-66 (1993); David E. Rosenbaum, "The Budget Struggle; House Passed Budget Plan, Backing Clinton By 218-216 After Hectic Maneuvering," *New York Times*, August 6, 1993, https://www.nytimes.com/1993/08/06/us/budget-struggle-house-passes-budget-plan-backing-clinton-218-216-after-hectic.html; David E. Rosenbaum, "The Budget Struggle; Clinton Wins Approval of His Budget as Gore Votes to Break Senate," *New York Times*, August 7, 1993, https://www.nytimes.com/1993/08/07/us/budget-struggle-clinton-wins-approval-his-budget-plan-gore-votes-break-senate.html. On Republican opposition to Clinton's health care plan, see Dana Priest and Michael Weisskopf, "Health Care Reform: The Collapse of a Quest," *Washington Post*, October 11, 1994, https://www.washingtonpost.com/archive/politics/1994/10/11/health-care-reform-the-collapse-of-a-quest/038a045b-3eef-4063-be19-5aa0bc090348/. On the 1994 elections, see Gary C. Jacobson, "The 1994 House Elections in Perspective," *Political Science Quarterly* 11, no. 2 (1996): 203–223.

23. David E. Rosenbaum, "Republicans Offer Voters a Deal for Takeover of House," *New York Times*, September 28, 1994, https://www.nytimes.com/1994/09/28/us/republicans-offer-voters-a-deal-for-takeover-of-house.html; Don Gonyea, "The Longest Government Shutdown In History, No Longer—How 1995 Changed Everything," NPR, January 12, 2019, https://www.npr.org/2019/01/12/683304824/the-longest-government-shutdown-in-history-no-longer-how-1995-changed-everything; Henry J. Aaron, "Death and Taxes: Now's Hardly the Time to Favor the Richest Among Us," Brookings Institution, May 4, 1997, https://www.brookings.edu/opinions/death-and-taxes-nows-hardly-the-time-to-favor-the-richest-among-us/.

24. Quoted in Tom Dickinson, "How the GOP Became the Party of the Rich," *Rolling Stone*, November 9, 2011, https://www.rollingstone.com/politics/politics-news/how-the-gop-became-the-party-of-the-rich-237247/.

25. David Maraniss and Michael Weisskopf, *Tell Newt to Shut Up: Prize-Winning Washington Post Journalists Reveal How Reality Gagged the Gingrich Revolution* (New York: Touchstone, 1996), 111.

26. Jon A. Shields and Joshua M. Dunn, *Passing on the Right* (New York: Oxford University Press, 2016), 39; Lou Dubose and Jan Reid, *The Hammer Comes Down: The Nasty, Brutish, and Shortened Political Life of Tom DeLay* (New York: PublicAffairs, 2005), 171.

27. Jacob S. Hacker and Paul Pierson, *American Amnesia: How the War on Government Led Us to Forget What Made America Prosper* (New York: Simon & Schuster, 2016), 216–217; Michael Weisskopf, "Lobbyists Shift Into Reverse," *Washington Post*, May 13, 1994, https://www.washingtonpost.com/archive/politics/1994/05/13/lobbyists-shift-into-reverse/7e8ba3e4-d034-4805-a328-b59868fbeac1/. See also Jack Nelson, "Conservatives Strain GOP, Chamber of Commerce Ties," *Los Angeles Times*, April 9, 1993, https://www.latimes.com/archives/la-xpm-1993-04-09-mn-20998-story.html; Alyssa Katz, *The Influence Machine: The U.S. Chamber of Commerce and the Corporate Capture of American Life* (New York: Penguin Random House, 2015), 62.

28. Dubose and Reid, *The Hammer*, 134.

29. Matthew Continetti, *The K Street Gang: The Rise and Fall of the Republican Machine* (New York: Doubleday, 2006), 61.

30. Steven M. Teles, "Conservative Mobilization against Entrenched Liberalism," in *The Transformation of American Politics: Activist Government and the Rise of Conservatism*, ed. Paul Pierson and Theda Skocpol (Princeton, NJ: Princeton University Press, 2007), 160–188.

31. Ken-Hou Lin and Donald Tomaskovic-Devey, "Financialization and U.S. Income Inequality, 1970–2008," *American Journal of Sociology* 118, no. 5 (March 2013): 1284–1329.

32. Gabriel Zucman, "Global Wealth Inequality," *Annual Review of Economics* 11 (August 2019): 109–138.

33. Benjamin I. Page, Jason Seawright, and Matthew J. Lacombe, *Billionaires and Stealth Politics* (Chicago: University of Chicago Press, 2018), 82.

34. Page, Seawright, and Lacombe, *Billionaires and Stealth Politics*, 25–76.

35. See also Benjamin Page and Cari Lynn Hennessy, "What Affluent Americans Want from Politics," paper presented at the American Political Science Association annual meeting, 2010; Nolan McCarty, Keith T. Poole, and Howard Rosenthal, "Political Polarization and Income Inequality," https://www.princeton.edu/~nmccarty/ineqpold.pdf; Page, Seawright, and Lacombe, *Billionaires and Stealth Politics*, 82, 116.

36. Martin Gilens and Benjamin I. Page, "Testing Theories of American Politics: Elites, Interest Groups, and Average Citizens," *Perspectives on Politics* 12, no. 3 (September 2014): 564–581; Jeffrey A. Winters, "Wealth Defense and the Limits of Liberal Democracy," Annual Conferences of the American Society of Political and Legal Philosophy (August 2014).

37. David Broockman, Greg F. Ferenstein, and Neil Malhotra, "The Political

Behavior of Wealthy Americans: Evidence from Technology Entrepreneurs," Stanford Graduate School of Business working paper no. 3581 (December 2017); Farhad Manjoo, "Silicon Valley's Politics: Liberal, With One Big Exception," *New York Times*, September 6, 2017, https://www.nytimes.com/2017/09/06/technology/silicon-valley-politics.html.

38. Benjamin I. Page, Larry M. Bartels, and Jason Seawright, "Democracy and the Policy Preferences of Wealthy Americans," *Perspectives on Politics* 11, no. 1 (March 2013): 51–73.

39. Broockman, Ferenstein, and Malhotra, "Political Behavior of Wealthy Americans"; Sahil Chinoy, "What Happened to America's Political Center of Gravity?" *New York Times*, June 26, 2019, https://www.nytimes.com/interactive/2019/06/26/opinion/sunday/republican-platform-far-right.html, using data from The Manifesto Project, version 2018b, https://manifesto-project.wzb.eu.

40. Jacob S. Hacker and Paul Pierson, "Confronting Asymmetric Polarization," in *Solutions to Political Polarization in America*, ed. Nathaniel Persily (New York: Cambridge University Press, 2015), 59–72; Thomas E. Mann and Norman J. Ornstein, *It's Even Worse Than It Looks: How the American Constitutional System Collided with the New Politics of Extremism* (New York: Basic Books, 2012); Christopher Ingraham, "This Astonishing Chart Shows How Moderate Republicans Are an Endangered Species," *Washington Post*, June 2, 2015, https://www.washingtonpost.com/news/wonk/wp/2015/06/02/this-astonishing-chart-shows-how-republicans-are-an-endangered-species/.

41. See Jacob S. Hacker and Paul Pierson, "Abandoning the Middle: The Bush Tax Cuts and the Limits of Democratic Control," *Perspectives on Politics* 3, no. 1 (March 2005): 33–53; Steve Benen, "Ten-to-One Isn't Good Enough for the GOP," *Washington Monthly*, August 12, 2011, https://washingtonmonthly.com/2011/08/12/ten-to-one-isnt-good-enough-for-the-gop/.

42. John Cassidy, "The Ringleader: How Grover Norquist Keeps the Conservative Movement Together," *New Yorker*, July 24, 2005, https://www.newyorker.com/magazine/2005/08/01/the-ringleader.

43. John M. Broder and Don Van Natta Jr., "Perks for Biggest Donors, and Pleas for More Cash," *New York Times*, July 30, 2000, https://archive.nytimes.com/www.nytimes.com/learning/students/pop/073000wh-donate.html; "The Bush Money Machine: Fundraising's Rewards," *Washington Post*, May 16, 2004, A17, http://www.washingtonpost.com/wp-srv/politics/pioneers/network_graphic.pdf.

44. Robert Scheer, "Enron's Enablers," *Nation*, October 25, 2006, https://www.thenation.com/article/enrons-enablers-0/; Broder and Van Natta, "Perks for Donors"; Charles Lewis, "Right on the Money: The George W. Bush Profile," Center for Public Integrity, July 8, 2003, https://publicintegrity.org/federal-politics/right-on-the-money-the-george-w-bush-profile/; Glen Justice, "The 2004 Campaign: Fund-Raising; Financial Firms Are Bush's Biggest Donors, Study Reports," *New York Times*, January 9, 2004, https://

www.nytimes.com/2004/01/09/us/2004-campaign-fund-raising-financial
-firms-are-bush-s-biggest-donors-study.html.

45. Don Van Natta Jr., "McCain Gets Big Payoff On Web Site," *New York Times*, February 4, 2000, https://www.nytimes.com/2000/02/04/us/the
-2000-campaign-the-money-game-mccain-gets-big-payoff-on-web-site
.html; Walter Shapiro, "How John McCain Almost Made the GOP the Party of Campaign Finance Reform," Brennan Center, August 25, 2018, https://www.brennancenter.org/our-work/analysis-opinion/how-john
-mccain-nearly-made-gop-party-campaign-finance-reform.

46. Alison Mitchell, "Campaign 2000: McCain on Taxes; Entering Fray on Republicans' Issue of Choice, the Senator Pitches His Tax Proposal," *New York Times*, January 12, 2000, https://www.nytimes
.com/2000/01/12/us/campaign-2000-mccain-taxes-entering-fray-repub
licans-issue-choice-senator.html.

47. Richard Gooding, "The Trashing of John McCain," *Vanity Fair*, September 24, 2008, https://www.vanityfair.com/news/2004/11/mccain200411; Jennifer Steinhauer, "Confronting Ghosts of 2000 in South Carolina," *New York Times*, October 19, 2007, https://www.nytimes.com/2007/10
/19/us/politics/19mccain.html.

48. Daniel J. Balz and Ronald Brownstein, *Storming the Gates: Protest Politics and the Republican Revival* (Boston: Little, Brown, 1996), 244; "Transcript of Debate Between Vice President Gore and Governor Bush," *New York Times*, October 4, 2000, https://www.nytimes.com/2000/10/04/
us/2000-campaign-transcript-debate-between-vice-president-gore-gov
ernor-bush.html; Adam Nagourney, "Bush and Gore Mix Jokes and Barbs at Smith Dinner," *New York Times*, October 20, 2000, https://
www.nytimes.com/2000/10/20/nyregion/bush-and-gore-mix-jokes-and
-barbs-at-smith-dinner.html.

49. Hacker and Pierson, "Abandoning the Middle," 33.

50. Alvin Chung, "100 Years of Tax Brackets, In One Chart," Vox, April 16, 2018, https://www.vox.com/policy-and-politics/2018/4/16/17215874/tax
-brackets-100-years-chart; Emmanuel Saez and Gabriel Zucman, *The Triumph of Injustice: How the Rich Dodge Taxes and How to Make Them Pay* (New York: W. W. Norton, 2019). Saez and Zucman also claim that the combined tax rate of the top 400 is lower than the combined rate paid by lower-income Americans—a claim that is controversial among economists. But the controversy is mainly about how to estimate the share of income devoted to taxes by the nonaffluent. There's no question that taxes on the very rich have come down dramatically since World War II. See Matthew Yglesias, "The Debate Over Whether the Very Rich Pay More Taxes Than You, Explained," Vox, November 4, 2019, https://www.vox
.com/policy-and-politics/2019/11/4/20938229/zucman-saez-tax-rates
-top-400; "Emmanuel Saez and Gabriel Zucman's New Book Reminds Us that Tax Injustice Is a Choice," Institute on Taxation and Economic Policy, October 15, 2019, https://itep.org/emmanuel-saez-and-gabriel
-zucmans-new-book-reminds-us-that-tax-injustice-is-a-choice/.

51. Hacker and Pierson, "Abandoning the Middle," 34, 38.

52. Andrew Prokop, "In 2005, Republicans Controlled Washington. Their Agenda Failed. Here's Why," Vox, January 9, 2017, https://www.vox .com/policy-and-politics/2017/1/9/13781088/social-security-privatiza tion-why-failed; James T. Patterson, "Transformative Economic Policies: Tax Cutting, Stimuli, and Bailouts," in *The Presidency of George W. Bush: A First Historical Assessment*, ed. Julian Zelizer (Princeton, NJ: Princeton University Press, 2010), 127.

53. Jane Mayer, *Dark Money: The Hidden History of the Billionaires Behind the Rise of the Radical Right* (New York: Doubleday, 2016), 4.

54. Hacker and Pierson, *American Amnesia*, 228.

55. Hacker and Pierson, *American Amnesia*, 228; Andrew Prokop, "The Koch Network Plans to Spend Nearly $1 Billion on the 2016 Elections," Vox, January 26, 2015, https://www.vox.com/2015/1/26/7917917/koch -billion-2016.

56. Adam Bonica, Nolan McCarty, Keith T. Poole, and Howard Rosenthal, "Why Hasn't Democracy Slowed Rising Inequality?" *Journal of Economic Perspectives* 27, no. 3 (Summer 2013): 103–124. The latest statistics are at Adam Bonica, Twitter post, June 4, 2019, https://twitter .com/adam_bonica/status/1136067959858712576. Figures for Adelson can be found at Geoff West, "Sheldon Adelson Donates $30 Million for House Republicans," Open Secrets: Center for Responsive Politics, July 16, 2018, https://www.opensecrets.org/news/2018/07/sheldon-adelson -donates-30-million-for-house-republicans/.

57. Andy Kroll, "The Secrets of a Right-Wing Dark-Money Juggernaut— Revealed," *Rolling Stone*, October 29, 2019, https://www.rollingstone.com/ politics/politics-features/dark-money-republican-party-americans-for-job -security-peter-thiel-devos-904900/; Andy Kroll, "California's Biggest 'Campaign Money Laundering' Scheme, Revealed—Kinda," *Mother Jones*, November 5, 2012, https://www.motherjones.com/politics/2012/11/ california-americans-responsible-leadership-donation-jerry-brown/; Michela Tindera, "At Least 20 Billionaires Behind 'Dark Money' Group That Opposed Obama," October 26, 2019, https://www.forbes.com/sites/michelatindera /2019/10/26/at-least-20-billionaires-behind-dark-money-group-that-opposed -obama/#18e83b486c66.

58. Alexander Hertel-Fernandez, Theda Skocpol, and Jason Sclar, "When Political Mega-Donors Join Forces: How the Koch Network and the Democracy Alliance Influence Organized U.S. Politics on the Right and Left," *Studies in American Political Development* 32, no. 2 (October 2018): 128.

59. Joshua Green, *Devil's Bargain: Steve Bannon, Donald Trump, and the Nationalist Uprising* (New York: Penguin, 2017), 119–136.

60. Alexander Hertel-Fernandez, *State Capture: How Conservative Activists, Big Businesses, and Wealthy Donors Reshaped the American States—and the Nation* (New York: Oxford University Press, 2019), 6.

61. Hertel-Fernandez, *State Capture*, 6.

62. According to careful research by the political scientists Theda Skocpol and Alexander Hertel-Fernandez, "the AFP federation has been able to penetrate GOP career ladders"—not only recruiting "knowledgeable Republican staffers, usually young men in their thirties or forties," but also moving them into high-level Republican positions after their time at AFP, helping "to drag the Republican Party as a whole further to the right on political-economic issues." See Skocpol and Hertel-Fernandez, "The Koch Network and Republican Party Extremism," *Perspectives on Politics* 14, no. 3 (September 2016): 692.

63. The next three paragraphs draw on Hacker and Pierson, *American Amnesia*, 213–227.

64. David Roberts, "The GOP Is the World's Only Major Climate-Denialist Party. But Why?" Vox, December 2, 2015, https://www.vox.com /2015/12/2/9836566/republican-climate-denial-why; Theda Skocpol, "Naming the Problem: What It Will Take to Counter Extremism and Engage Americans in the Fight against Global Warming," Politics of America's Fight Against Global Warming Symposium, Harvard University, February 14, 2013.

65. Roberts, "The GOP Is the World's Only Major Climate-Denialist Party. But Why?"; Anthony Deutsch, "Surge In Young Republicans Worried About the Environment: Survey," Reuters, August 29, 2019, https://www .reuters.com/article/us-environment-poll-republicans/surge-in-young -republicans-worried-about-the-environment-survey-idUSKCN1VJ17V.

66. Chinoy, "What Happened to America's Political Center of Gravity?"

67. Alexander Hertel-Fernandez, Theda Skocpol, and Daniel Lynch, "Business Associations, Conservative Networks, and the Ongoing Republican War Over Medicaid Expansion," *Journal of Health Politics, Policy and Law* 41, no. 2 (April 2016): 239–286; "Data Note: 10 Charts About Public Opinion on Medicaid," Kaiser Family Foundation, June 27, 2017, https://www.kff.org/medicaid/poll-finding/data-note-10-charts-about -public-opinion-on-medicaid/.

68. Morton Kondracke and Fred Barnes, *Jack Kemp: The Bleeding-Heart Conservative Who Changed America* (New York: Sentinel, 2015), 257; Arthur Delaney and Michael McAuliff, "Paul Ryan Wants 'Welfare Reform Round 2,'" HuffPost, March 20, 2012, https://www.huffpost .com/entry/paul-ryan-welfare-reform_n_1368277.

69. Harry Enten, "What Paul Ryan Has That Kevin McCarthy and John Boehner Don't," FiveThirtyEight, October 22, 2015, https://fivethirty eight.com/features/what-paul-ryan-has-that-kevin-mccarthy-and-john -boehner-dont/; L. T. James, "House Speakers and Polarization," Medium, September 5, 2018, https://medium.com/be-sad-with-me/ house-speakers-polarization-3c38827e753b; Paul Ryan, *The Way Forward: Renewing the American Idea* (New York: Twelve, 2014), 156–157.

70. Jake Sherman, "Bulk of Ryan's Fundraising Haul in $50k-Plus Chunks," *Politico*, April 13, 2016, https://www.politico.com/story/2016/04/paul -ryan-fundraising-analysis-221920; Megan Janetsky, "As Paul Ryan

Rose through the House, His Money Rose with Him," Open Secrets, April 11, 2018, https://www.opensecrets.org/news/2018/04/as-paul-ryan -retires/; Kristina Peterson and Siobhan Hughes, "Paul Ryan's Fundraising to Be Used to Push GOP Agenda," *Wall Street Journal*, December 21, 2016, https://www.wsj.com/articles/paul-ryans-fundraising-to-be -used-to-push-gop-agenda-1482348497; Leonard E. Burman, James R. Nunns, Benjamin R. Page, Jeffrey Rohaly, and Joseph Rosenberg, "Analysis of the House GOP Tax Plan," *Columbia Journal of Tax Law* 8 (2017).

71. Robert Shogan, "A Liberated Kemp Now Free to Shape Public Policy," *Los Angeles Times*, May 12, 1999, 5; Kondracke and Barnes, *Jack Kemp*, 294; Jack Kemp, "A Letter to My Grandchildren," RealClearPolitics, November 12, 2008, https://www.realclearpolitics.com/articles/2008/11 /a_letter_to_my_grandchildren.html; Jack Kemp, "Immigration Reform Will Help Keep This Nation Strong," Townhall, July 17, 2006, https:// townhall.com/columnists/jackkemp/2006/07/17/immigration-reform -will-help-keep-this-nation-strong-n946512.

Chapter 3: **ORGANIZING THROUGH OUTRAGE**

1. Nancy Tatom Ammerman, *Baptist Battles: Social Change and Religious Conflict in the Southern Baptist Convention* (New Brunswick, NJ: Rutgers University Press, 1990), 52. The number is closer to 50,000 today. Dalia Fahmy, "7 Facts about Southern Baptists," Pew Research Center, June 7, 2016, https://www.pewresearch.org/fact-tank/2019/06/07/7-facts -about-southern-baptists/.

2. Yochai Benkler, Robert Faris, and Hal Roberts, *Network Propaganda: Manipulation, Disinformation, and Radicalization in American Politics* (Oxford, Eng.: Oxford University Press, 2018), 320.

3. Frances FitzGerald, "A Disciplined, Charging Army," *New Yorker*, May 18, 1981, https://www.newyorker.com/magazine/1981/05/18/a-disciplined -charging-army.

4. Frances FitzGerald, *The Evangelicals: The Struggle to Shape America* (New York: Simon and Schuster, 2017), 411.

5. FitzGerald, *The Evangelicals*, 444.

6. Daniel K. Williams, *God's Own Party: The Making of the Christian Right* (Oxford, Eng.: Oxford University Press, 2010), 166.

7. Quoted in Daniel Schlozman, *When Movements Anchor Parties: Electoral Alignments in American History* (Princeton, NJ: Princeton University Press, 2015), 85.

8. FitzGerald, *The Evangelicals*, 283, 266–267; Williams, *God's Own Party*, 162.

9. For good discussions see FitzGerald, *The Evangelicals*; Schlozman, *When Movements Anchor Parties*; Robert P. Jones, *The End of White*

Christian America (New York: Simon and Schuster, 2016); Williams, *God's Own Party*, 156–158.

10. Williams, *God's Own Party*, 164.

11. FitzGerald, *The Evangelicals*, 290, 304; Williams, *God's Own Party*, 86.

12. David Karol, *Party Position Change in American Politics: Coalition Management* (Cambridge, Eng.: Cambridge University Press, 2009), 64, 66, 68.

13. FitzGerald, *The Evangelicals*, 332, 333.

14. Ibid., 436–437.

15. Schlozman, *When Movements Anchor Parties*; FitzGerald, *The Evangelicals*, 518–519.

16. FitzGerald, *The Evangelicals*, 508, 528, 532; David Domke and Kevin Coe, *The God Strategy: How Religion Became a Political Weapon in America* (Oxford, Eng.: Oxford University Press, 2008).

17. FitzGerald, *The Evangelicals*, 422–425.

18. Schlozman, *When Movements Anchor Parties*, 21; Dan Gilgoff, *The Jesus Machine: How James Dobson, Focus on the Family, and Evangelical America Are Winning the Culture War* (London: Macmillan Publishers, 2007); FitzGerald, *The Evangelicals*, 500.

19. Gilgoff, *The Jesus Machine*.

20. Jones, *The End of White Christian America*, 243; Schlozman, *When Movements Anchor Parties*, 90.

21. Paul A. Djupe and Brian Calfano, *God Talk: Experimenting with the Religious Causes of Public Opinion* (Philadelphia: Temple University Press, 2013), 28–29; Geoffrey Layman and Mark Brockway, "Evangelical Activists in the GOP: Still the Life of the Party?" in *The Evangelical Crackup? The Future of the Evangelical-Republican Coalition*, ed. Paul A. Djupe and Ryan L. Classen (Philadelphia: Temple University Press, 2018), 37; Kevin den Dulk, "Evangelical Elites and the Challenge of Pluralism," in *The Evangelical Crackup?*, 72.

22. Jones, *The End of White Christian America*, 217.

23. Karol, *Party Position Change*.

24. On these events, see Adam Winkler, *Gunfight: The Battle Over the Right to Bear Arms in America* (New York: W. W. Norton & Company, 2011); Scott Melzer, *Gun Crusaders: The NRA's Culture War* (New York: New York University Press, 2009); Joel Achenbach, Scott Higham, and Sari Horowitz, "How NRA's True Believers Converted a Marksmanship Group Into a Mighty Gun Lobby," *Washington Post*, January 12, 2013, https://www.washingtonpost.com/politics/how-nras -true-believers-converted-a-marksmanship-group-into-a-mighty-gun -lobby/2013/01/12/51c62288-59b9-11e2-88d0-c4cf65c3ad15_story.html.

25. As with many movement organizations it is hard to be sure of the NRA's true membership, since it is the only real source of information, "membership" may be ambiguous, and the organization has good incentives to exaggerate. See Dave Gilson, "The NRA Says It Has 5 Million Members. Its Magazines Tell Another Story," *Mother Jones*, March 7, 2018, https:// www.motherjones.com/politics/2018/03/nra-membership-magazine-num

bers-1/, which suggests based on magazine subscription data that membership estimates are likely modestly exaggerated. There is no particular reason to think that estimates have become less accurate over time. It seems safe to guess that while the NRA might have fewer than the 5 million members it currently claims, it likely has at least 3 million members. Melzer, *Gun Crusaders*, 67. Author's calculations for inflation adjustments.

26. Melzer, *Gun Crusaders*, 104–106.
27. All quotes from Melzer, *Gun Crusaders*, 55, 73, 105.
28. Jennifer Carlson, *Citizen-Protectors: The Everyday Politics of Guns in an Age of Decline* (Oxford, Eng.: Oxford University Press, 2015), 21, 22.
29. Melzer, *Gun Crusaders*, 18, 85.
30. Melzer, *Gun Crusaders*, 85.
31. Daniel J. Balz and Ronald Brownstein, *Storming the Gates: Protest Politics and the Republican Revival* (Boston: Little, Brown, 1996), ch. 4.
32. Pew Research Center, "America's Complex Relationship with Guns," June 22, 2017, https://www.pewsocialtrends.org/2017/06/22/americas -complex-relationship-with-guns/.
33. Melzer, *Gun Crusaders*, 41.
34. Melzer, *Gun Crusaders*, 237; Richard Cowan, "NRA Gun Rights Group Pours Money into Republican U.S. Senate Campaigns," Reuters, October 7, 2016, https://www.reuters.com/article/us-usa-election-guns/ nra-gun-rights-group-pours-money-into-republican-u-s-senate-cam paigns-idUSKCN1270YO.
35. Mike Spies, "The Making of Donald Trump and the NRA's Marriage of Convenience," *The Trace*, April 28, 2017, https://www.thetrace .org/2017/04/donald-trump-nra-convention/.
36. Thomas B. Rosenstiel, "It's Rush Night for GOP Lawmakers-in-Waiting," *Los Angeles Times*, December 11, 1994, https://www.latimes.com/ archives/la-xpm-1994-12-11-mn-7794-story.html.
37. Jackie Calmes, "'They Don't Give a Damn About Governing': Conservative Media's Influence on the Republican Party," Shorenstein Center on Media, Politics and Public Policy, discussion paper D-96, Harvard University, July 2015.
38. Kevin Arceneaux, Martin Johnson, Rene Lindstädt, and Ryan J. Vander Wielen, "The Influence of News Media on Political Elites: Investigating Strategic Responsiveness in Congress," *American Journal of Political Science* 60, no. 1 (January 2016): 5–29; Gregory J. Martin and Ali Yurukoglu, "Bias in Cable News: Persuasion and Polarization," *American Economic Review* 107, no. 9 (2017): 2565–2599; Alexander Hertel-Fernandez, Matto Mildenberger, and Leah C. Stokes, "Legislative Staff and Representation in Congress," *American Political Science Review* 113, no. 1 (2019): 1–18.
39. Benkler, Faris and Roberts, *Network Propaganda*, 321, 322.
40. Nicole Hemmer, *Messengers of the Right: Conservative Media and the Transformation of American Politics* (Philadelphia: University of Pennsylvania Press, 2016).

41. Hemmer, *Messengers of the Right*.

42. Hemmer, *Messengers of the Right*, 324–325.

43. Hemmer, *Messengers of the Right*, 324.

44. Amy Mitchell, Katie Simmons, Katerina Eva Matsa, and Laura Silver, "Publics Globally Want Unbiased News Coverage, but Are Divided on Whether Their News Media Deliver," Pew Research Center, January 11, 2018, https://www.pewresearch.org/global/2018/01/11/publics-globally -want-unbiased-news-coverage-but-are-divided-on-whether-their-news -media-deliver/.

45. Joanne M. Miller, Kyle L. Saunders, and Christina E. Farhart, "Conspiracy Endorsement as Motivated Reasoning: The Moderating Roles of Political Knowledge and Trust," *American Journal of Political Science* 60, no. 4 (October 2016): 824–844; *The Colbert Report*, October 17, 2005.

46. Tim Alberta, *American Carnage: On the Front Lines of the Republican Civil War and the Rise of President Trump* (New York: HarperCollins Publishers, 2019), 190.

47. Elliot Ash and Michael Poyker, "Conservative News Media and Criminal Justice: Evidence from Exposure to Fox News Channel," Columbia Business School research paper, May 3, 2019, https://papers.ssrn.com/ sol3/papers.cfm?abstract_id=3381827.

48. Benkler, Faris, and Roberts, *Network Propaganda*, 46–60.

49. Theda Skocpol and Vanessa Williamson, *The Tea Party and the Remaking of Republican Conservatism* (Oxford, Eng.: Oxford University Press, 2012), 132.

50. Jonathan Mahler and Jim Rutenberg, "How Rupert Murdoch's Empire of Influence Remade the World," *New York Times Magazine*, April 3, 2019.

51. Joshua Green, *Devil's Bargain: Steve Bannon, Donald Trump, and the Nationalist Uprising* (London: Penguin Publishing, 2017), 177.

52. Benkler, Faris, and Roberts, *Network Propaganda*, 57–65; Green, *Devil's Bargain*, 171–174.

53. Alberta, *American Carnage*, 255.

Chapter 4: **IDENTITY AND PLUTOCRACY**

1. Erin Blakemore, "How the Willie Horton Ad Played on Racism and Fear," *History*, November 2, 2018, https://www.history.com/news/george-bush -willie-horton-racist-ad; "Politics 1984 [Lee Atwater Reports, 1983] (2)," in Richard G. Darman Files, Ronald Reagan Presidential Library Digital Library Collections.

2. Darman, "Politics 1984," 38; James Boyd, "Nixon's Southern Strategy," *New York Times*, May 17, 1970, https://www.nytimes.com/1970/05/17/ archives/nixons-southern-strategy-its-all-in-the-charts.html.

3. Darman, "Politics 1984," 38–39.

4. Darman, "Politics 1984," 41, 59; Eric Schickler, *Racial Realignment:*

The Transformation of American Liberalism, 1932–1965 (Princeton, NJ: Princeton University Press, 2016).

5. "Exclusive: Lee Atwater's Infamous 1981 Interview on the Southern Strategy," YouTube, November 13, 2012, https://www.youtube.com/watch?v=X_8E3ENrKrQ.

6. Angie Maxwell and Todd Shields, *The Long Southern Strategy: How Chasing White Voters in the South Changed American Politics* (Oxford, Eng.: Oxford University Press, 2019); Christopher Caldwell, "The Southern Captivity of the GOP," *Atlantic Monthly*, June 1998, https://www.theatlantic.com/magazine/archive/1998/06/the-southern-captivity-of-the-gop/377123/.

7. Margit Tavits and Joshua D. Potter, "The Effect of Inequality and Social Identity on Party Strategies," *American Journal of Political Science* 59, no. 3 (July 2015): 744–758.

8. Phillip Connor and Gustavo Lopez, "5 Facts about the U.S. Rank in Worldwide Migration," Pew Research Center, May 18, 2016, https://www.pewresearch.org/fact-tank/2016/05/18/5-facts-about-the-u-s-rank-in-worldwide-migration/.

9. David Masci and Gregory A. Smith, "5 Facts about U.S. Protestant Evangelicals," Pew Research Center, March 1, 2018, https://www.pewresearch.org/fact-tank/2018/03/01/5-facts-about-u-s-evangelical-protestants/; Avidit Acharya, Matthew Blackwell, and Maya Sen, *Deep Roots: How Slavery Still Shapes Southern Politics* (Princeton, NJ: Princeton University Press, 2018); Kim Parker, Juliana Menasce Horowitz, Ruth Igielnik, J. Baxter Oliphant, and Anna Brown, "The Demographics of Gun Ownership," Pew Research Center, June 22, 2017, https://www.pewsocialtrends.org/2017/06/22/the-demographics-of-gun-ownership/; "American Views: Trust, Media and Democracy," A Gallup/Knight Foundation Survey, Knight Foundation, last modified 2018, https://www.politico.com/f/?id=00000160-fbcc-dcd4-a96b-ffeddf140001; John Nichols, "When the Republicans Really Were the Party of Lincoln," Moyers, July 2, 2014, https://billmoyers.com/2014/07/02/when-the-republicans-really-were-the-party-of-lincoln/; Maxwell and Shields, *The Long Southern Strategy*, 2; Ilyana Kuziemko and Ebonya Washington, "Why Did the Democrats Lose the South? Bringing New Data to an Old Debate," *American Economic Review* 108, no. 10 (October 2018): 2830–2867.

10. Ken Mehlman, "Ken Mehlman Remarks at NAACP National Convention," kenmehlman.com, accessed September 25, 2019, http://kenmehlman.com/ken-mehlman-remarks-at-naacp/; Maxwell and Shields, *Long Southern Strategy*, 26; Marisa Abrajano and Zoltan L. Hajnal, *White Backlash: Immigration, Race, and American Politics* (Princeton, NJ: Princeton University Press, 2015), 92.

11. Kuziemko and Washington, "Why Did the Democrats Lose the South," 2830–2867.

12. Katherine J. Cramer, *The Politics of Resentment: Rural Consciousness in Wisconsin and the Rise of Scott Walker* (Chicago: University of Chicago Press, 2016), 6; Thomas Frank, *What's the Matter with Kansas?:*

How Conservatives Won the Heart of America (New York: Henry Holt, 2004), 5.

13. Jeffrey M. Jones, "Obama Job Approval Ratings Most Politically Polarized by Far," Gallup, January 25, 2017, https://news.gallup.com/poll/203006/obama-job-approval-ratings-politically-polarized-far.aspx; James M. Glaser and Jeffrey M. Berry, "Compromising Positions: Why Republican Partisans Are More Rigid than Democrats," *Political Science Quarterly* 133, no. 1 (2018): 99–126; Matt Grossmann and David A. Hopkins, "Ideological Republicans and Group Interest Democrats: The Asymmetry of American Party Politics," *Perspectives on Politics* 13, no. 1 (2015): 119–139.

14. Marc Hetherington and Thomas Rudolph, "Why Don't Americans Trust the Government? Because the Other Party Is In Power," *Washington Post*, January 30, 2014, https://www.washingtonpost.com/news/monkey-cage/wp/2014/01/30/why-dont-americans-trust-the-government-because-the-other-party-is-in-power/; Josh Clinton and Carrie Roush, "Poll: Persistent Partisan Divide Over 'Birther' Question," NBC News, August 10, 2016, https://www.nbcnews.com/politics/2016-election/poll-persistent-partisan-divide-over-birther-question-n627446; "The Presidential Square Wave Through the 113th Congress," voteviewblog.com, August 4, 2016, https://voteviewblog.com/2016/08/04/the-presidential-square-wave-through-the-113th-congress/; Chris Cillizza, "Is President Obama the Most Liberal President Ever?" *Washington Post*, February 4, 2016, https://www.washingtonpost.com/news/the-fix/wp/2014/02/04/is-barack-obama-the-most-liberal-president-ever/.

15. Seth J. Hill and Chris Tausanovitch, "Southern Realignment, Party Sorting, and the Polarization of American Primary Electorates, 1958–2012," *Public Choice* 176, no. 1–2 (July 2018): 107–132; David E. Broockman, Nicholas Carnes, Melody Crowder-Meyer, and Christopher Skovron, "Having Their Cake and Eating It, Too: Why Local Party Leaders Don't Support Nominating Centrists," forthcoming, *British Journal of Political Science*, last accessed October 1, 2018; Danielle M. Thomsen, "Ideological Moderates Won't Run: How Party Fit Matters for Partisan Polarization in Congress," *Journal of Politics* 76, no. 3 (2014): 786–797.

16. Lane Kenworthy, Sondra Barringer, Daniel Duerr, and Garrett Andrew Schneider, "The Democrats and Working-Class Whites" (unpublished, 2007), 1–53, https://www.researchgate.net/profile/Lane_Kenworthy/publication/228479856_The_Democrats_and_Working-Class_Whites/links/55df14c508ae7983897e834a/The-Democrats-and-Working-Class-Whites.pdf; Maxwell and Shields, *Long Southern Strategy*; Thomas M. Carsey and Geoffrey C. Layman, "Changing Sides or Changing Minds? Party Identification and Policy Preferences in the American Electorate," *American Journal of Political Science* 50, no. 2 (2006): 464–477; Clem Brooks and Jeff Manza, "A Great Divide? Religion and Political Change in US National Elections, 1972–2000," *Sociological Quarterly* 45, no. 3 (2004): 421–450; Robert Griffin, "Party Hoppers: Understanding Vot-

ers Who Switched Partisan Affiliation," Voter Study Group, December 2017, https://www.voterstudygroup.org/publication/party-hoppers; Lilliana Mason, *Uncivil Agreement: How Politics Became Our Identity* (Chicago: University of Chicago Press, 2018).

17. Tali Mendelberg, "Executing Hortons: Racial Crime in the 1988 Presidential Campaign," *Public Opinion Quarterly* 61, no. 1 (Spring 1997): 134–157; Nicholas Valentino, Vincent Hutchings, and Ismail White, "Cues That Matter: How Political Ads Prime Racial Attitudes during Campaigns," *American Political Science Review* 96, issue 1 (March 2002): 75–90; Ian Haney-Lopez, *Dog Whistle Politics: How Coded Racial Appeals Have Reinvented Racism and Wrecked the Middle Class* (New York: Oxford University Press, 2015).

18. Kuziemko and Washington, "Why Did the Democrats Lose the South," 2830–67; Michael S. Lewis-Beck, Charles Tien, and Richard Nadeau, "Obama's Missed Landslide: A Racial Cost?" *PS: Political Science and Politics* 43, no. 1 (January 2010): 69–76; Spencer Piston, "How Explicit Racial Prejudice Hurt Obama in the 2008 Election," *Political Behavior* 32, issue 4 (December 2010): 431–451.

19. Tali Mendelberg, *The Race Card: Campaign Strategy, Implicit Messages, and the Norm of Equality* (Princeton, NJ: Princeton University Press, 2001).

20. Jacob S. Hacker and Paul Pierson, *American Amnesia: How the War on Government Led Us to Forget What Made America Prosper* (New York: Simon & Schuster, 2016); Alexandra Filandra and Noah Kaplan, "Not Just About Performance: The Racial Antecedents of Whites' Public Mistrust and Hostility to Government," paper presented at the annual meeting of the American Political Science Association, Washington, DC, 2019.

21. Quoted in Maxwell and Shields, *The Long Southern Strategy*, 40.

22. Martin Gilens, *Why American Hate Welfare: Race, Media, and the Politics of Antipoverty Policy* (Chicago: University of Chicago Press, 1999); Emily Badger, "The Outsize Hold of the Word 'Welfare' on the Public Imagination," *New York Times*, August 6, 2018, https://www.nytimes.com/2018/08/06/upshot/welfare-and-the-public-imagination.html; Theda Skocpol and Vanessa Williamson, *The Tea Party and the Remaking of American Conservatism* (Oxford, Eng.: Oxford University Press, 2016); Arlie Russell Hochschild, *Strangers in Their Own Land: Anger and Mourning on the American Right* (New York: The New Press, 2018); Cramer, *The Politics of Resentment*; Suzanne Mettler, *The Government-Citizen Disconnect* (New York: Russell Sage Foundation, 2018), 101–116.

23. Ryan D. Enos, "Causal Effect of Intergroup Contact on Exclusionary Attitudes," *Proceedings of the National Academy of Sciences* 111, no. 10 (March 2014): 3699–3704; Ryan D. Enos, *The Spaces Between Us: Social Geography and Politics* (New York: Cambridge University Press, 2017), ch. 5.

24. Matt Barreto and Gary M. Segura, *Latino America: How America's*

Most Dynamic Population is Poised to Transform the Politics of the Nation (New York: Public Affairs, 2014); "Modern Immigration Wave Brings 59 Million to U.S., Driving Population Growth and Change Through 2065: Views of Immigration's Impact on U.S. Society Mixed," Pew Research Center, September 28, 2015, https://www.pewresearch .org/hispanic/2015/09/28/modern-immigration-wave-brings-59-mil-lion-to-u-s-driving-population-growth-and-change-through-2065/; "Hispanic Heritage Month 2017," Census Bureau, August 31, 2017, https://www.census.gov/newsroom/facts-for-features/2017/hispanic -heritage.html.

25. See, e.g., Walter G. Stephan, Oscar Ybarra, and Kimberly Rios Morrison, "Intergroup Threat Theory," in *Handbook of Prejudice, Stereotyping, and Discrimination*, ed. Todd D. Nelson (New York: Taylor & Francis, 2009), 43–60.

26. Richard Alba, "The Likely Persistence of a White Majority," *American Prospect*, January 11, 2016, https://prospect.org/civil-rights/likely -persistence-white-majority/.

27. See, for example, Maureen A. Craig and Jennifer A. Richeson, "Information about the US Racial Demographic Shift Triggers Concerns about Anti-White Discrimination among the Prospective White 'Minority'," *PLoS One*, published online September 27, 2017, https://doi.org/10.1371/ journal.pone.0185389.

28. Nate Silver, "The Effects of Union Membership on Democratic Voting," FiveThirtyEight, February 26, 2011, https://fivethirtyeight.com/features/ the-effects-of-union-membership-on-democratic-voting/.

29. Alvin Rabushka and Kenneth Shepsle, *Politics in Plural Societies: A Theory of Democratic Instability* (Columbus, OH: Charles E. Merrill Publishing Company, 1972); Kanchan Chandra, "Ethnic Parties and Democratic Stability," *Perspectives on Politics* 3, no. 2 (June 2005): 235–252; Stuart J. Kaufman, "Spiraling the Ethnic War: Elites, Masses, and Moscow in Moldova's Civil War," *International Security* 21, no. 2 (Fall 1996): 108–138; Zack Beauchamp, " 'Ethnic Outbidding': The Academic Theory That Helps Explain Trump's Anti-Muslim Rhetoric," Vox, December 10, 2015, https://www.vox.com/world/2015/12/10/9881876/trump-muslims -ethnic-outbidding; Shiping Tang, "The Onset of Ethnic War: A General Theory," *Sociological Theory* 33, issue 3 (October 2015): 256–279.

30. Ezra Klein, "The Hard Question Isn't Why Clinton Lost—It's Why Trump Won," Vox, November 11, 2016, https://www.vox.com/policy -and-politics/2016/11/11/13578618/why-did-trump-win.

31. Anthony York, "The GOP's Latino Strategy," Salon, January 13, 2000, https://www.salon.com/2000/01/13/latinos/; Patricia Hart, "George W. Es Muy Bueno," *TexasMonthly*, June 30, 2000, https://www.texas monthly.com/articles/george-w-es-muy-bueno/; Samantha L. Hernandez, "Virtually Shaking Hands and Kissing Babies: Congressional Candidates and Social Media Campaigns," in *Latinas in American Politics*, ed. Sharon

A. Navarro, Samantha L. Hernandez, and Leslie A. Navarro (Lanham, MD: Lexington Press), 83–96.

32. Nancy LeTourneau, "Republicans Can't Generate Enough Angry White Guys," *Washington Monthly*, December 11, 2018, https://washington monthly.com/2018/12/11/republicans-cant-generate-enough-angry -white-guys/.

33. Gabriel R. Sanchez, F. Chris Garcia, and Melina Juárez, "Latino Public Policy Opinions," in *The Oxford Handbook of Racial and Ethnic Politics in the United States*, ed. David L. Leal, Taeku Lee, and Mark Sawyer, published online August 2014, https://www.oxfordhandbooks .com/view/10.1093/oxfordhb/9780199566631.001.0001/oxfordhb -9780199566631-e-15.

34. Margaret E. Peters, *Trading Barriers: Immigration and the Remaking of Globalization* (Princeton, NJ: Princeton University Press, 2017). See also Elaine Kamarck and Christine Stenglein, "Can Immigration Reform Happen? A Look Back," Brookings Institution, February 11, 2019, https://www.brookings.edu/blog/fixgov/2019/02/11/can-immigration -reform-happen-a-look-back/.

35. Sam Stein, "Bachmann on Immigration: Deport All the Undocumented," *HuffPost*, December 3, 2011, https://www.huffpost.com/entry/bachmann -immigration-deport-undocumented-_n_1127533; Robert Costa, "Bachmann: Obama Turning 'Illiterate' Immigrants into Democratic Voters," *Washington Post*, November 19, 2014, https://www.washingtonpost.com /news/post-politics/wp/2014/11/19/bachmann-obama-turning-illiterate -immigrants-into-democratic-voters/.

36. Skocpol and Williamson, *Tea Party*; Christopher Parker, "The (Real) Reason Why the House Won't Pass Comprehensive Immigration Reform," Brookings Institution, August 4, 2014, https://www.brook ings.edu/blog/fixgov/2014/08/04/the-real-reason-why-the-house-wont -pass-comprehensive-immigration-reform/.

37. Parker, "The (Real) Reason." See also Christopher S. Parker and Matt A. Barreto, *Change They Can't Believe In: The Tea Party and Reactionary Politics in America* (Princeton, NJ: Princeton University Press, 2013).

38. "Growth & Opportunity Project," Republican National Committee, last accessed September 26, 2019, 7–8, https://assets.documentcloud.org/ documents/623664/republican-national-committees-growth-and.pdf.

39. Jonathan Martin, "Eric Cantor Defeated by David Bratt, Tea Party Challenger, in G.O.P. Primary Upset," *New York Times*, June 10, 2014, https:// www.nytimes.com/2014/06/11/us/politics/eric-cantor-loses-gop-primary .html; Sean Trende, "The Case of the Missing White Voters," RealClear Politics, November 8, 2012, https://www.realclearpolitics.com/articles /2012/11/08/the_case_of_the_missing_white_voters_116106.html.

40. Kyle Cheney, "Trump Kills GOP Autopsy," *Politico*, March 4, 2016, https://www.politico.com/story/2016/03/donald-trump-gop-party -reform-220222.

41. John Sides, Lynn Vavrek, and Michael Tesler, *Identity Crisis: The 2016 Presidential Campaign and the Battle for the Meaning of America* (Princeton, NJ: Princeton University Press, 2018), 21–22.

42. Harry Enten, "We've Never Known Less About an Incoming President's Ideology," FiveThirtyEight, November 28, 2016, https://fivethirty eight.com/features/trump-ideology/; Tara Golshan, "Trump Said He Wouldn't Cut Medicaid, Social Security, and Medicare. His 2020 Budget Cuts All 3," Vox, March 12, 2019, https://www.vox.com/policy-and -politics/2019/3/12/18260271/trump-medicaid-social-security-medicare -budget-cuts; Scott Pelley, "Trump Gets Down to Business on *60 Minutes*," *60 Minutes*, September 27, 2015, https://www.cbsnews.com/news/ donald-trump-60-minutes-scott-pelley/.

43. Jonathan Chait, "The GOP's Age of Authoritarianism Has Only Just Begun," *New York*, October 30, 2016, http://nymag.com/intelligencer/ 2016/10/the-gops-age-of-authoritarianism-has-only-just-begun.html.

44. Danielle Paquette, "The Unexpected Voters Behind the Widest Gender Gap in Recorded Election History," *Washington Post*, November 9, 2016, https://www.washingtonpost.com/news/wonk/wp/2016/11/09 /men-handed-trump-the-election/; Jeffrey M. Jones, "Gender Gap in 2012 is Largest in Gallup's History," Gallup, November 9, 2012, https:// news.gallup.com/poll/158588/gender-gap-2012-vote-largest-gallup -history.aspx; Angie Maxwell, "Why Southern White Women Voted against Feminism," *Washington Post*, September 10, 2019, https://www .washingtonpost.com/outlook/2019/09/10/why-southern-white-women -vote-against-feminism/. These numbers are based on exit polls, which may differ slightly from data validated by election returns. Some analysts measure the gender gap as simply the difference between the share of male voters backing the winning candidate and the share of women backing the winning candidate; the trends do not appreciably differ if that approach is used.

45. Nate Cohn, "The Obama-Trump Voters Are Real. Here's What They Think," *New York Times*, August 15, 2017, https://www.nytimes .com/2017/08/15/upshot/the-obama-trump-voters-are-real-heres-what -they-think.html; Jeff Guo, "Death Predicts Whether People Vote for Donald Trump," *Washington Post*, March 4, 2016, https://www.wash ingtonpost.com/news/wonk/wp/2016/03/04/death-predicts-whether -people-vote-for-donald-trump/; Torben Iversen and David Soskice, *Democracy and Prosperity: Reinventing Capitalism through a Turbulent Century* (Princeton, NJ: Princeton University Press, 2019).

46. David Autor, David Dorn, Gordon Hanson, and Kaveh Majlesi, "Importing Political Polarization? The Electoral Consequences of Rising Trade Exposure," National Bureau of Economic Research, working paper no. 22637, December 2017, https://www.nber.org/papers/w22637.

47. Keith Boag, "Money Man," CBC, 2018, https://www.cbc.ca/news2/ interactives/sh/wex94ODaUs/trump-robert-mercer-billionaire/.

Chapter 5: **A VERY CIVIL WAR**

1. Tim Alberta, "Inside Trump's Feud with Paul Ryan," *Politico Magazine*, July 16, 2019, http://politico.com/magazine/story/2019/07/16/donald -trump-paul-ryan-feud-227360.

2. Ezra Klein, "How Democracies Die, Explained," Vox, February 2, 2018, http://vox.com/policy-and-politics/2018/2/2/16929764/how-demo cracies-die-trump-book-levitsky-ziblatt.

3. Marty Cohen, David Karol, Hans Noel, and John Zaller, *The Party Decides: Presidential Nominations Before and After Reform* (Chicago: University of Chicago Press, 2008).

4. Tim Alberta, *American Carnage: On the Front Lines of the Republican Civil War and the Rise of President Trump* (New York: Harper, 2019), 243.

5. Jane Mayer, "The Danger of President Pence," *New Yorker*, October 16, 2017, http://newyorker.com/magazine/2017/10/23/the-danger-of -president-pence.

6. Grover Norquist, "Speech to the American Conservative Union," C-SPAN, February 11, 2012, http://c-span.org/video/?304376-9/grover -norquist-remarks.

7. Matt Ford, "The Banality of Lindsey Graham," *New Republic*, July 22, 2019, http://newrepublic.com/article/154501/banality-lindsey-graham -biggest-trump-supporter-congress.

8. Ewan Palmer, "CNN's Don Lemon Cracks Up While Reading Donald Trump Staffers' Old Quotes about the President," *Newsweek*, http:// newsweek.com/video-cnn-don-lemon-reading-donald-trump-staff -quotes-1262446; Brakkton Booker, "Rubio Backs Trump, but Stands By Calling Him a 'Con Man,'" NPR, August 16, 2016, http://npr .org/2016/08/16/490222799/rubio-backs-trump-but-stands-by-calling -him-a-con-man; Heather Caygle, "Ryan: Trump's Comments 'Text- book Definition' of Racism," *Politico*, June 7, 2016, http://politico.com/ story/2016/06/paul-ryan-trump-judge-223991.

9. Alberta, *American Carnage*, 600; Paul Ryan, "Welcome to the Dawn of a New, Unified Republican Government," YouTube, November 15, 2016, http://youtube.com/watch?v=3F5uRcA_nok.

10. Anthony Damico, Rachel Garfield, and Kendal Orgera, "The Unin- sured and the ACA: A Primer," Kaiser Family Foundation, 2019; Sarah Kliff, "How Congress Paid for Obamacare (in Two Charts)," *Wash- ington Post*, August 30, 2012, http://washingtonpost.com/news/wonk/ wp/2012/08/30/how-congress-paid-for-obamacare-in-two-charts/.

11. Data on Medicaid enrollment provided by the Centers for Medicare & Medicaid Services, as of August 2019; Paul Ryan, "Speaker Paul Ryan at National Review Institute Ideas Summit," C-SPAN, March 17, 2017, http://c-span.org/video/?425555-6/national-review-institute -ideas-summit-speaker-paul-ryan.

12. Jacob S. Hacker and Paul Pierson, "The Dog That Almost Barked: What the ACA Repeal Fight Says about the Resilience of the American Wel-

fare State," *Journal of Health Politics, Policy and Law* 43, no. 4 (August 2018): 561, 571–572; Edwin Park, "Trump Budget Cuts Medicaid Even More than House Health Bill, Showing Danger of Per Capita Cap," Center on Budget and Policy Priorities, May 23, 2017, http://cbpp.org/blog/trump-budget-cuts-medicaid-even-more-than-house-health-bill-showing-danger-of-per-capita-cap.

13. Scott Clement and Emily Guskin, "Republicans' Obamacare Repeal Was Never Really That Popular," *Washington Post*, July 28, 2017, https://www.washingtonpost.com/news/the-fix/wp/2017/07/28/republicans-obamacare-repeal-was-never-really-that-popular. Had any senator who voted against the bill switched their allegiance, Vice President Mike Pence would have broken the tie, almost certainly in favor of the legislation. Other proposed Republican legislation would have left even more Americans uninsured. See Haeyoun Park, "The 'Skinny' Repeal Republicans Hope to Pass Would Leave Huge Numbers Uninsured," *New York Times*, July 27, 2017, http://nytimes.com/interactive/2017/07/27/us/cbo-score-of-skinny-repeal.html.

14. Donald Trump, "I Was the First," Twitter post, May 7, 2015, https://twitter.com/realDonaldTrump/status/596338364187602944; David Beier, Bryan King, and Robert Kocher, "The Midterm's Biggest Winners: Medicaid and Rural America," *Health Affairs*, January 25, 2019, http://healthaffairs.org/do/10.1377/hblog20190124.621253/full; Robert Pear, "Repeal of Health Law Faces a New Hurdle: Older Americans," *New York Times*, March 5, 2017, https://www.nytimes.com/2017/03/05/us/politics/health-care-law-obamacare-repeal-older-americans.html; Vann R. Newkirk II, "How the American Health Care Act Leaves Near-Elderly People Behind," *Atlantic Monthly*, March 14, 2017, https://www.theatlantic.com/politics/archive/2017/03/ahca-trumpcare-older-sicker-voters/519423/.

15. Donald Trump, "Trump: 'Wiretap Covers a Lot of Different Things,'" interview by Tucker Carlson, Fox News, March 15, 2017, http://video.foxnews.com/v/5361147496001/#sp=show-clips.

16. Peter Cary and Allan Holmes, "The Secret Saga of Trump's Tax Cuts," Center for Public Integrity, April 30, 2019, http://publicintegrity.org/business/taxes/trumps-tax-cuts/the-secret-saga-of-trumps-tax-cuts.

17. "Distributional Analysis of the Conference Agreement for the Tax Cuts and Jobs Act," Tax Policy Center, December 18, 2017, 5, 8.

18. Laura Davison, "Making Trump's Tax Cuts Permanent Would Cost Nearly $920B," Bloomberg, July 9, 2019, https://www.bloomberg.com/news/articles/2019-07-08/making-trump-s-tax-cuts-permanent-would-cost-nearly-920-billion; Chye-Ching Huang, "Fundamentally Flawed 2017 Tax Law Largely Leaves Low- and Moderate-Income Americans Behind," statement on behalf of Center on Budget and Policy Priorities to House Budget Committee, 116th Cong., 1st Sess. (February 27, 2019) http://congress.gov/116/meeting/house/108985/witnesses/HHRG-116-BU00-Wstate-HuangC-20190227-U1.pdf.

19. Harry Enten, "The GOP Tax Cuts Are Even More Unpopular Than Past

Tax Hikes," FiveThirtyEight, November 29, 2017, https://fivethirtyeight
.com/features/the-gop-tax-cuts-are-even-more-unpopular-than-past
-tax-hikes/; "Top Frustrations with Tax System: Sense That Corporations, Wealthy Don't Pay Fair Share," Pew Center for the People and
the Press, April 14, 2017, https://www.people-press.org/2017/04/14/
top-frustrations-with-tax-system-sense-that-corporations-wealthy
-dont-pay-fair-share/.

20. Kali Holloway, "Five Times Republicans Admitted They Work for Rich
Donors," Salon, November 20, 2017, http://salon.com/2017/11/20/5
-times-republicans-admitted-they-work-for-rich-donors_partner/.

21. Dan Alexander, "Inside the $400 Million Fortune of Trump's Treasury
Secretary Steve Mnuchin," *Forbes*, July 22, 2019, https://www.forbes
.com/sites/danalexander/2019/07/22/inside-the-400-million-fortune-of
-trumps-treasury-secretary-steve-mnuchin/#5b1a0e5c6333; Antoine Gara,
"Trump Taps Steve Schwarzman, Jamie Dimon and Mary Barra for Advice on
Job Creation, Growth," *Forbes*, December 2, 2016, https://www.forbes.com
/sites/antoinegara/2016/12/02/trump-taps-steve-schwarzman-jamie-dimon
-and-mary-barra-for-advice-on-job-creation-growth/#542d46ca4359/.

22. Data on roll-call votes accessible through Voteview, hosted by UCLA's
Department of Political Science and Social Sciences Computing.

23. Mayer, "The Danger of President Pence."

24. Ibid.

25. Ibid.

26. Ibid; Jonathan Mahler, "How One Conservative Think Tank Is Stock-
ing Trump's Government," *New York Times Magazine*, June 20, 2018,
https://www.nytimes.com/2018/06/20/magazine/trump-government
-heritage-foundation-think-tank.html.

27. Danielle Ivory and Robert Faturechi, "The Deep Industry Ties of
Trump's Deregulation Teams," *New York Times*, July 11, 2017, http://
nytimes.com/2017/07/11/business/the-deep-industry-ties-of-trumps-de
regulation-teams.html; Matthew Yglesias, "Trump Has Granted More
Lobbyist Waivers in Four Months than Obama Did in Eight Years," Vox,
June 1, 2017, http://vox.com/2017/6/1/15723994/trump-ethics-waivers.

28. Jacob S. Hacker and Paul Pierson, *American Amnesia: How the War on
Government Led Us to Forget What Made America Prosper* (New York:
Simon & Schuster, 2016), 290–291.

29. Margaret Talbot, "Scott Pruitt's Dirty Politics: How the EPA Became
the Fossil Fuel Industry's Best Friend," *New Yorker*, March 26, 2018,
https://www.newyorker.com/magazine/2018/04/02/scott-pruitts
-dirty-politics; Joe Davidson, "Trump Transition Leader's Goal Is
Two-Thirds Cut in EPA Employees," *Washington Post*, January 30, 2017,
https://www.washingtonpost.com/news/powerpost/wp/2017/01/30/
trump-transition-leaders-goal-is-two-thirds-cut-in-epa-employees/; Steven Mufson, "Trump's Energy Policy Team Includes Climate Change
Skeptic, Free-Market Advocate," *Washington Post*, November 29, 2016,
https://www.washingtonpost.com/business/economy/trumps-energy

-policy-team-includes-climate-change-skeptic-free-market-advocate
/2016/11/29/86e52004-b5a4-11e6-b8df-600bd9d38a02.story.html.

30. Rebecca Leber, "Making America Toxic Again," *Mother Jones*, March/
April 2018, https://www.motherjones.com/politics/2018/02/scott-pruitt
-profile-epa-trump/; Lisa Friedman, "Bill Wehrum, an Architect of
E.P.A. Rollbacks, Faces New Ethics Inquiry," *New York Times*, July 22,
2019, https://www.nytimes.com/2019/07/22/climate/william-wehrum
-epa-inquiry.html; Annie Snider, "Former Koch Official Runs EPA
Chemical Research," *Politico*, February 4, 2019, https://www.politico
.com/story/2019/02/04/former-koch-official-runs-epa-chemical-re
search-1136230; Emily Holden and Anthony Adragna, "Major Trump
Donor Helped Pruitt Pick EPA Science Advisers," *Politico*, June 8, 2018,
https://www.politico.com/story/2018/06/08/doug-deason-trump-donor
-helped-pruitt-pick-epa-science-advisers-603450.

31. "Corporate Impunity: 'Tough on Crime' Trump Is Weak on Corporate Crime and Wrongdoing," Public Citizen, July 2018; Umair
Irfan, "Trump's EPA Just Replaced Obama's Signature Climate Policy with a Much Weaker Rule," Vox, June 19, 2019, https://www.vox
.com/2019/6/19/18684054/climate-change-clean-power-plan-repeal-af
fordable-emissions; Robinson Meyer, "How the Carmakers Trumped
Themselves," *Atlantic Monthly*, June 20, 2018, https://www.theatlan
tic.com/science/archive/2018/06/how-the-carmakers-trumped-them
selves/562400; Brady Dennis and Juliet Eilperin, "Under Trump, EPA
Inspections Fall to a 10-year Low," *Washington Post*, February 8, 2019,
https://www.washingtonpost.com/climate-environment/2019/02/08/
under-trump-epa-inspections-fall-year-low/; Coral Davenport, "Trump
to Revoke California's Authority to Set Stricter Auto Emissions
Rules," *New York Times*, September 17, 2019, https://www.nytimes
.com/2019/09/17/climate/trump-california-emissions-waiver.html;
"Corporate Impunity: 'Tough on Crime' Trump Is Weak on Corporate
Crime and Wrongdoing," Public Citizen.

32. Lance Williams, "Recording Reveals Oil Industry Execs Laughing at
Trump Access," *Politico Magazine*, March 23, 2019, https://www.polit-
ico.com/magazine/story/2019/03/23/trump-big-oil-industry-influence
-investigation-zinke-226106.

33. "Corporate Impunity: 'Tough on Crime' Trump Is Weak on Corporate
Crime and Wrongdoing," Public Citizen; Michael Cohn, "IRS Keeps
Cutting Back on Audits of Millionaires and Big Businesses," *Account-
ing Today*, March 7, 2019, https://www.accountingtoday.com/news/irs
-keeps-cutting-back-on-audits-of-millionaires-and-big-businesses.

34. David Montgomery, "Conquerors of the Courts," *Washington Post*, January 2, 2019, http://washingtonpost.com/news/magazine/wp/2019/01/02/
feature/conquerors-of-the-courts/.

35. Russell Wheeler, "Trump's Judicial Appointments Record at the August
Recess: A Little Less than Meets the Eye," Brookings, August 8, 2019,
http://brookings.edu/blog/fixgov/2019/08/08/trumps-judicial-appoint

ments-record-at-the-august-recess-a-little-less-than-meets-the-eye; Jake Holland, "U.S. Appeals Court Vacancies Fall to Four After Phipps Confirmed," Bloomberg Law, July 16, 2019, https://www.bloomberglaw .com/document/XCP31C8G000000?bna_news_filter=us-law-week &jcsearch=BNA%25200000016bfb4dd60eaf6bfb5fdbbf0000#jcite.

36. Jon Green, "The Ideology of Trump's Judges," Data for Progress, May 10, 2019, http://filesforprogress.org/memos/Trump%20Judges %20Memo%20-%20Demand%20Justice%20-Final.pdf.

37. David Montgomery, "Conquerors of the Courts," *Washington Post*, January 2, 2019, http://washingtonpost.com/news/magazine/wp/2019/01/02/ feature/conquerors-of-the-courts/.

38. Jay Michaelson, "The Secrets of Leonard Leo, the Man behind Trump's Supreme Court Pick," Daily Beast, July 24, 2018, http://thedailybeast.com/ the-secrets-of-leonard-leo-the-man-behind-trumps-supreme-court-pick.

39. Hacker and Pierson, *American Amnesia*, 215–226.

40. Sabeel Rahman and Kathleen Thelen, "The Role of Law in the American Political Economy," paper presented at the MIT Conference on American Political Economy in Comparative Perspective, 2019.

41. Heather Timmons, "How White House Lawyer Don McGahn Helped Break the U.S. Election System," Quartz, September 1, 2018, http://qz .com/1375949/how-white-house-lawyer-don-mcgahn-helped-break -the-us-election-system.

42. Robert O'Harrow Jr. and Shawn Boburg, "A Conservative Activist's Behind-the-Scenes Campaign to Remake the Nation's Courts," *Washington Post*, May 21, 2019, http://washingtonpost.com/graphics/2019/ investigations/leonard-leo-federalists-society-courts/; Andrew Perez, "Conservative Legal Interests Funneled $2.7 Million to NRA, Freedom Partners around Gorsuch Fight," MapLight, January 7, 2019, https:// maplight.org/story/conservative-legal-interests-funneled-2-7-million-to -nra-freedom-partners-around-gorsuch-fight/; Mark Joseph Stern, "What the Koch Brothers' Money Buys," *Slate*, May 2, 2018, https://slate .com/news-and-politics/2018/05/we-now-know-how-the-koch-brothers -and-leonard-leo-buy-special-favors.html.

43. Viveca Novak and Peter Stone, "The JCN Story: Building a Secretive GOP Judicial Machine," Center for Responsive Politics, March 23, 2015, http:// opensecrets.org/news/2015/03/the-jcn-story-building-a-secretive-gop -judicial-machine; Andrew Perez and Margaret Sessa-Hawkins, "Tax Returns Identify Dark Money Organization As Source of GOP Supreme Court Attacks," MapLight, November 21, 2017, https://maplight.org/ story/tax-returns-identify-dark-money-organization-as-source-of-gop -supreme-court-attacks; Anna Massoglia and Andrew Perez, "Secretive Conservative Legal Group Funded by $17 Million Mystery Donor before Kavanaugh Fight," MapLight, May 17, 2019, http://maplight .org/story/secretive-conservative-legal-group-funded-by-17-million -mystery-donor-before-kavanaugh-fight/.

44. Donald Trump, "Remarks in New York City Accepting Election as the

45th President of the United States," The American Presidency Project, November 9, 2016, http://presidency.ucsb.edu/node/318972.

45. Alexander Hamilton, Federalist No. 68, "The Mode of Electing the President," *New-York Packet*, March 12, 1788.

46. Ben Casselman and Ana Swanson, "Survey Shows Broad Opposition to Trump Trade Policies," *New York Times*, September 19, 2019, http://nytimes.com/2019/09/19/business/economy/trade-war-economic-concerns.html; Jason Lemon, "Trump Adviser Calls Reduced China Tariffs 'Christmas Present to the Nation' Despite Claiming They Didn't Hurt Consumers," *Newsweek*, August 14, 2019, http://newsweek.com/trump-adviser-china-tariffs-christmas-present-nation-1454368; Taylor Telford, "Trump's Trade War Comes for Consumers: Tariffs Could Cost U.S. Families Up to $1,000 a Year, JPMorgan Forecasts," *Washington Post*, August 20, 2019, http://washingtonpost.com/business/2019/09/20/trumps-trade-war-comes-consumers-tariffs-will-cost-us-families-year-jp-morgan-forecasts.

47. Joseph Parilla and Max Bouchet, "Which US Communities are Most Affected by Chinese, EU, and NAFTA Retaliatory Tariffs?" Brookings, October 2018, http://brookings.edu/research/which-us-communities-are-most-affected-by-chinese-eu-and-nafta-retaliatory-tariffs/.

48. Sifan Liu and Mark Muro, "Another Clinton-Trump Divide: High-Output America vs Low-Output America," Brookings, November 29, 2016, https://www.brookings.edu/blog/the-avenue/2016/11/29/another-clinton-trump-divide-high-output-america-vs-low-output-america; Maggie Fox, "Where 'Despair Deaths' Were Higher, Voters Chose Trump," NBC News, September 5, 2018, https://www.nbcnews.com/health/health-news/where-despair-deaths-were-higher-voters-chose-trump-n906631; Robert Reich, "How Blue States Help Red States," Salon, November 16, 2018, http://salon.com/2018/11/16/how-blue-states-help-red-states_partner.

49. Sarah Miller et al., "Medicaid and Mortality: New Evidence from Linked Survey and Administrative Data," National Bureau of Economic Research, working paper no. 26081, 2019; Alexander Hertel-Fernandez, Theda Skocpol, and Daniel Lynch, "Business Associations, Conservative Networks, and the Ongoing Republican War Over Medicaid Expansion," *Journal of Health Politics, Policy and Law* 41, no. 2 (2016): 239–286.

50. Julia Lurie, "The Senate Just Passed a Sweeping Opioid Bill. It's Still Not Nearly Enough," *Mother Jones*, September 17, 2018, http://motherjones.com/politics/2018/09/the-senate-just-passed-a-sweeping-opioid-bill-its-still-not-nearly-enough-2.

51. Ben Steverman, Dave Merrill, and Jeremy C. F. Lin, "A Year After the Middle Class Tax Cut, the Rich Are Winning," Bloomberg, December 18, 2018, http://bloomberg.com/graphics/2018-tax-plan-consequences.

52. Nicole Goodkind, "Mitch McConnell Calls for Social Security, Medicare, Medicaid Cuts After Passing Tax Cuts, Massive Defense Spending," *Newsweek*, October 16, 2018, http://newsweek.com/deficit-budget-tax-plan-social

-security-medicaid-medicare-entitlement-1172941; Joel Friedman and Richard Kogan, "House GOP Budget Retains Tax Cuts for the Wealthy, Proposes Deep Program Cuts for Millions of Americans," Center for Budget and Policy Priorities, June 28, 2018, http://cbpp.org/research/federal-budget/house-gop-budget-retains-tax-cuts-for-the-wealthy-proposes-deep-program-cuts.

53. Christopher Leonard, *Kochland: The Secret History of Koch Industries and Corporate Power in America* (New York: Simon & Schuster, 2019), 557, 563.

54. Quinnipiac University Poll, August 14, 2018, https://poll.qu.edu/images/polling/us/us08142018_unvt25.pdf/; Alberta, *American Carnage*, 504.

55. Sabrina Siddiqui, "Republican Attack Ads Echo Trump's Anti-Immigration Message to Whip Up Fear Among Supporters," *Guardian*, October 18, 2018, http://theguardian.com/us-news/2018/oct/18/republicans-immigration-attack-ads-trump; Ashley Parker, Philip Rucker, and Josh Dawsey, "Trump and Republicans Settle on Fear—and Falsehoods—as a Midterm Strategy," *Washington Post*, October 22, 2019, http://washingtonpost.com/politics/trump-and-republicans-settle-on-fear--and-falsehoods--as-a-midterm-strategy/2018/10/22/1ebbf222-d614-11e8-a10f-b51546b10756_story.html.

56. Allan Smith, "Nancy Pelosi Gives Impassioned Speech to Vote Down AHCA Minutes Ahead of the Vote: You Will Glow in the Dark," *Business Insider*, May 4, 2017, https://www.businessinsider.com/nancy-pelosi-ahca-speech-vote-2017-5.

57. Alberta, *American Carnage*, 499.

58. Tim Alberta, "Inside Trump's Feud with Paul Ryan," *Politico Magazine*, July 16, 2019, http://politico.com/magazine/story/2019/07/16/donald-trump-paul-ryan-feud-227360; Barbara Weinger, "Former Speaker Paul Ryan Joins Fox Corp. Board," Directors and Boards, April 4, 2019, http://directorsandboards.com/news/former-speaker-paul-ryan-joins-fox-corp-board; Amy Goldstein, *Janesville: An American Story* (New York: Simon & Schuster, 2017); Jennifer Steinhauer, "Even as House Speaker, Paul Ryan Sleeps in His Office," *New York Times*, November 10, 2015, http://nytimes.com/2015/11/11/us/politics/speaker-paul-ryan-sleeps-in-office.html; Natasha Korecki and Jake Sherman, "Paul Ryan Is Moving His Family to Washington from Wisconsin," *Politico*, August 20, 2019, https://www.politico.com/story/2019/08/20/paul-ryan-returns-to-washington-1468994.

Chapter 6: **TYRANNY OF THE (WEALTHY AND EXTREME) MINORITY**

1. Donald Trump, "Big Win," Twitter post, November 7, 2018, https://twitter.com/realdonaldtrump/status/1060141780878979072?lang=en.

2. Steven Levitsky and Daniel Ziblatt, *How Democracies Die* (New York: Crown, 2018).

3. Daniel Ziblatt, *Conservative Parties and the Birth of Democracy* (New York: Cambridge University Press, 2017).

4. James Madison, Federalist No. 10, *New-York Packet*, November 22, 1787; James Madison, "Observations on Jefferson's Draft of a Constitution for Virginia," National Archives, ca. October 15, 1788, https://founders.archives.gov/documents/Madison/01-11-02-0216. See also Paul Pierson and Eric Schickler, "Madison's Constitution Under Stress: A Developmental Analysis of Political Polarization," *Annual Review of Political Science*, forthcoming.

5. Ganesh Sitaraman, *The Crisis of the Middle-Class Constitution: Why Economic Inequality Threatens Our Republic* (New York: Vintage Books, 2018); Drew R. McCoy, *The Last of the Fathers: James Madison and the Republican Legacy* (New York: Cambridge University Press, 1989).

6. Alexander Hamilton, Federalist No. 1, *New-York Packet*, October 27, 1787.

7. William Edward Hartpole Lecky, *Democracy and Liberty* (London: Longmans, Green and Company, 1896; Indianapolis: Liberty Fund, 1981), 24.

8. Ed Kilgore, "Conservatives Want a 'Republic' to Protect Privileges," *New York*, August 28, 2019, https://www.nymag.com/intelligencer/2019/08/conservatives-want-a-republic-to-protect-privileges.html; Jamelle Bouie, "Alexandria Ocasio-Cortez Understands Democracy Better Than Republicans Do," *New York Times*, August 27, 2019, https://www.nytimes.com/2019/08/27/opinion/aoc-crenshaw-republicans-democracy.html.

9. Rand described this as the "original meaning" of democracy. Ayn Rand, "How to Read (and Not to Write)," in *The Voice of Reason: Essays in Objectivist Thought*, ed. Leonard Peikoff (New York: Meridian, 1990), 133–134.

10. Will Wilkinson, "How Libertarian Democracy Skepticism Infected the American Right," Niskanen Center, November 3, 2017, https://www.niskanencenter.org/libertarian-democracy-skepticism-infected-american-right.

11. Chrisopher Leonard, *Kochland: The Secret History of Koch Industries and Corporate Power in America* (New York: Simon & Schuster, 2019), 34–40; Dwight D. Eisenhower to Edgar Newton Eisenhower, November 8, 1954, in *The Papers of Dwight David Eisenhower*, Volume XV—The Presidency: The Middle Way, Part VI: Crises Abroad, Party Problems at Home; September 1954 to December 1954, Chapter 13: "A new phase of political experience."

12. Wilkinson, "How Libertarian Democracy Skepticism Infected the American Right."

13. Andrew Clark, "Blackstone Billionaire Is Sorry for Nazi Jab Against Obama's Tax Policies," *Guardian*, August 17, 2010, https://www.theguardian.com/business/andrew-clark-on-america/2010/aug/17/privateequity-secondworldwar; Chrystia Freeland, "Super-Rich Irony," *New Yorker*, October 1, 2012, https://www.newyorker.com/magazine

/2012/10/08/super-rich-irony; Sam Gustin, "Tom Perkins Says the Rich Should Get More Votes in Elections," *Time*, February 14, 2014, https://time.com/8466/tom-perkins-taxes.

14. Peter Thiel, "The Education of a Libertarian," *Cato Unbound*, April 13, 2009, https://www.cato-unbound.org/2009/04/13/peter-thiel/education-libertarian.

15. Andrew Kaczynski and Paul LeBlanc, "Trump's Fed Pick Stephen Moore Is a Self-Described 'Radical' Who Said He's Not a 'Big Believer in Democracy,'" CNN, April 13, 2019, https://www.cnn.com/2019/04/12/politics/stephen-moore-kfile/index.html.

16. Carol Anderson, *One Person, No Vote: How Voter Suppression Is Destroying Our Democracy* (New York: Bloomsbury, 2018).

17. Keith G. Bentele and Erin E. O'Brien, "Jim Crow 2.0? Why States Consider and Adopt Restrictive Voter Access Policies," *Perspectives on Politics* 11, no. 4 (2013): 1088–1116; Zoltan Hajnal, Nazita Lajevardi, and Lindsay Nielson, "Voter Identification Laws and the Suppression of Minority Votes," *Journal of Politics* 79, no. 2 (2017). See also the symposium in a July 2018 special issue of *The Journal of Politics*, which highlights the difficulty of pinpointing the causal effects of particular vote restrictions. Nonetheless, there is a long tradition of research suggesting that the ease of voter registration affects turnout. See, e.g., Christopher Ingraham, "Low Voter Turnout Is No Accident, According to a Ranking of the Ease of Voting in All Fifty States," *Washington Post*, October 22, 2018, https://www.washingtonpost.com/business/2018/10/22/low-voter-turnout-is-no-accident-according-ranking-ease-voting-all-states/; João Cancela and Benny Geys, "Explaining Voter Turnout: A Meta-Analysis of National and Subnational Elections," *Electoral Studies* 42 (2016): 264–275.

18. It is difficult to differentiate the effects of Republican gerrymandering from the effects of the geographic concentration of Democratic votes, in part because that concentration facilitates Republican gerrymandering. However, the simulations of Jonathan Rodden suggest gerrymandering's effects are substantial. See his *Why Cities Lose* (New York: Basic Books, 2019). See also David Wasserman, "The Congressional Map Has a Record-Setting Bias against Democrats," FiveThirtyEight, August 7, 2017, https://fivethirtyeight.com/features/the-congressional-map-is-historically-biased-toward-the-gop/. A rough estimate of the effect of gerrymandering can be calculated by assessing the basic GOP advantage (commonly calculated as the difference between the Republican presidential margin in the national popular vote and the Republican presidential margin in the median congressional district), and then comparing that advantage for elections before and after decennial redistricting. Wasserman calculates a bias of approximately six points in favor of Republicans in 2016; his estimates show the bias averaged around three points in elections between 2000 and 2010. Hence the "roughly half" estimate. FiveThirtyEight's Atlas of Redistricting (https://projects.fivethirtyeight.com/redistricting-maps/) calculates that a highly pro-Democratic gerrymander would have resulted in 184 seats for Republicans after the 2016 election, as compared with their actual 236.

19. Miles Parks, "Redistricting Guru's Hard Drives Could Mean Legal, Political Woes For GOP," NPR, June 6, 2019, https://www.npr.org/2019 /06/06/730260511/redistricting-gurus-hard-drives-could-mean-legal -political-woes-for-gop; Alan Greenblat, "How Democracy Died in North Carolina," *American Prospect*, September 12, 2019, https://prospect .org/power/democracy-died-north-carolina.

20. Russ Choma, "GOP Paid Millions to Gerrymandering Expert Behind Census Citizenship Question," *Mother Jones*, June 5, 2019, https://www .motherjones.com/politics/2019/06/gop-paid-millions-to-gerrymander ing-expert-behind-census-citizenship-question; Charles S. Clark, "The Exhausting Ordeal of the Census Bureau's Top Scientist," *Government Executive*, April 22, 2019, https://www.govexec.com/management/ 2019/04/exhausting-ordeal-census-bureaus-top-scientist/156467/; J. David Brown, Misty Heggeness, Suzanne Dorinski, Lawrence Warren, and Moises Yi, "Predicting the Effects of Adding a Citizenship Question to the 2020 Census," *Demography* 56 (July 2019): 1173–1194. The authors of the last article are Census Bureau researchers. The "exceed 8 million" figure updates the Census's original estimates of 6.5 million to reflect the higher nonresponse rate predicted in the article.

21. Ari Berman, "Architect of GOP Gerrymandering Was Behind Trump's Census Citizenship Question," *Mother Jones*, May 30, 2019, https:// www.motherjones.com/politics/2019/05/architect-of-gop-gerrymandering -was-behind-trumps-census-citizenship-question. The Hofeller files are available at https://www.commoncause.org/wp-content/uploads/2019/05 /2019-05-30-Letter-Motion-dckt-587_1.pdf.

22. Michael Wines, "Deceased G.O.P. Strategist's Hard Drives Reveal New Details on the Census Citizenship Question," *New York Times*, May 30, 2019, https://www.nytimes.com/2019/05/30/us/census-citizenship-question -hofeller.html.

23. Jack Shafer, "How the Court Imitates the World Series," *Slate*, September 13, 2005, https://slate.com/news-and-politics/2005/09/the-supreme-court -imitates-the-world-series.html. See also see Mark Joseph Stern, "A New *Lochner* Era," *Slate*, June 29, 2018, https://slate.com/news-and-politics /2018/06/the-lochner-era-is-set-for-a-comeback-at-the-supreme-court.html.

24. Adam Feldman, "Empirical SCOTUS: The Big Business Court," SCOTUSblog, August 8, 2018, https://www.scotusblog.com/2018/08 /empirical-scotus-the-big-business-court/; Lee Epstein, William M. Landes, and Richard A. Posner, "How Business Fares in the Supreme Court," *Minnesota Law Review* 97 (2012): 1431–1472.

25. David A. Graham, "John Roberts Says Partisan Gerrymandering Is Not His Problem," *Atlantic Monthly*, June 27, 2019, https://www.theatlantic .com/ideas/archive/2019/06/partisan-gerrymandering-supreme-court-north -carolina/592741.

26. Camila Domonoske, "Supreme Court Declines Republican Bid To Revive North Carolina Voter ID Law," NPR, May 15, 2017, https://www.npr .org/sections/thetwo-way/2017/05/15/528457693/supreme-court-declines

-republican-bid-to-revive-north-carolina-voter-id-law; Adam Liptak, "Supreme Court Invalidates Key Part of Voting Rights Act," *New York Times*, June 25, 2013, https://www.nytimes.com/2013/06/26/us/supreme -court-ruling.html; Ari Berman, "The Country's Worst Anti-Voting Law Was Just Struck Down in North Carolina," *Nation*, July 29, 2016, https://www.thenation.com/article/the-countrys-worst-anti-voting-law -was-just-struck-down-in-north-carolina/.

27. Alexander Hertel-Fernandez, *Politics at Work: How Companies Turn Their Workers into Lobbyists* (New York: Oxford University Press, 2018).

28. Alexander Hertel-Fernandez, "American Employers as Political Machines," *Journal of Politics* 79, no. 1 (2017): 105–117.

29. Anna Harvey and Taylor Mattia, "Does Money Have a Conservative Bias? Estimating the Causal Impact of Citizens United on State Legislative Preferences," *Public Choice* (2019); Alexander Hertel-Fernandez, Matto Mildenberger, and Leah C. Stokes, "Legislative Staff and Representation in Congress," *American Political Science Review* 113, no. 1 (2019): 1–18.

30. Todd N. Tucker, "Fixing the Senate: Equitable and Full Representation for the 21st Century," Roosevelt Institute, March 2019, http://rooseveltin stitute.org/wp-content/uploads/2019/03/RI_Fixing-The-Senate_report _201903.pdf; Adam Liptak, "Smaller States Find Outsize Clout Grow- ing in Senate," *New York Times*, March 11, 2013, http://archive.nytimes .com/www.nytimes.com/interactive/2013/03/11/us/politics/democracy -tested.html. The House of Lords is not considered in these analyses, since its powers have been highly limited since the Parliament Act of 1911.

31. Wasserman, "The Congressional Map Has a Record-Setting Bias against Democrats."

32. Michael Geruso, Dean Spears, and Ishaana Talesara, "Inversions in US Presidential Elections: 1836–2016," National Bureau of Eco- nomic Research, working paper no. 26247, September 2019; David M. Drucker, "Republicans Resigned to Trump Losing 2020 Popular Vote but Confident about Electoral College," *Washington Examiner*, March 22, 2019, https://www.washingtonexaminer.com/news/campaigns /republicans-resigned-to-trump-losing-2020-popular-vote-but-confident -about-electoral-college.

33. Sarah A. Binder, "The History of the Filibuster," Brookings, April 22, 2010, https://brookings.edu/testimonies/the-history-of-the-filibuster. Data on Senate filibusters are available at https://www.senate.gov/legislative/clo ture/clotureCounts.htm.

34. "With Kavanaugh Vote, the Senate Reaches a Historic Low in Dem- ocratic Metric," *GovTrack Insider*, October 7, 2018, https://govtrack insider.com/with-kavanaugh-vote-the-senate-reaches-a-historic-low-in -democratic-metric-dfb0f5fa7fa. The analysis covered all non-unanimous Senate roll call votes from 1901 to the present in which yes votes outnum- bered no votes. The *GovTrack Insider* write-up notes that some of these votes did not succeed because a super-majority was required.

35. Mike Abramowitz, "Democracy in Retreat: Freedom in the World 2019,"

Freedom House, February 5, 2019, https://freedomhouse.org/report/freedom-world/freedom-world-2019/democracy-in-retreat.

36. Tim Alberta, *American Carnage: On the Front Lines of the Republican Civil War and the Rise of President Trump* (New York: HarperCollins, 2019).

37. "21 Grahams," *Harper's*, November 2018, https://www.harpers.org/archive/2018/11/lindsey-graham-describes-donald-trump/.

38. Alberta, *American Carnage*.

39. Carl Hulse, "A Blaring Message in Republicans' Muted Criticism: It's Trump's Party," *New York Times*, July 15, 2019, https://www.nytimes.com/2019/07/15/us/politics/republicans-trump-tweet.html.

40. Li Zhou, "11 Senate Republicans Voted to Block Trump's Border Wall Emergency Declaration," Vox, September 25, 2019, https://www.vox.com/2019/9/25/20880248/senate-republicans-trump-border-wall. Twelve Republicans voted against Trump's declaration in March 2019, but Republican Senator Marco Rubio of Florida was absent during the second vote in September.

41. Publius Decius Mus, "The Flight 93 Election," *Claremont Review of Books*, September 5, 2016, claremont.org/crb/basicpage/the-flight-93-election; Philip Wegman, "Publius Pulls the Ripcord and Michael Anton Bails Out of 'Flight 93,'" *Washington Examiner*, April 9, 2018, https://www.washingtonexaminer.com/opinion/publius-pulls-the-ripcord-and-michael-anton-bails-out-of-flight-93.

42. Justin Baragona, "Fox News Host Jeanine Pirro: Dems Plotting to 'Replace American Citizens With Illegals,'" Daily Beast, August 29, 2019, https://www.thedailybeast.com/fox-news-host-jeanine-pirro-democrats-plotting-to-replace-american-citizens-with-illegals.

43. Tara Golshan, "North Carolina Wrote the Playbook Wisconsin and Michigan Are Using to Undermine Democracy," Vox, December 5, 2018, https://www.vox.com/policy-and-politics/2018/12/5/18125544/north-carolina-power-grab-wisconsin-michigan-lame-duck.

44. Steve Benen, "Wisconsin and the 'If Only Those People Weren't Here' Phenomenon," MSNBC, December 7, 2018, https://msnbc.com/rachel-maddow-show/wisconsin-and-the-if-only-those-people-werent-here-phenomenon; Charles P. Pierce, "Republicans Have a Problem With Democrats. But More So With Democracy," *Esquire*, December 5, 2018, https://esquire.com/news-politics/politics/a25411459/republicans-wisconsin-democracy-governor-early-voting.

CONCLUSION

1. David Gelles and David Yaffe-Belany, "Shareholder Value Is No Longer Everything, CEOs Say," *New York Times*, August 19, 2019, https://www.nytimes.com/2019/08/19/business/business-roundtable-ceos-corporations.html.

2. Jeffrey Sonnenberg, "CEOs Fire Back on Guns—A New American Revolution," *Chief Executive*, September 12, 2019. https://chiefexecutive .net/ceos-fire-back-on-guns-a-new-american-revolution/; Griffin Dix, "Walmart's Doug McMillon Is a Corporate Hero," Hill, September 11, 2019, https://thehill.com/opinion/finance/460950-walmarts-doug-mc millon-is-a-corporate-hero.

3. Maggie Severns, "The Next Koch Doesn't Like Politics," *Politico Magazine*, December 14, 2018, https://www.politico.com/magazine/story /2018/12/14/koch-brothers-chase-charles-next-generation-223099.

4. Jacob S. Hacker and Paul Pierson, *American Amnesia: How the War on Government Made Us Forget What Made America Prosper* (New York: Simon & Schuster, 2016). The next few paragraphs draw on chapter 7 of the book.

5. Christina Prignano, "Poll Finds 90 Percent of Voters Support Background Checks. But Respondents Don't Expect Congress to Act," *Boston Globe*, September 9, 2019, https://www.bostonglobe.com/news/politics /2019/09/09/poll-finds-percent-voters-support-background-checks-but -respondents-don-expect-congress-act/UwqCqWCT1aqOyAo5ZOtrvK /story.html.

6. Jake Grumbach and Paul Pierson, "Are Large Corporations Politically Moderate? Using Money in Politics to Infer the Preferences of Business," UC Berkeley (working paper, July 13, 2019); Alexander Hertel-Fernandez, *State Capture: How Conservative Activists, Big Businesses, and Wealthy Donors Reshaped the American States—and the Nation* (New York: Oxford University Press, 2019). Though we should distinguish between companies' stances and those of their CEOs, a recent analysis of CEO political contributions is revealing. Looking at the nearly 4,000 executives who served as CEOs of Standard & Poor's 1500 companies between 2000 and 2017, the study found that 57 percent of CEOs devoted two-thirds or more of their donations to Republican candidates, compared with 19 percent who devoted two-thirds or more to Democratic candidates. Moreover, CEOs who favored Republicans headed companies with almost twice the asset value of companies headed by CEOs who favored Democrats, and the companies they led were less transparent to investors about corporate political spending. Alma Cohen, Moshe Hazan, Roberto Tallarita, and David Weiss, "The Politics of CEOs," *Journal of Legal Analysis* 11 (2019): 1–45.

7. Ed Conard, "How Free Market Advocates Can Regain Control of the GOP," https://www.edwardconard.com/2016/08/17/ed-conard-at-mitt -romneys-2016-offsite-how-free-market-advocates-can-regain-control -of-the-gop/.

8. Carla Maranucci, "California Republicans Hit Rock Bottom," *Politico*, May 30, 2018, https://www.politico.com/story/2018/05/30/california -republicans-third-party-status-613568/. For a skeptical view of Proposition 187's effects, see Iris Hui and David O. Sears, "Reexamining the Effect of Racial Propositions on Latinos' Partisanship in California," *Political Behavior* 40, no. 1 (2018): 149–174.

9. Ronald Brownstein, "Donald Trump's Coalition of Restoration," *Atlantic Monthly*, June 23, 2016, https://www.theatlantic.com/politics/archive/2016/06/donald-trumps-coalition-of-restoration/488345/.

10. Stanley B. Greenberg, *RIP GOP: How the New America is Dooming the Republicans* (New York: Thomas Dunne, 2019).

11. Quoted in Tim Alberta, *American Carnage: On the Front Lines of the Republican Civil War and the Rise of President Trump* (New York: HarperCollins, 2019), 546.

12. The relationship between racial progress and political instability is an underlying theme in Steven Levitsky and Daniel Ziblatt, *How Democracies Die* (New York: Crown, 2018). See also Richard M. Valelly, *The Two Reconstructions: The Struggle for Black Disenfranchisement* (Chicago: University of Chicago Press, 2004); Robert Mickey, Steven Levitsky, and Lucan Way, "Is America Still Safe for Democracy? Why the United States Is in Danger of Backsliding," *Foreign Affairs*, May–June 2017, https://www.foreignaffairs.com/articles/united-states/2017-04-17/america-still-safe-democracy.

13. Joshua Green, *Devil's Bargain: Steve Bannon, Donald Trump, and the Nationalist Uprising* (New York: Penguin, 2017), 8.

14. Patrick Gleason, "Blue State Republican Governors Are Among the Nation's Most Popular Politicians," *Forbes*, September 30, 2019, https://www.forbes.com/sites/patrickgleason/2019/09/30/blue-state-republican-governors-are-among-the-nations-most-popular-politicians/#1854e7db4239. The article is based on the Morning Consult poll of gubernatorial approval from the fourth quarter of 2019.

EPILOGUE

1. Caitlin Oprysko, "In Grievance Filled Speech, St. Louis Couple Warns of Chaos in the Suburbs if Democrats Elected," *Politico*, August 24, 2020, https://www.politico.com/news/2020/08/24/mccloskey-convention-speech-guns-suburbs-401297.

2. Morgan Chalfant, "Trump: 'The Only Way We're Going to Lose this Election is if the Election is Rigged,'" *The Hill*, August 17, 2020, https://thehill.com/homenews/administration/512424-trump-the-only-way-we-are-going-to-lose-this-election-is-if-the; Danny Hakim, Stephanie Saul, Nick Corasaniti and Michael Wines, "Trump Renews Fears of Voter Intimidation as G.O.P. Poll Watchers Mobilize," *New York Times*, September 30, 2020, https://www.nytimes.com/2020/09/30/us/trump-election-poll-watchers.html.

3. Anna Lührmann and Staffan I. Lindberg, "A Third Wave of Autocratization Is Here: What Is New About It?," *Democratization* 26:7 (2019): 1095-1113; Anna Lührmann, Juraj Medzihorsky, Garry Hindle, and Staffan I. Lindberg, "New Global Data on Political Parties: V-Party," V-Dem Institute, October 26, 2020, https://www.v-dem.net/media/filer_public/b6/55/b6553f85-5c5d-45ec-be63-a48a2abe3f62/briefing_paper_9.pdf.

4. Ella Koeze, "Counties That Suffered Higher Unemployment Rates Voted for Biden," *New York Times*, November 16, 2020, https://www.nytimes.com/interactive/2020/11/16/business/economy/unemployment-election-counties.html.

5. Jesse Drucker, "Bonanza for Rich Real Estate Investors, Tucked Into Stimulus Package," *New York Times,* March 26, 2020, https://www.nytimes.com/2020/03/26/business/coronavirus-real-estate-investors-stimulus.html; John Wagner, "McConnell Takes Flak After Suggesting Bankruptcy for States Rather than Bailouts," *Washington Post,* April 23, 2020, https://www.washingtonpost.com/powerpost/mcconnell-takes-flak-after-suggesting-bankruptcy-for-states-rather-than-bailouts/2020/04/23/f70311fe-8560-11ea-a3eb-e9fc93160703_story.html.

6. Chuck Collins, Omar Ocampo, Sara Mycklebust, Bianca Agustin, and Jonathan Heller, "Report: Billionaire Wealth vs. Community Health," *Inequality.org,* November 18, 2020, https://inequality.org/great-divide/billionaire-wealth-community-health/.

7. Center for Political Accountability (CPA), *Conflicted Consequences* (Washington, DC: CPA, 2020), https://politicalaccountability.net/hifi/files/Conflicted-Consequences.pdf.

8. Federal contribution data from OpenSecrets.org, focusing on donations from the Chamber's PACs (https://www.opensecrets.org/orgs/us-chamber-of-commerce/summary?id=D000019798)

9. Byron Tau, "Obama: Republican 'Fever' will Break after Election," *Politico,* June 1, 2012, https://www.politico.com/blogs/politico44/2012/06/obama-republican-fever-will-break-after-the-election-125059.

10. Mark Joseph Stern, "Lindsey Graham's Alleged Attempt to Toss Georgia Ballots Is Felony Election Fraud," *Slate,* November 19, 2020, https://slate.com/news-and-politics/2020/11/lindsey-graham-brad-raffensperger-georgia-election-fraud.html.

11. Jerry Taylor, "What Democrats Can Learn from the Republicans about Political Power," August 10, 2020, https://www.niskanencenter.org/what-democrats-can-learn-from-the-republicans-about-political-power/

12. James Madison, "Notes of Debates in the Federal Convention of 1787," May 31, 1787, https://avalon.law.yale.edu/18th_century/debates_531.asp.

13. Ronald Brownstein, "Democrats' Real Liability in the House," *Atlantic*, November 27, 2020, https://www.theatlantic.com/politics/archive/2020/11/bidens-popular-vote-win-didnt-help-house-democrats/617211/.

14. Brownstein, "Democrats' Real Liability in the House."

15. Corwin D. Smidt, "Polarization and the Decline of the American Floating Voter," American Journal of Political Science, 61:2 (2015): 365–81.

16. Peter Nicholas, "The Republican Plan for the Next Four Years Isn't Normal," *Atlantic*, December 6, 2020, https://www.theatlantic.com/politics/archive/2020/12/trump-will-reign-atop-gop-until-2024/617300/.

INDEX